FAMOUS TRIALS
of HISTORY

THE RT. HONOURABLE THE EARL OF BIRKE...

P. C., D. L., D. C. L., LL. D.

High Steward of Oxford University

Fellow of Wadham and Merton Colleges

FAMOUS TRIALS
OF HISTORY

THE STAR SERIES

GARDEN CITY PUBLISHING CO., INC.

.GARDEN CITY, NEW YORK

FAMOUS TRIALS OF HISTORY

I dedicate this book to Sir Edward Clarke, and, in doing so, recommend his standard and methods of advocacy to young gentlemen fitting themselves for practice at the Bar.

PREFACE

Let me begin by an attempt to disarm an obvious criticism. This book is called "Famous Trials of History." But it contains (it may be said) some trials in which the author was himself engaged for which it cannot be claimed that they fall within this description. This is perfectly true. And if it be asked: "Why, then, do you so dignify them?" I can only reply that I was quite unable to think of a compendious title which would cover both really famous trials and others which, interesting or not, are unlikely to become historical. *Habetis confitentem reum.*

The treatment of the cases is throughout untechnical, so that the narratives may easily be comprehended by laymen. They belong to very different periods of English history, some of which are now remote and curious. If they amuse an idle hour I am content.

BIRKENHEAD.

Charlton, 1926.

CONTENTS

THE TRIAL OF
MARY QUEEN OF SCOTS

THE TRIAL OF MARY QUEEN OF SCOTS

THE trial and execution of Mary Queen of Scots form the culmination of her long rivalry with Elizabeth. Fate brought the two women into inevitable conflict, and their struggle, commenced with almost equal chances, forms a record of intrigue on both sides in which the less skilful player, always with the inferior hand, gradually lost the advantage and paid the forfeit with her life.

The story is a long one. Even before she took refuge in England in 1568, Mary had challenged her cousin's right to the throne, and her escape from Scotland added one more difficulty to the many that beset Elizabeth and England

The English Queen had reigned for nearly ten years. As the daughter of Anne Boleyn, she was regarded by many worthy people as illegitimate and therefore a usurper. To this she added the additional disqualification that she favoured the Protestant settlement. Her legitimacy had been affirmed by statute, but a status thus acquired could, if circumstances allowed, as readily be disaffirmed, especially if the Pope decided, as indeed he did later, to release all Catholics from any religious obligation to render her allegiance. She had a perilous upbringing. While yet an infant her mother had fallen a victim to her consort's suspicious jealousy. When Edward VI succeeded she was growing to a marriageable age and was coveted as a pawn in the game by ambitious men. Delivered from more than one particular peril by Edward's early death, she encountered thereafter worse dangers. She could not but be an object of dislike and suspicion to her sister, to whom she was a living reminder of the wrongs done to the unfortunate Catharine of Aragon. Yet, if the union of Philip and Mary proved sterile, as it did in fact, Elizabeth was the obvious successor to the Crown. As such, her name could plausibly be used by any rebel bidding for popular support. When Wyatt's rebellion broke out, she was suspected of complicity and for a time in the gravest peril of life. Throughout the reign of Philip and Mary she was under close surveillance. Spies scrutinised her every act, and had she made a false move, it would probably have sealed her doom. It is small wonder, having regard to her wonderful education and her natural abilities, which included all the Tudor aptitude for dissimulation, that her early life made her a mistress of intrigue, while weakening in the process her perception of principle.

When, after Mary's short reign, Elizabeth ascended the throne, a new era seemed about to dawn. But clouds threatened storms from many quarters. To steer a safe course between the shoals demanded the highest skill and the keenest foresight. It was to that task that Elizabeth thenceforth devoted her dominating life.

The first and perhaps the most fateful problem was as to the form of religion. Henry's changes had divorced the realm from Catholicism without making the people Protestants. But for the bigotry with which schism was attacked in the reign of Mary it might have been possible to reunite England permanently to Rome. When Elizabeth succeeded, it was too late; the general sense of the nation had definitely hardened against union with Rome. The decision had to be taken at once, and by that decision the second change of religion within a few years was brought about, and the Church of England had to be built anew. This threw the Catholics into opposition. It made many hypocrites, for now numbers made their second or third *volte-face* according to the solution favoured by the Government for the time being. As time wore on the Catholics in the Continent made their plots against the Queen, the repressive legislation turned almost every English Catholic into a potential rebel, while numbers who conformed to the Established Church were ready on a change of fortune to make a fresh recantation. It was not easy to choose an adviser upon whom to rely; the period is remarkable for the facility with which information could be obtained from men on whom no breath of suspicion could seem rightly to rest. Traitors swarmed round every Court.

The four countries with which England had to reckon were Spain, France, Scotland and Ireland. The Spanish monarch had only just ceased to rule in England. As a descendant of John of Gaunt, Philip II had claims to England, which were only less strong than those of a few others. It is perhaps due to the fact that the nearest of these, Mary Queen of Scots, was the wife of the Dauphin that Philip allowed Elizabeth to succeed without a struggle, contenting himself with the suggestion of himself as her husband. Spain was the source from which the Counter-Reformation took its origin. She appeared to be the strongest European power. Few then realised how fatal it was for her, with a new world fallen to her share, to have warred against the Moors, the Jews and the Protestants in Spain; and thus, at a time calling for the greatest national effort, to have deprived the realm of the flower of its wealthy, industrious and labouring classes. Not content with that, the King had roused his subjects in the Netherlands, and turned a race of seamen into enemies. Had they been kept loyal, the history of England would have been different.

France was also a danger. Mary and her husband had assumed the style and arms of King and Queen of England. Less strong apparently than Spain, three factions within the realm were striving for the mastery. United to France, England would be an invaluable support. In the hands of Spain, she might prove a fatal enemy.

Scotland had passed through a phase of Reformation more sweeping than in England. She was distinctly a Protestant power, but her Queen was Catholic, the relations with France were of the closest, and if the turn of events threw France and Scotland together against England, the attack might well come from two quarters at once.

Ireland, unlike the other three countries, was part of the English dominions. She had not adopted the Reformation, and was more in the position of a conquered country held by a garrison against a hostile population than a source of strength.

Any power that could hold the sea could land in Ireland and be sure of support against England.

Amid these dangers Elizabeth walked warily. She was compelled to play for time. When problems called for urgent solution, every way out might prove to be the path into other and worse perils. To put off the evil day, to "wait and see" whether events would not bring about the safest decision was the policy to which she adhered, even in cases where that policy was the least wise of those that offered. When she ascended the throne, England had lost prestige; the people were divided; difficulties were great; counsellors deceitful. It is her glory that she lived to be the head of a united nation which had taken its true place in the world.

One of her most difficult problems was the succession. Unless she married and had issue, there was no obvious successor. It is significant that there always was a doubt whether any of the numerous marriage negotiations was really serious. To offer the chance of matrimony to those who coveted her throne was an obvious method of preventing them from resorting to force. The fact that she could bestow her hand to a prince of a rival power was a potent reason for each of the contending powers to refrain from declaring war upon England. The realm was safer with her alone, but marriage might be a small sacrifice if an ally were urgently needed. But unless she produced a child, then Mary Queen of Scots was the nearest of the possible claimants. Parliament from time to time urged Elizabeth to name a successor, but she declined, perceiving clearly that such a successor might rise in rebellion against her, or else, if a more remote one were preferred, her choice might provoke a nearer expectant heir to try the fortune of war. In all her measures Elizabeth from the commencement of her reign had always to take into account Mary Queen of Scots.

That ill-fated Queen had succeeded her father, James V, Elizabeth's cousin, when a babe a week old. In her tenderest infancy Henry VIII had coveted her for his son, and had sent an army into Scotland to seize her. He failed, but the attempt caused her to be sent to France at the age of six. She was brought up with the French royal family as a Catholic, and at that Court witnessed the disputes and intrigues of the three contending factions, a bad training for a child as true a Tudor as Elizabeth herself. She naturally lost all touch with Scotland, where during her absence, in the most impressionable years of her life, the Scottish people passed through a bigoted Protestant movement. When sixteen she married the Dauphin and her future seemed bound up in France. On Elizabeth's accession she became at once a menace. Her succession at that date would have added strength to the French, and Spain could not allow it. Soon, however, her husband died and in August, 1561, she returned to Scotland alone, a stranger in her own country. Her subjects were in no mood to accept her rule. They were fierce, turbulent and grasping, and she was alien in religion and sympathy. She might and did gain the love and devotion of a few, but she failed, unlike Elizabeth, to put herself at the head of the national movement and so unite the factions in a common loyalty to the throne. But in Scotland she was always a danger, and the turn of events might at any time enable her to strike a decisive blow. Her difficulties were accordingly enhanced by the English agents in Scotland. They were focuses of discontent and supplied fruitful sources of opposition.

It was soon obvious that she could not stand alone, and her marriage became a pressing question, in which Elizabeth's seeming opposition obtained a diplomatic victory. The chosen spouse was a Protestant, Henry Lord Darnley, whose claims to both thrones were not to be despised. Had he not been a headstrong, vain and foolish man, he might have afforded Mary the counsel and support this brilliant and beautiful woman so urgently needed. The Scottish nobility soon perceived his weak points, and, playing upon his jealousy, procured his estrangement from her by his participation in the murder of Rizzio in her presence. The breach, though sought to be concealed, was complete. Soon after their son James was born, he was murdered in circumstances which threw some suspicion upon Mary. Within three months of the murder she fell into the hands of the Earl of Bothwell, who married her in indecent

haste and with doubtful legality. The opposing factions united
to take up arms against this unnatural union and within a
month she was a captive and he an exile. Abdication was imposed upon her; her infant son was proclaimed King; and she
was imprisoned in Lochleven Castle. She seemed to have
become negligible, but in the following year, 1568, she escaped.
Her forces were defeated and she fled into England where she
appealed to Elizabeth for aid.

The English Queen was in a quandary. Mary was indeed
in her power, but was a queen and no subject, and moreover
had given no cause for a trial in England, even if a subject.
While in England she must inevitably be a focus of rebellion.
Out of England she would be beyond Elizabeth's control. The
first step taken was to discredit Mary in the eyes of the
world. A conference, called of York, though it afterwards
adjourned to Westminster, was occupied from October, 1568,
to January, 1569, in investigating the charges made against
her by the Scots. Delegates named by Elizabeth met delegates from Scotland and Mary's agents. Elizabeth had the
good excuse that she could not receive her until the charges
were disposed of. The Conference effected nothing—perhaps
it was never intended to; but, when the Scottish delegates
returned home, much dirty linen had been washed in public,
and Mary's good name had been for all time besmirched.
Whether she was rightly accused or not depends upon the
authenticity of the Casket Letters. The historical mystery
connected with them will probably never be solved, as they
were not published and have disappeared. If they were hers
and contained what was alleged, then she was guilty. No one
can say with certainty, and she is at least entitled to the benefit
of the doubt. Enough was done, however, to enable the
Regent in Scotland to retain his power and to justify Elizabeth in keeping Mary at a distance. The unfortunate Queen
remained in England a prisoner in the guise of a guest.

Her confinement lasted for eighteen long and poignant years.
All that time her energies were devoted to attempts to escape
from durance. She intrigued to supplant, or to be associated
with, her son in Scotland; she strove to placate or overthrow

Elizabeth; she appealed to France, to Spain and to the Pope for aid. Sometimes she seemed ready to change her religion. At other times her faith was the ground upon which she made her appeals. These appeals were the less readily listened to because her suggestion of a change of religion made her sincerity suspect. Nor did the European situation assist her designs. The Pope feared the Jesuits, who worked in favour of Spain; and, while France and Spain might come to blows over England, a united crusade for the faith was impossible. Besides, Spain was not ready. Though the wealth of America was flowing into her coffers, her economic position was precarious and Philip was forced, not merely to connive at the trade, but to encourage English food cargoes to come to Spain. The powers therefore rather preferred to await a successful plot in order to gather an advantage, if opportunity offered them, than to run the risks in which a decided course of action might involve them. Nevertheless plot after plot was formed against Elizabeth, many of which had as the central idea the rescue of Mary and her accession to the throne. In 1570 the Pope excommunicated Elizabeth and thereafter her Catholic subjects were released from any religious obligation of allegiance. The first danger came when the Duke of Norfolk planned to marry Mary and thereby become the ruler of England. It is significant that while no one was sure that Elizabeth would ever marry, it was always assumed that Mary would, and she certainly had no celibate prejudice. Perhaps she realised that she could not rule without a husband, and her experiences with the feeble Francis, the jealous Darnley and the brutal Bothwell had made her profoundly indifferent to the identity of a spouse for whom she was unlikely to feel the love of a wife for her husband. The Duke's plot was discovered and he was executed in 1572.

The machinations of the Catholic plotters continued, and the consequent repressive measures against them tended to drive all Catholics into opposition to Elizabeth. Protestants too were becoming embittered. The massacre of St. Bartholomew in 1572 caused them to be apprehensive lest they should share the fate of the Huguenots. Feeling was rising, and it was perceived that the assassination of Elizabeth would plunge the nation into the horrors of a disputed succession, which might lead to foreign invasion and the placing of a Catholic on the throne. Plot followed plot, and it was believed that Mary was not innocent of participation. She had not been discreet. She hardly could be. Once even, under the guise of reporting slander, she had written to Elizabeth detailing all the infamous stories she had heard about her. She did not trouble to conceal her opinion that she was unjustly kept from the throne by Elizabeth. In time that monarch, who had never been blind to the advantages that would accrue from Mary's death, was brought to believe that the disadvantages might not be so formidable as she had sometimes feared. Mary was the natural heir to the throne. She might marry and then, if she had children, they would be Catholics. Legislation could deprive James of his heirship and England would then have a Catholic dynasty. On the other hand, if she were dead, all the claimants except Philip of Spain were Protestants. No Catholic would seek to dethrone Elizabeth for another Protestant. Few, if any, Englishmen would lend any countenance to schemes in Philip's interest. Meanwhile Elizabeth was in imminent danger, and those of her subjects who perceived that the continuance of Mary's life was a menace to them did not share their Queen's scruples. At last, when several assassination plots had been brought to light, Elizabeth's Ministers brought her to the opinion that if Mary gave just cause she would be justified in proceeding to the last extremity.

There were grave risks. The trial of a monarch was a threat to all crowned heads. James must inevitably be deeply offended at an attempt on his mother's life. Any king who sought for an excuse for war could find one in such a trial. Unless Mary's complicity in treason was manifest, there was no justification or excuse, and even then there would be no small legal doubt whether any Court had jurisdiction. Nevertheless events were moving to such a crisis that either Elizabeth or Mary would fall, and Elizabeth's advisers were determined that their mistress, having a powerful offensive in her hand, should not be the victim.

And now began the closing scenes of the tragedy. The nation was thoroughly roused, and at the news that a new plot had been discovered against their Sovereign, began to act. In November, 1584, the Protestants of England formed an association pledge to defend and avenge her. By the Act of Association they bound themselves, their "bodies, lives and goods," to withstand "by force of arms as by all other means of revenge" all who should attempt to harm her. And if any such attempt should succeed they declared that they would never accept the successor on whose behalf the attempt was made, and would pursue the offenders to death.

The first Statute of the ensuing session of Parliament was an Act for the Security of Her Majesty's Royal Person (27 Eliz. c. 1). It provided means whereby a Commission of twenty-four Peers and Privy Councillors might be appointed to investigate any future conspiracy or attempt to bring about an invasion or rebellion or anything tending to the hurt of the Queen "by any person or with the privity of any person that shall or may pretend title to the Crown of this realm." If such Commission gave sentence or judgment against anyone, then upon proclamation of the sentence or judgment under the Great Seal two consequences would follow. First, that the claimant should be for ever disabled to have or succeed to the Crown, and secondly that anyone might lawfully put to death the person or persons declared to be guilty. The Act could only have been aimed at one person, and only one trial was held under it. Mary realised the object and offered to sign the Act of Association, but that, of course, was not allowed. Once the measure became law, Elizabeth, or maybe only some of her advisers, began to take steps to secure that the desired enquiry should have evidence to justify it. In 1585-6 Mary was at Chartley corresponding in cypher through her secretaries with foreign princes. Her object was to procure her release, and she was seemingly indifferent as to the means, if only they proved effectual. She was prepared to cede to the King of Spain her title to the English throne, and apparently would have welcomed an armed invasion intended to set her free. But if the proceedings at her trial are to be believed, she also stooped to countenance treason and murder. Anthony Babington and his associates were plotting the assassination of Queen Elizabeth and the accession of Mary as a Catholic Queen, and they confessed that they had corresponded with the royal captive. These confessions, with the admissions of her secretaries and copies of the incriminating letters, have been made known. Taken at their face, the evidence of her complicity in the plot is complete. Cecil and Walsingham had been watching the hatching of the plot and reading the letters as they passed. Some say indeed that Walsingham had organised the plot in order to accomplish his designs. At a convenient moment Babington and his friends were seized, tried and executed. By 21st September, 1586, the last of them had paid the penalty, and there remained one only, but that one the noble quarry, at last to be brought to bay.

Whether Elizabeth desired her rival's death, or was overpersuaded to sanction the various stages, is a question which, in all probability, can never receive an authoritative answer. That the necessary steps were taken, and taken with her sanction, cannot be denied. But even with evidence clearly pointing to Mary's guilt, there were serious doubts what procedure could be followed. Mary had been Queen of Scotland, and her abdication was a forced one, repudiated by her when she escaped from Lochleven Castle in 1568. It is the received doctrine that a foreign sovereign is immune from all process of law. If such a visitor violates the law, the proper remedy is to bring about his or her departure. If Mary was exempt, then the English ministers were in a dilemma. To expel her would let loose upon the realm undefined but plain disasters. To retain her in custody, as she had been for nineteen years, would merely continue an intolerable situation. While in this country she was a prize coveted by every conspirator, and a counter of value to the diplomatists of neighbouring realms. If she were to survive Elizabeth, she, almost beyond doubt, would plunge England into civil war: almost certainly Scotland would involve herself, and the bait thus offered to France and Spain would be likely to prove too much for one or the other, if not both. Her death would cut this Gordian knot.

The lawyers were set busy. They pondered over the weighty questions whether Mary was a sovereign, and whether as a sovereign she could be tried by the State in which she happened to be. It was even suggested that the Queen of England as the feudal superior of the Scottish monarch, had jurisdiction over her, though Bannockburn had given a decisive negative to that contention nearly three hundred years before. The precedents were few and the writings of the learned of little value, but it mattered less. The legal answer was predetermined and the lawyers were merely engaged in finding reasons for upholding that answer, and not, as they should have been, in finding what the true answer was. It was averred, with some support, at least from common sense, that a monarch who abused the hospitality of another country by treasonable practices was amenable to the laws of that country. The flaw in the reasoning was twofold. First, Mary was a prisoner, and secondly the remedy is expulsion. Nevertheless the conclusion that she was amenable to the jurisdiction was pleasing in the eyes of those who had the power, if not the right, to try her, and the way was clear for the next legal problem. With what offence and before what tribunal was she to be tried? It might be suggested that she was guilty of treason and could therefore be hauled before the appropriate Court for trying treason. The difficulties of that course are greater than would appear at first sight. Mary was not born a subject of the English Crown, nor had she sworn allegiance or been denizated. She was not even voluntarily present in the country. Besides, who was to try her? She was not a peer, and yet, if not tried by the Lords, the only recourse was to a common jury, though she was of higher rank than a lord. But in England all accused persons were entitled to be tried by their peers, i.e., equals, and of her peers there was only one—Elizabeth herself. Obviously in taking advantage of the Act of Association and legalising an enquiry, Elizabeth's advisers had been finding a way out, and had avoided the glaring strain on the ordinary law which any other course would necessarily have involved. The Act was precise and clear.

Mary was arrested and taken to Fotheringhay in the custody

of Sir Amyas Paulet. A Commission was issued to the Archbishop of Canterbury, the Lord Chancellor, Lord Burghley, the Marquess of Winchester, the Earls of Oxford, Shrewsbury, Kent, Derby, Worcester, Rutland, Warwick, Pembroke, Leicester and Lincoln, Viscount Montague, Lords Howard, Hunsdon, Abergavenny, Zouch, Morley, Cobham, Stafford Grey of Wilton, Lumley, Stourton, Sandes, Mordaunt, St. John of Bletsoe, Buckhurst, Compton and Cheyney, Sir Francis Knowles, Sir James Croft, Sir Christopher Hatton and Sir Francis Walsingham, William Davison, Sir Ralph Sadleir, Sir Walter Mildmay, Sir Amyas Paulet and John Wolley, all the Commissioners being Privy Councillors, and to Lord Chief Justice Wray, Lord Chief Baron Anderson, Mr. Justice Gawdy and Mr. Justice Periam. Their task was set out in few words. It was alleged that, since the Statute was passed, Mary and others by her privity had engaged in conspiracy tending to Her Majesty's hurt and the Commissioners were to hear evidence and give sentence accordingly. There was no need for delay. The Commissioners included the Ministers who had prepared the case against Mary, and her gaoler. On 11th October, 1587, they arrived at Fotheringhay with their counsel and with documents prepared for immediate action.

Queen Elizabeth had on the 6th written a letter informing Mary of the charge and intimating that as she lived within the Queen's protection, and thereby subject to the laws of the realm, she could be brought to trial and requesting her to answer the charge. Sir Amyas Paulet and a notary public waited upon her and delivered her letter. Having read it, she expressed her regret that the Queen should be misinformed and recalled that, after the Association and the Act confirming it, she had foreseen that, whatever happened, she would bear the whole blame, having, as she well knew, mortal enemies at Court. She then asserted that as a Queen she was not amenable to trial and would do nothing to prejudice herself or others of her rank or her son. She then complained that she was ignorant of the laws of England, did not know who were to be the judges, all her papers and notes had been taken and no man dared step forth to be her advocate, and ended: "I am clear of all crime against the Queen. I have excited no man against her and I am not to be charged but by my own word or writing which cannot be produced against me. Yet can I not deny but I have commended myself and my cause to foreign princes."

On the next day her answer was shewn written down and she accepted it as accurate, but added that she did not enjoy the protection and benefit of the laws of England since she had come into England to crave aid, and had ever since been detained in prison. Her denial of the authority of the Commissioners caused trouble, and some of the Commissioners, with the Crown lawyers and advocates, came to see her. She maintained her objection and said that she would listen to their arguments against the objection but by way of interlocution and not judicially. These discussions appear to have lasted two days. She would, she said, answer in a full Parliament so that she might be declared next to the succession, but "to the judgment of mine adversaries amongst whom I know all defence of mine innocency will be barred, flatly, I will not submit myself." In vain they threatened to proceed in her absence, but eventually on the 14th it was agreed that, if her protest were received but not accepted, she would appear, "being anxious to refute the charge."

Thereupon the Commissioners took their places according to an elaborate scheme and ceremonial that had been settled in advance. A chair had been placed on the daïs for the Queen of England who was not present. Mary's chair was in the middle opposite the Queen's chair. As she came in she exclaimed, "I am a Queen by right of birth and my place should be there under the daïs." She repeated her protest. She was denied counsel and papers. Mr. Justice Gawdy then opened the case, speaking as a counsel for the prosecution would. He maintained that she knew of Babington's conspiracy, approved, promised assistance and showed the ways and means. Thereupon she denied all knowledge of Babington and all communication with him and demanded production of her own writing if that were to be proved. Extracts were then read from Babington's confession, whereupon she said that letters had

desperate, I am fully resolved not to reject foreign aid."
Finally she asked to be heard in a full Parliament or to speak
with the Queen and with the Council.

This ended the proceedings at Fotheringhay and the Commission adjourned to the Star Chamber at Westminster where
they reassembled on 25th October. Mary was not present and
the only business was to call Nan and Curle, her secretaries,
to prove the letters and copy letters. Thereupon the Commissioners pronounced the charge against Mary to be true. Nan
afterwards protested that he had not betrayed his mistress,
but on the contrary had given evidence in her favour. The
records do not bear out this assertion. Although the findings
would only affect Mary herself, it was thought advisable to
declare that the sentence in no way affected King James. It
was important to keep him from a personal grievance, and
active steps were now taken to prevent his taking up arms to
rescue or avenge his mother. To his eternal disgrace he contented himself with verbal remonstrances.

When the findings were published, a curious episode occurred. Some would have it that the whole of what happened
afterwards was an elaborate pretence, to make a cold, deliberate purpose of putting Mary to death. Others see in the
incidents the machination of Elizabeth's advisers to trick her
into consenting to her cousin's death against her will. Probably the truth is that she was vacillating, as was her wont, and
her advisers were seeking to force her to a definite decision.
There seems to be no reason to doubt that, having decided,
Elizabeth sought to change that decision and still keep matters
in suspense. With her habit of mind it would be easy for her
to come to the honest belief that she never really did consent.
Parliament confirmed the sentence and then both Houses presented a humble Supplication to her, desiring in stately language
that Mary's execution should be decreed. Elizabeth's answer
was evasive, and after twelve days she returned a final reply,
which she herself described as an "answer answerless." The
Lord Chancellor and the Speaker procured an audience to give
reasons why Parliament should adhere to their resolutions,
though she had desired them to find another solution. She de-

clined to commit herself and prorogued Parliament. Meanwhile the diplomatists were busy and the French Ambassador was especially active in his efforts to prevent the execution. The Queen would not give a decisive answer. She even wrote to Amyas Paulet to relieve her of the necessity by himself killing Mary, but he refused. The incident is not quite so atrocious as is generally assumed. It can at least be suggested with some plausibility that the publication of the findings, by the very terms of the Statute, deprived the killing of the legal aspects of murder. However that may be, the suggestion was disingenuous and must always cast deserved discredit upon Elizabeth. Eventually she signed the warrant and Davison the Secretary of State sent it off. After it had gone, Elizabeth desired (or pretended she did) to recall it, but it was too late. Whether she knew that it had gone and acted in order to save her face with other countries is a matter for conjecture, but the request supplied her with a convenient scapegoat, for Davison bore the whole brunt of the blame.

The execution was a touching scene. Whatever faults Mary had committed, she bore herself in this last ordeal with courage and dignity. In all she said and did she cast lustre on her fame and by the last act of her life largely redeemed its previous crimes. She went to the block as a Queen confident of her cause, and her memory still lives as that of a beautiful, radiant and unfortunate woman sacrificed to the policy of an envious rival.

Was she really guilty? I answer that none who reads the protests against her secretaries' confessions and acts being received as evidence can resist the conclusion that her whole defence was based upon the fallacy that what she implied but did not personally do was no proof against her. She was cruelly treated at her trial. Without aid of counsel, a lonely woman was confronted by the best brains of England. She defended herself steadfastly and brilliantly, weakened as she was by long years of imprisonment; but she was done to death.

THE TRIAL OF
THOMAS WENTWORTH
(EARL OF STRAFFORD)

THE TRIAL OF THOMAS WENTWORTH
(EARL OF STRAFFORD)

WHEN the Earl of Strafford was informed that the King had consented to his death, he is said to have quoted with bitterness, "Put not your trust in Princes." And indeed, whether Charles wished to preserve his honour unsullied, or intended to pursue his policy, his failure to save his Minister was a convincing proof of incapacity.

The Commons knew Strafford better than he. They realised that in that Minister Charles possessed a servant who was able to bring to fruition the designs of a master who aimed at despotism. At him they struck, and when the King yielded to their attack, they learned from his surrender that victory in the constitutional struggle must in the end rest with them.

The Stuarts misconceived their duties as grossly as they mistook the temper of their subjects. They forgot, what the Tudors had never forgotten, that their title was Parliamentary and conceived that they reigned by Divine Right, being responsible to God alone. The great Tudors were more unscrupulous and more tyrannous than they, but preserved an outward deference for Parliamentary forms. Warned by rebellion and disaffection, they realised that a King must be the leader of the nation, and when Elizabeth died she left to James the loyalty of a united people. That nation did not change because the Stuarts had replaced the Tudors. The new King might have had all the loyalty that Elizabeth had won, but "the wisest fool in Christendom" chose a policy running counter to the traditions and prejudices of the nation, while confiding in favourites whose unworthiness was a public scandal. But James did not live to see civil war. Under his rule, the struggle lay in the Courts, and his subjects viewed with apprehension the attempt to subvert the rights and liberties given by law. He died, and his young son became King. He could have stayed the conflict, for the nation would have welcomed with enthusiasm a change of monarch and of policy. One thing, however, it intended to secure—that the money which it granted should neither be fooled nor frittered away. Give them good government and they were satisfied. But Charles, like his father, fell under the spell of Buckingham, the one man whose hands Parliament was determined to keep from the public purse.

On his accession, Charles followed the usual practice of summoning a Parliament, the short-lived Parliament of 1625. The Commons demanded that supplies should be managed by persons in whom they could confide, and the affronted King at once dissolved Parliament. Conspicuous on the popular side in the debates was Sir Thomas Wentworth, the head of a notable Yorkshire family. Parnell, centuries later, had some of this man's qualities. He was a passionate and ambitious man, of swarthy countenance and harsh expression, bent on avenging his real or fancied slights at the hands of Buckingham. The favourite had thwarted Wentworth's natural ambition to hold the offices open to men of position in his county; a rival and enemy was preferred. So Wentworth ranged himself in opposition and added weight to that opposition.

Dissolution without grants did not solve Charles's financial problem, and so in 1626 a fresh Parliament was summoned. To silence opposition, many of the late Members were made sheriffs, which would at least prevent them from taking their seats. Wentworth, Coke and others were honoured by this attention, but the device was a failure, and the second Parliament was also dissolved, leaving all the problems unrelieved, with embittered feeling on both sides.

Buckingham had projected an expedition to the Isle of Rhé, and to finance it Charles resorted to the easy but illegal method of exacting forced loans. Wentworth, Eliot and others resisted the imposition, and were imprisoned. But the expedition miscarried; the money was spent; and in 1628 Charles summoned a third Parliament, which was certain to challenge the King's illegal actions. Wentworth desired an accommodation. It was not agreeable to any Englishman to see the realm weakened by disputes which could be avoided by tact and diplomacy. He proposed to Charles a measure which would declare the recent exactions illegal, but the King rejected it and thereby offended Wentworth and left the field free for Eliot, who, with the aid of Coke and Selden, forced on the King the Petition of Right, which asserted the illegality of those practices in a manner still more obnoxious to the monarch. So ended the first session.

Most Englishmen were satisfied, and many became reconciled to the Crown, especially as Buckingham's murder, in August, 1628, removed a grave cause of offence. Wentworth had been taken into favour in July, 1628. In quick succession he was created a baron, then a viscount and made President of the Council of the North. The Council had been created by Henry VIII after the Pilgrimage of Grace, and it exercised vague, but extensive, executive and judicial functions in the five northern counties. Its legality had been challenged, but Wentworth now held unquestioned authority in the North.

Next year a final breach occurred, and for eleven years Charles achieved the astonishing feat of reigning without a Parliament. Taxes were levied without legislative sanction; old feudal dues and rights were revived; and all classes were made to groan under exactions which were not the less resented because the payers believed, and with reason, that they were illegal.

Wentworth's trial has perhaps been the reason why the blame is so often put upon his shoulders, but he was not the King's sole, or even chief, adviser. Weston, the Lord Treasurer, succeeded to Buckingham's position as chief Minister, and when he died Wentworth was in Ireland. He became a Privy Councillor in 1629, and in 1632 he became Lord Deputy of Ireland, where he usually resided until 1639. He retained his English offices and remained in close contact with the English administration. Under his rule, Ireland began to prosper. He knew the art of managing a Parliament, and the body which met in 1634 was induced to make grants of such liberality that he was practically free from the need to summon it again.

He encouraged and developed trade, and has the credit for establishing the linen industry. But he was harsh and over-bearing, and by his imperious insistence on his own way alienated the English and Scottish settlers. His servants were held to their duty and given few opportunities for plunder, though the Lord Deputy had secured to himself an adequate share of the revenues. By his satellites in Council he exercised all administrative functions, and even claimed legislative and judicial powers. Dissentients were tried by court-martial. While thus alienating the settlers, he also alarmed them by raising forces from among the Irish and using them to enforce his decrees.

But next he roused the Irish. Under Elizabeth and James they had experienced the woes of being ejected to make way for settlers. Connaught, however, had escaped. Wentworth now laid claim to that province on the King's behalf. By practising on the judges, and packing and intimidating the juries he succeeded, in 1635 and the following years, in obtaining verdicts for the Crown. At the last moment, however, the project of a land settlement was abandoned. Affairs in Scotland had reached a crisis. In England they were rapidly approaching the critical stage, and there was no need to fling Ireland into the cauldron. Nevertheless, rebellion had become inevitable. But as it did not flare up until he lay in his grave, his responsibility was forgotten. Men only recalled that in his day he had maintained peace with a high hand and that under him the land had known prosperity.

All along Wentworth had been following with attention the course of events in England and Scotland. His chief correspondent was Laud, who became Archbishop of Canterbury in 1633. Between them they evolved the policy of "Thorough," and Wentworth sent a constant stream of advice and comment across St. George's Channel. There is no doubt that he realised his own high competence, and devoted it to the service of the King. He was no enemy of Parliaments, but by now he had reduced them in his mind to the rôle of a legislative body to whom was entrusted the task of providing the money that the administration needed. But in his opinion the function of Parliament, like the rule of law, was only for times of peace. When crises arose and the country was in danger from within or without, the King's will became supreme, over-riding all inconvenient forms or rules. Though he limited this special function to times of stress, it was not difficult for him to slide into the opinion that Parliamentary opposition to the King's views might itself afford such an occasion, and in any case his statement of the rule left it entirely to the King to decide when such an emergency had arisen or had ceased. But both he and Laud forgot that their policy of "Thorough" demanded as a condition of success that the royal support should be equally thorough, and Charles was not a companion upon whom a discriminating man would rely for the purpose of hunting the tiger.

By 1639 Wentworth had became necessary in England. The system of personal government was breaking down. With Laud's assistance Charles had as a sideshow been imposing an episcopal system upon the Scots, and Scotland was on the brink of revolt. No other Minister was so able as Wentworth. He was at once sent for. He was created Earl of Strafford, and in fact, if not in name, became the King's chief adviser. He counselled Charles to summon a Parliament. He had called one in Ireland himself, and it was a success, but in England the Commons, meeting early in 1640, demanded redress before supply, and were promptly dismissed. This, the fourth Parliament, earned the name of the Short Parliament. The Scots, who had taken up arms and come to an understanding, again began hostilities, defeating the King's forces and capturing Newcastle. Strafford had by now become Lieutenant-General—he never seems to have resigned any office he obtained—and shared the disgrace. He again advised a Parliament, and the Long Parliament came into being in 1640. Charles was in extremities, and the popular leaders, realising their opportunity, carried a motion to impeach Strafford and Laud. The haughty Lord-Deputy was arrested on his arrival from Ireland, and the two accused were lodged in safe custody in the Tower.

Impeachment was then the appropriate method of bringing a delinquent Minister to justice. The Commons prosecuted, by Members named by them as managers, and the Lords sat as judges. The tribunal was capable of resisting any royal influence.

The procedure adopted was to frame Articles of Accusation, to which the accused made a written reply. In this instance, the Commons accused Strafford of treason, by seven articles in general terms which were supplemented and explained by twenty-eight further articles which formed the statement of the charges made. They may be grouped under five heads. First, statements of policy and advice given, subversive of the fundamental laws of the realm and designed to bring about arbitrary government. Next he was accused of procuring a new and illegal commission to the Council of the North, and of using his powers to vex and oppress the people living within its district. Thirdly, there was Ireland, and the charges relating thereto were numerous. Instances were adduced of interfering with the administration of justice, of exercising martial law in time of peace, of treating disobedience to illegal orders of the Privy Council as crimes, of ejecting men from their estates without process of law and imprisoning such as resisted, of exacting taxes and enforcing decrees by the quartering of soldiers, of manipulating the Customs for his own profit to the detriment of traders, of enforcing his illegal and arbitrary exactions by fines, imprisonment and whipping, and of raising an army of Papists to be used in England. Fourthly, as to Scotland, he was accused of endeavouring to stir up strife between the English and Scots, and to break the Pacification between Charles and the Scots. Lastly came a series of charges relating to recent events: that he had advised the King that he was released from all rules; that he was a party to the exaction of Ship Money and other imposts; that he was concerned in the illegal jurisdiction of the Star Chamber; that in July, 1640, he advised the King to seize the bullion at the Mint, which belonged to private owners, and to debase the coinage; that in August, 1640, he had taxed Yorkshire to maintain his troops; that he had threatened the City of London in order to enforce a loan; and, finally, that he had procured the defeat of the army and the loss of Newcastle to stir up strife between England and Scotland. In short, nothing that had happened since 1628 had occurred except by his advice and procurement.

Strafford's reply is more interesting from its admissions than from its denials. Much he did deny; for many things he had the King's own command or express approval; for others he could point to many precedents. But as to Ireland, his answers are illuminating. Granting that the law was different, that martial law was always in force, that troops were habitually used to collect taxes and enforce decrees, the impression remains that in Ireland his will was supreme; that no law, custom or rule was strong enough to curb his actions. His explanations as to the Customs are plausible. A farmer of the Customs might safely rely upon his contentions, but for the Lord-Deputy to be that farmer was indefensible, and fraught with evident risk of irregularity and extortion.

As to the main charge that by counsel and advice he had assisted the endeavour to subvert the fundamental laws of the realm and to introduce arbitrary and tyrannical government against the law, his answer is of the utmost interest. He said (in effect): "What advice I gave I gave honestly, and it was my duty to the King to say what I honestly thought. It is true that I have at times given different advice, but no man can always be consistent. Further consideration often convinces one of error. But remarks of mine have been taken, in a mutilated form without any mention of the circumstances or of the necessary qualifications. Therefore I state now my doctrine of the Prerogative, viz., 'That in a case of absolute and unavoidable necessity, which neither would nor could be prevented by ordinary remedies provided by the laws, . . . His Majesty was absolved from ordinary rules and might use (in a moderate way as the necessity of the cause would permit) all ways and means for the defence of himself and his Kingdom: for in such extremity *Salus populi* was *suprema Lex*, provided it were not colourable nor anything demanded employed to other use, nor drawn into example when law and justice might take place, and that when peace was settled reparation was to be given to particular men, otherwise it would be unjust.' What is alleged misses out all my qualifications and the circumstances with regard to which it was spoken."

One may test this doctrine by the undoubted fact that he justified on this principle the levying of Ship Money in time of peace, when the need arose merely because the King and Parliament differed as to the terms on which a money grant should be made. His correspondence with Laud shows clearly that the law and lawyers were obnoxious to him; insistence upon obedience to due form hampered and circumscribed his domineering activities. How far he was to be trusted may be seen in the case of Loftus, Lord Chancellor of Ireland, whom he deprived of office and imprisoned. The cause alleged was disobedience to an Order in Council. This order was a command to execute a suitable settlement on Loftus's son on the occasion of his marriage. The bride was a lady with whom Strafford had an affair, for, like Wilkes, who was much uglier, the harsh and forbidding Viceroy was a notorious gallant. In short, it came to this: Loftus was imprisoned and deprived of office because he declined to sanction and subsidise his son's marriage with the Deputy's late mistress.

The time now came for the trial. Westminster Hall was fitted up for the occasion, with a throne for the King and seats for the Lords, the Judges and the bystanders. A curious structure adjoined the throne, a wooden room or cabinet wherein unseen the King and his young son (for the Queen soon wearied of the technical arguments) sat day by day hearing the tale of Strafford's tyranny and his constant proof that the King had commanded or approved the acts so denounced. On 22nd March, 1641, at 7 a.m., Strafford left the Tower by water escorted by six barges with 50 pairs of oars and 100 soldiers. At Westminster he was taken to the Hall by a guard of 200 of the train band. At 9 o'clock the King and Queen came, but did not show themselves. Various explanations were attempted for this attendance, unseen but not unknown. It would have been far better for them to come openly or stay away altogether. The Earl of Arundel was Lord High Steward, presiding over the Lords present. The Judges attended to advise the House, and the Commons were present in large numbers. The managers, of course, had special places assigned for them; the other Members had merely seats reserved for such as cared to come. The whole day, from 9 till 2, was occupied in reading the accusation and the answers. Two hours of this proved enough for the Queen, but Charles and his son sat it out till the end. Next day serious business began. Pym led for the Commons, assisted by Glyn, Maynard, Whitlock, Lord Digby, St. John, Palmer, Sir Walter Earle, Stroud, Selden and Hampden. Most of them were lawyers of repute. Pym opened the case in a long speech, and then Strafford made a short answer, speaking of his services to the State. After that Pym sprang a surprise by bringing forward three new Articles of Accusation. Strafford, not unnaturally, objected, but offered to waive objections if he could have time to make his answer. The Lords deliberated, and decided at length that though Strafford's objection and request were well founded in principle, the new articles were neither so numerous nor so weighty that he could not reply at once. The ground given is surprising in view of their nature, but no more was heard of them.

The three new charges were:

1. Withdrawing from the Exchequer in Ireland £40,000 for his own use.

2. Maintaining garrisons in Ireland at the cost of England.

3. Advancing Papists and infamous persons to high places in the Church of Ireland.

Strafford's surprise appears to have been merely forensic, for in answer to the first of them he produced on the spot the King's letter authorising the transaction and bearing the marks of the auditor who had passed the payment.

To the second he replied that he had so decreased the burden which existed before his time that he deserved thanks, and to the third that he acted on the advice of the best and wisest of the clergy. This closed the second day's proceedings.

On the third day, the Commons attempted to prove their accusations one by one. These were the 28 Articles, and each of the lawyers took charge of a group. Glyn began to prove

the treasonable words.   The first of these was that he said
at York Assizes in 1632 "That the King's little finger should
be heavier than the loins of the law."

It is unlikely that Strafford would, in the early days of a
young King, model his language so closely upon that of the
advice of the young men to Rehoboam.   His version is more
reasonable—that, on an occasion when some penalties imposed
by law were remitted, he had remarked that the little finger
of the law was heavier than the King's loins.   One witness
said he heard the President make the statement alleged when
he was nine yards away, and it was at once proved that for
years he had been too deaf to hear what was said three yards
away.   Strafford objected to Sir David Foulis as a witness on
the ground that he was a personal enemy, but the objection was
rightly overruled.   Such an objection is not to the admissibility
of his evidence, but to his being believed.   On the Thursday,
Glyn proceeded to prove that Strafford had said at Dublin,
in 1633, that Ireland was a conquered nation, and that the
King could do with it what he pleased.   Strafford explained
that he had pointed out that as Ireland was a conquered country
the King could have done what he pleased, but had determined
to give it the benefit of the laws; and admitted that he had
stated that the King's sentence was law in matters not determined by Act of Parliament.   But, as he pointed out, it did
not matter what the real version was, for a thousand such expressions would not make one felony, to say nothing of treason,
which was the charge against him.

On Friday came the proof of his saying: That he would
not suffer his ordinances to be disputed by lawyers before
inferior judicatories, and that he would make an Act of State
equivalent to an Act of Parliament.   Strafford retorted that
what he had said was: That he would not have his ordinances
contemned; and that obedience was due to Acts of State as
well as Acts of Parliament.   This concluded the proof of his
sayings, and on Saturday the Commons took up the particular
acts alleged.   The first was that he had sentenced Lord Mount-
morres to death by court-martial for resisting orders ejecting
him from his estates.   The fact was clear, and the defence set

up was that martial law was the accustomed course in Ireland, that the Court had acted without interference from him though he was present; and, furthermore, that he had the particular commands of His Majesty. In any event, it could not be high treason. This concluded the first week's proceedings.

Next week Glyn took up the sixth, eighth, ninth, tenth, and eleventh Articles, omitting the seventh, and then Maynard dealt with the twelfth. Palmer then followed with the second part of the fifteenth Article, saying nothing about the thirteenth, fourteenth and first part of the fifteenth, and concluded his part by taking the witnesses as to the sixteenth Article. Then Whitlock dealt with the nineteenth Article, omitting the two between, and the second week of the trial concluded. On Monday, 5th April, Whitlock proposed to take Articles 20 and 24 together. Strafford objected. Tuesday was a blank day, and on the Wednesday, Whitlock resumed with the twenty-fifth Article. The prisoner objected that what was alleged was not treason. Whitlock replied that they relied on the cumulative effect of all. To this Strafford retorted that talking in such a way was as much as to say "No treason at all," and he objected to the heaping of things together in order to bolster up an unfounded charge. Then came the evidence as to the twenty-sixth and twenty-seventh Articles, and the twenty-eighth was abandoned. This, charging him with responsibility for defeat and the loss of a fortress, would, if true, have supported a charge of treason, but it was manifestly absurd. Then Sir Walter Earl took up the twenty-second Article, but was so roughly handled that Lord Digby ended it by saying that their evidence was not ready, a statement which throws light on Whitlock's attempt to group Articles 20 and 24 together. On Friday, Strafford was ill. On Saturday, Glyn proposed to take the evidence on the twenty-second Article. The Lords refused; a deadlock ensued, and the Court adjourned. Sunday was a day of rumours, but when the fourth week began the two Houses were in conference, and eventually the evidence on both sides on the disputed Articles was waived. On Tuesday, 13th April, Strafford was called on for his defence. He stated his constitutional principle to be that the "Prerogative must be used, as

God doth his omnipotence, upon extraordinary occasion. The laws must have place at other times." He went through all the charges, denying and explaining and commenting upon the charges which had not been supported by evidence. Eventually he paused and confessed that he was unable to go on. Nature was exhausted. Pym replied, and this concluded the speeches on the evidence. So far Strafford had been alone against the Commons. In criminal trials prisoners were not allowed the aid of counsel on questions of fact. The Commoners who appeared were nearly all lawyers of tried worth, and they had managed the case as a team. Nevertheless, Strafford had held his own, and the next event was the argument on the legal question whether the facts given in evidence constituted treason. Upon that question counsel for the prisoner would be heard, and the Commons began to be afraid of their position. On Wednesday the House met, and it was proposed to proceed by Bill of Attainder. The suggestion was made that the offence was clearly treason within the words of the Statute of Treasons. Selden, Holborne and Bridgman pointed out that the words relied upon had been repealed, and treason depended upon the enacting words of the Statute. In spite of, or perhaps, indeed, because of, this objection, the Commons decided to proceed by Bill. On Thursday the two Houses met in conference. The Lords were inclined to continue the trial by hearing Strafford's counsel, but the Commons insisted upon the Bill and threatened a rupture. Friday saw the deadlock continue, but, as the Lords remained of the same mind, they resumed on the Saturday, when the managers attended, but sat as spectators among their colleagues. The prisoner's counsel were Lane, the Attorney-General to the Prince of Wales, Gardiner, the Recorder of London, Lee and Lightfoot. Lane argued at length that the evidence disclosed no treason. Gardiner followed, but pointed out the inconvenience of separating law from fact. They did not know what conclusions of fact had been arrived at, and until they did were unable to consider the evidence. On this the Lords adjourned, and the fourth week ended. Several days passed, and on Thursday, 29th April, a conference was held at which St. John endeavoured to satisfy the Lords that the most appropriate procedure was by Bill of Attainder. The King and Queen were present. The only speaker was St. John. Next day Strafford petitioned the Lords for his counsel to be heard again. On Saturday, 1st May, the King intervened. Addressing the Commons in person, he assured them that there was no project to bring the Irish army to England, nor had he been advised to establish arbitrary government. He declared that there was nothing against Strafford that deserved censure, and he was fit to hold any office. Charles ended by declaring that he would never in heart or hand concur with them to punish Strafford as a traitor.

Nevertheless, by 204 votes against 59 the Commons passed the Bill. On the 3rd May the unusual course was adopted of blacklisting the minority. Someone offered in Old Palace Yard a list of 55 "Straffordians" who voted against the Bill. All were not supporters of Strafford. Indeed, two of the managers, Lord Digby and Selden, figure in this list.

It is not easy to determine what was the real motive of the Commons' change of front, but there must have been some very cogent reason. One may conjecture that the object was, to remove the scruples of the Lords. There was an active minority devoted to the Court, and much influence was being brought to bear. On an impeachment, they would decide judicially, or should endeavour to do so, and the advice of the judges would weigh heavily. But on a Bill of Attainder the Lords were only called on to act legislatively, and scruples as to the law would not have the same weight. A peer might well be convinced on the evidence that Strafford deserved condign punishment, and yet hesitate to pronounce him guilty of treason. Such a doubter could perhaps vote for death on the Bill, but might vote for acquittal on the impeachment.

While the matter was pending in the Lords, Charles made a fatal move. He planned to seize the Tower and rescue his Minister. The Commons were well informed. Pym revealed the plot. The populace rose, and threatened the Queen and the Royal Family. In the excitement the Lords met to consider the Bill. It was a thin house, for a number stayed away from motives of prudence or fear. The Bill passed by 26 to 19, and it was left to Charles to decide whether to assent or not.

It is said, and perhaps with truth, that Strafford wrote to Charles, urging him to pass the Bill if he might thereby bring about an accord with his subjects. Yet, when the victim heard that the King had yielded and that he was to die, he received the news with surprise and bitterness. Once his fate was decided little time was lost, and on Wednesday, the 12th May, 1641, Strafford's head fell on the scaffold. His body was taken to Yorkshire for burial.

Was Strafford guilty of treason? The answer in strict law must clearly be in the negative. Treason is an offence against the allegiance due to the Sovereign in aid and counsel. The underlying theory of the Commons that there were fundamental laws, and that to aim at overturning them was treason, is erroneous. In legal theory there are in this country no laws, not even the Act of Settlement or the Act of Union, which Parliament may not alter as easily as a Statute providing for byelaws in a country parish. To break the law is a crime. To break the laws upon which civil liberty depends is a high crime. But to call treason that which falls clearly outside the terms of the Statute of Treason does not justify a conviction. He was charged with treason, but at best the evidence proved offences, heinous indeed to the last degree, but not treasonable. Nevertheless, if one sets aside the purely legal aspect of the case and regards it from the wider standpoint, there can be little doubt that Charles and his advisers were working to substitute arbitrary government for the rule of law. Strafford had shown himself to be a grave menace to the constitution, and in that untechnical sense he was a traitor.

Why did Charles abandon his Minister? He had declared in public that he would never do so. It is commonly said that he was moved by the clamour of the mob or by fear lest harm befall the Queen and her children. But even if it be true that Henrietta Maria disliked Strafford—and it is certain that the courtiers detested him—that would not be an explanation. It is true that the Commons demanded his life, but that was because he had ruthlessly carried out the King's policy, and the sacrifice would be in vain if that policy were not abandoned.

Yet Charles had no intention of giving up his aims, and to further them he needed able, resolute men, whom the memory of Strafford would thereafter deter from entering boldly upon a course which might evidently lead them to the scaffold.   Personal honour and clear policy demanded that the struggle should be determined then and for ever.   But Charles was a weak man, and he gave way.   Thereby not only did he lose his honour, but he signed his own death warrant.   The one man who could have carried out his policy was sacrificed, but the policy was continued.

"Put not your trust in Princes."

THE MAN WHO STOLE
THE KING'S CROWN

THE MAN WHO STOLE THE KING'S CROWN

Colonel Thomas Blood is believed to have been born in Ireland, so perhaps it is appropriate that his trial never took place at all. It is remarkable that this man, caught in the act in a daring crime with which the whole town rang, was pardoned before his examination was completed, and thus cheated the gallows. His audacity saved him. Charles II loved a daring scoundrel, and Blood played a last card when he bluffed his captors into bringing him before the King. He left the audience a free man, not only pardoned but with his estates restored.

The days of the Merry Monarch were noted for the good fortunes of the nimble witted adventurer. The Restoration had by a turn of the wheel changed Charles from a claimant to a King, and re-action set in from the stern rule of public conduct enjoined by the Puritan régime. Men and women seemed to devote their time and energy to the pursuit of wanton pleasure, and the monarch led the dance and set the pace. But Blood was not of this stamp. He had been a Cromwellian and to his dying day was ranked as a Presbyterian. The Restoration which had confirmed the fortunes of the Monks and Montagues was the cause of his ruin. He refused to rally round the throne, plunged into treason, raised rebellion and made himself known as a daring opponent ready at all times and places to strike a blow for vengeance. The gates of Dublin Castle, a lonely road near Doncaster, and St. James's Street in London, had all been scenes of exploits which had made him famous before he set the seal on his consummate audacity by depriving the King of his Crown in 1671.

It is not quite certain when or where he was born. Some authorities say that it was in 1618 in Ireland, and those data

will serve.   His father was a blacksmith in Ireland, but a prosperous one, for he acquired iron works.   When the Civil War
broke out, Thomas Blood was a vigorous young man and he
joined the Parliamentary forces.   He rose rapidly and when
fighting ceased he was a Colonel.   He went to Ireland with
the Army when the "curse of Cromwell" fell upon that unhappy country, and was one of the mainstays of the Cromwellian rule there.   Henry Cromwell rewarded him with grants
of forfeited estates, so that when the King came to his own
again, Blood lost an income of £500 a year and was thrown
into opposition and poverty at one stroke.   He made no attempt at reconciliation but was marked as a "sectary"—a
dangerous man, "bloody, bold and resolute" who needed careful
watching.

For a time the Puritan party in Ireland remained quiet,
biding their opportunity.   By 1663 they thought the chance
had come.   The Duke of Ormonde ruled Ireland for the King,
and the King needed money for his pleasures too urgently to
pay for the necessary services.   An army was essential if Ireland was to be held, but the soldiers, like the civil officials,
were allowed to be in arrears with their pay, and discontent
grew among the very men whose loyalty was an indispensable'
condition for the maintenance of government.   The "Sectaries"
thought that the season was at hand and planned a rising.
Some practised upon the Members of Parliament in Dublin,
others on the troops.   But something more was needed.   It
was essential to seize Ormonde and Dublin Castle in order to
capture the whole machinery of government.   To do so, a
body of desperate men was needed, and above all an able,
resolute leader.   To the conspirators it seemed that Blood was
the right man for this enterprise, and he entered into the
design with zest and zeal.   All was prepared and the rising
was planned for 9th March, 1663, when, a week before that
date, one Arden betrayed the plot, and Ormonde began to prepare reprisals.   Many men would have fled, but Blood was not
of that stamp.   The Lord Lieutenant knew the date; well then,
nothing was more simple than to throw him out by altering the
date to the 5th, and so it was arranged.   There were more

informers than one, however, and Ormonde struck on the 4th. Many were arrested and afterwards tried, convicted and executed. Blood had received warning and got away. He did not go far. His brother-in-law had been seized, and Blood's first thought was to rescue him. He made the attempt and nearly succeeded. After this failure he lurked about in secret places in Ireland sheltering among the disaffected, but at last the pursuit became too close and he departed for Holland.

It is eloquent testimony to the difficulty of communication in those days that Charles did not learn of the plot until all was over. It was not till 1st June that Pepys visiting the King's Court found that the place was ringing with the news of Blood's plot, as it was called. By that time the enterprise was mere history, its leaders were in their graves, all but Blood, who was abroad. He did not remain long in foreign lands. It was soon found that he was in London associating with the Fifth Monarchy Men, a set of fanatics, who were conspiring to establish a republican theocracy in England. Their plot miscarried, but Blood again escaped. From now onwards he was a marked man, but the authorities could never find him. So often did he offend, so open was he in his daring, that suspicion grew. Perhaps they did not want to find him. He was known to be a desperate and ruined rebel. Every disaffected man in England knew that, and so did the Government. Blood had learned that there was one safe method of dabbling in treason, and that was to betray the traitors, and it is now believed that while in Holland he had come to an understanding with the Government and had purchased immunity by becoming a spy. Wherever revolt was threatened, there was Blood to be found. Perhaps he was always sincere in his political opinions, but there were two things that he desired above all others—to escape an ignominious death and to obtain restitution of his forfeited estates. To secure these objects, others might be sacrificed provided always they were not his relatives or friends, for to them, in an odd perverted way, he was loyal.

After the Fifth Monarchy Men had failed, Blood went to Scotland and joined the Covenanters. With them he served at the Battle of Pentland Hills on 27th November, 1666, and after that disastrous defeat he returned to England pursued by the royal officers who chased him into Ireland and thence back to England. His friend Captain Mason had been unlucky and was awaiting trial. The Assizes were about to be held in the North and Mason was sent from London under an escort of eight soldiers picked for the purpose by the Duke of York himself. All went well until the troop were nearing Doncaster, when on a lonely road they were suddenly attacked by Blood and three friends, who rescued Mason and left most of the escort dead on the field.

This exploit caused a fresh sensation and a price of £500 was set on Blood's head, but he removed quietly to Kent, where he lived for a long time as Thomas Allen, a physician.

In November, 1670, William Prince of Orange visited England and there were great celebrations at Court. James, Duke of Ormonde, was naturally one of the guests and attended the rejoicings. Years had passed since the Duke had dispossessed Blood and had crushed his Irish plot, but the latter had neither forgotten nor forgiven him. In November, 1670, the Duke left St. James's Palace in his coach and was driving up St. James's Street, when he was stopped by Blood with five others. They dragged the Duke from his coach, bound him and mounted him behind one of the party who began to gallop off to Tyburn. The object was to hang him on the gallows there as a common malefactor. Blood had gone hot foot to get the gallows ready, and was not in charge of the Duke. The prisoner did not lose his head. He struggled with his captor and just by Devonshire House succeeded in throwing him from the horse, but, being bound to him, the two fell together. While struggling on the ground, the Duke's coachman arrived and rescued his master. Again Blood escaped, and this time rumour had it that he had acquired a patron, the Duke of Buckingham, whose enmity towards Ormonde was notorious.

Another account is given of this outrage. It was suggested that Blood merely meant to hold the Duke to ransom until his estates were restored. It is difficult to accept this theory. The lands were in Ireland, the prisoner was in

England, hard to hold in captivity and as a captive highly dangerous to the safety of his captors. Moreover, once the Duke got free, he could with perfect lawfulness and propriety repudiate his deed and hang the man who had extorted it. A swift revenge alone was possible, and men of the time believed that Blood sought the Duke's life.

No one was arrested, though the affair had taken place in the highway near the fields of Mayfair. But Blood was not satisfied. He had been baulked of vengeance and his estates were still forfeited. A man without means has a hard life at best, and Blood had been brought up to the profession of arms. He meditated on his position, and one day he had a great idea—he would hold the King to ransom, not in person, but by means of his treasure.

The Crown Jewels were kept at the Tower. They were not numerous. Since John had lost the Regalia in the Wash, successive Kings had formed a store of jewels and from time to time the need of money had forced them to part with them. The Crown had been pawned at times. During the Civil War the furnishing of armies had led the first Charles to part with most of his jewels, and Cromwell had seized what were left. On the Restoration Charles II had succeeded to a scanty inheritance in that respect, and the gifts that he lavished on his favourites had prevented him from making many additions. Nevertheless he was possessed of all the ornaments necessary for a Coronation, the Crown, the Orb, the Sceptre and the other costly things. They were in charge of Mr. Talbot Edwards, Keeper of the Crown Jewels, an aged man who kept them in a strong room in his official residence at the Tower. To reach them it was necessary to pass the gateway and the guards, and the problem of abstracting them, now insoluble, was then difficult enough to daunt all but the most daring and skilful.

Sometimes the Keeper would shew his precious charges to the public, to whom the Tower has always been a place of interest. Early in 1671 he received two visitors who were anxious to see the Crown before they returned to their country home. One was a swarthy country parson in the flowing cloak that clergymen then wore, and the other was his wife. The parson was Blood on a reconnoitring expedition. Who the woman was no one could ever find out, for Blood would never say. It was not his wife, since she was lying sick at her parents' home in Lancashire. The two were shewn the Crown and the other things, but while they were admiring them the lady became faint and giddy. Edwards called his wife, who ran to administer aid to the poor woman. She was given restoratives and permitted to lie down on Mrs. Edwards' bed, while Edwards and the parson conversed in the Jewel Room. At length the lady revived and was escorted away by the parson, who was loud in his expression of thanks. Nor did he stop at words. Three or four days later he came again with a present of white gloves for Mrs. Edwards. Naturally, friendly relations were set up, especially as the parson was of such irreproachable loyalty, as his conversation showed. He saw the daughter, a young girl of great beauty, just of marriageable age. He was much impressed by her and eagerly enquired whether a husband had been found for her. As it happened, her parents were thinking about the matter, but as yet no candidate had been considered. This was indeed fortunate, for the good clergyman had a nephew, just come of age, who had succeeded to a nice landed estate and was looking for a wife. He must arrange for him to visit the young lady with a view to paying her addresses. The Edwards were charmed. They asked him to stay to dinner and were much edified by his pious conversation. He was now a friend of the family, perhaps soon to be related to them, and of course he was welcome to call whenever he pleased. The unsuspecting Edwards made much of him. Matters progressed rapidly, and soon it was arranged that the nephew should pay a *visite de cérémonie* on the 9th May, 1671. The hour was fixed at 7 a.m., for in those days, even without summer time, people were up and about their work long before this hour, which was late enough for such an important call.

The day came and, as the hour approached, Miss Edwards retired with her mother to be suitably attired for the all important first impression. Dressing was then, as now, a lengthy business, and they were safely out of the way when the reverend gentleman was announced with two friends of the family. A fourth member of the party was outside, but Edwards did not know this. One may explain at once that one of the two men with Blood was a man named Parrot, who was, it is believed, the man of that name who had been lieutenant to Major General Harrison, the regicide. Parrot was afterwards hanged, in 1685, for his part in Monmouth's rebellion. There must be a delay, explained the parson, his nephew could not come with them but was following on after. Perhaps Mr. Edwards could while away the time by shewing the friends the Crown Jewels. The old man had no reason for refusing to satisfy so innocent and loyal a curiosity, and accordingly they went to the Jewel Room, where the chest was unlocked and the glittering emblems of royalty were produced. The next stage was soon over. As soon as the jewels were produced, Edwards was seized and gagged. In spite of his surprise he struggled. Fearing that the noise would alarm the house, they struck him with mallets that had been concealed in their clothes. He still struggled, and endeavoured to raise an alarm, so Blood drew a sword from under his cloak and ran the poor man through. He fell apparently dead, and the three men proceeded to work. Blood seized the Crown and crushed it together to hide under his cloak. Parrot was wearing loose breeches and they formed a convenient bag in which to put the Orb. The sceptre had been taken by the other man. Blood had thought over the problem of the sceptre. It was too long to conceal, and he had adopted the plan of cutting it in half. A file was produced, and the third thief was busy filing it in two when the outpost raised an alarm.

He had been loitering outside for some time. Miss Edwards was naturally anxious to know what manner of man it was to whom her parents were thinking of giving her. She sent her maid to watch for his arrival and the girl saw the fourth man. She jumped to the conclusion that this was the nephew and went back to report to her mistress. This circumstance prevented the ladies being suspicious and gave them a fresh topic of conversation and so delayed them further. But while the miscreants were preparing to cut the Sceptre, young Talbot Edwards came up. He was newly arrived on leave from his regiment in Flanders. The watcher stopped him, much to his indignation, and he went off to find his mother and sister. They went to speak to Edwards and could not find him. As they were searching, he recovered consciousness and his daughter heard a voice in the Jewel Room feebly calling "Treason. The Crown is stolen." They burst in and found him lying bathed in blood. The Sceptre had been cast aside but the three men and the Crown and Orb had gone.

The news of young Edwards' approach had alarmed the confederates, and they departed from the Tower as rapidly as they dared, without alarming the guard. Hardly had they emerged on to Tower Hill when young Edwards came up with the captain of the guard and raised a hue and cry.

Parrot found the Orb was hindering him and abandoning it fled among the crowd and was lost. The other two men also found safety in flight. Blood with the Crown under his cloak had just remounted the horse upon which he had arrived. He set spurs to it and was all but beyond pursuit when his horse slipped and fell. Before he could rise his pursuers seized him, and at last he was in captivity. The Crown was retaken and the prisoner was brought back to the Tower. He had been in many tight corners before, but never so tight a one as this. He had committed a capital offence and that not merely against a private citizen, but against the King, and this after many years of plotting and treason with a price upon his head.

The news aroused the whole town, who looked forward to a sensational trial to be followed by a public execution with all the thrilling barbarities to which they had become accustomed by the execution of the regicides. They waited with expectancy, but no trial seemed to be pending, and then to everyone's astonishment Blood reappeared in public, attending at Court, prosperous and in favour. How was it done? Everyone was curious, and soon it was whispered that Blood's audacity had once more pulled him through.

As soon as he was taken, he was brought before Dr. Chamberlain, whose duty it was to interrogate him after the custom of the day. Not a word could he get out of Blood except that he would say nothing to anyone save Charles himself. In this fix, Dr. Chamberlain called in Sir William Waller. He too was met with the same reply. Charles was naturally curious and to him was repeated the prisoner's refusal to say anything but to the King himself. The monarch was interested, and decided to humour the prisoner. Accordingly, due precautions having been taken, Blood was ushered into the Presence.

The interview justified his hopes. He took a high line. The plan was his he admitted, and he had adopted it to revenge his wrongs. He refused to say who his associates were, but threatened Charles with their vengeance if ill befell their leader. The risk was great, he admitted, but then the prize was a Crown for which a man might well risk his life. This point would appeal to Charles, who, at Worcester, had risked his life for the Crown in another sense. As to the Ormonde outrage, Blood frankly admitted that he organised it for revenge. Then he played a master card. He told the King that he had gone to assassinate him while he was bathing at Battersea—then the Thames at that spot was a limpid stream—but had been restrained, though the King was at his mercy, because the sight of His Majesty had filled him with awe, and he was unable to do him harm. Charles admired the bold, unscrupulous adventurer, and granted him a pardon for all his offences. Moreover, he restored to him the forfeited estates. Thenceforth Blood was a man of means and of mark. He could appear openly in the streets where men would point at him with wonder. No one else had done so much and escaped the gallows. The Duke of Buckingham introduced him to Court, where he frequently appeared. Ministers invited him to dinner, and thus it is that we have a description of him by Evelyn, who met him later in the year at the Treasurer's house. The Treasurer was then the chief Minister of Finance. "This man," wrote Evelyn, "had not only a daring but a villainous, unmerciful look, a false countenance, but very well spoken and dangerously insinuating." This gives us a clue as to the reason why Charles took such an extraordinary view

of the crime. He was defied by an audacious flatterer, who
went just far enough to excite admiration without incurring
resentment. Evelyn mentions the belief that Blood owed his
previous immunity to being a spy, since otherwise it seemed
inexplicable.

Though received into favour, Blood did not turn his coat.
Throughout the rest of his life he was classed as a Presbyterian
and regarded as one who would take up arms if ever the extreme dissenting party raised a revolt. He was wont to asso-
ciate with congenial spirits at an inn in Westminster Market.
Most of them, like himself, had been officers in Cromwell's
Army, and then in 1679 Dangerfield thought fit to confess that
he had been suborned to invent a Presbyterian plot so as to
further Papist designs. Blood, he said, was down in the list as
the head of one section of the conspiracy, in charge of men who
until the occasion were to act as messengers, and on a call to
arms would lead the troops, when Blood was to be a Major-
General. It is not necessary to enter into an unravelling of
Dangerfield's testimony. It is at best suspect, but it does
prove that Blood was then counted as he always had been, an
active and determined Presbyterian.

He had been watched for years by men of less adventurous
life and courage to see when he would make that false step
which they felt sure would lead him to the gallows in the end.
In 1680 it seemed that the day was at hand. He had quar-
relled with Buckingham and was arrested on a charge of conspiring to charge his former patron with atrocious crimes. It
seemed that he was tricked into speaking when it would have
been wiser to remain silent. The Duke took proceedings and
claimed £10,000 damages. Blood was committed into custody
but found bail. Once more the town looked forward to a sensational trial, and once again was disappointed. The prisoner
fell ill, and after a short illness, died on 24th August, 1680. So
tame an ending to such a life seemed unnatural. The rumour
spread that the court was being deceived by a sham death and
burial. Consequently the coroner decided to hold an inquest.
The grave was opened and the dead body of Blood was found
lying in the coffin. At the inquest the body was duly identified,

and was re-buried.   No one had expected him to die a natural death, but throughout his life he had constantly disappointed expectations.

It remains to be stated that Edwards did not die.   The wound though dangerous was not mortal.   Charles rewarded his faithful servant, though not so generously as he did the assailant.   Nevertheless the public interest in the Crown jewels so nearly lost rewarded him with many perquisites and he lived to a ripe old age, repeating to every questioner the story of the man who stole the crown.

THE TRIAL OF GREEN AND OTHERS
FOR THE MURDER OF
SIR EDMUNDBURY GODFREY

THE TRIAL OF GREEN AND OTHERS FOR THE MURDER OF SIR EDMUNDBURY GODFREY

THE murder of Sir Edmundbury Godfrey was one of the great mysteries of crime, and though three men were convicted and hanged for his murder, many of its aspects remain mysterious to this day.

First as to the man himself. He was the eighth son of a family of twenty children, was educated at Christ Church, Oxford, and destined for the Bar. But though he entered at Grays Inn he was never called, because he became too deaf for active practice. Being thereby deprived of a career, he took to trade, and prospered greatly as a woodmonger, with a wharf at Westminster, near Charing Cross. During the Great Plague of 1665 his active benevolence to sufferers ruined by the desert which fear of infection had made of London was rewarded by a knighthood. He was chiefly renowned for his merits as a magistrate. At that time justices were expected to take an active part in the detection of crime and the apprehension of offenders. Godfrey, though some carped at him as being fussy, vain and interfering, had earned the reputation of being the best justice in England. In spite of his activities he was everywhere known as a good neighbour, and lived at peace with the world, at least with all law-abiding citizens, and he was noticeably on good terms with the Roman Catholics.

Such was the man who, in the late afternoon of the 12th October, 1678, went from his house near Charing Cross to make a prolonged call near St. Clement's Danes. He was never seen again alive. His prolonged absence caused well-grounded fears for his safety, and it was suggested that he had been murdered by the Roman Catholics. It was hinted that the object of the murder was to burke enquiry into their treasonable practices. When, on the morning of the 17th October, his corpse was found in a ditch by the fields at Primrose Hill, public suspicion became certainty. An attempt had been made to suggest suicide. The dead man's sword was in his body, as if he had deliberately fallen upon it. But this attempt only made matters worse. Even in those days surgical knowledge could pronounce with confidence that the wounds were inflicted after death, and that Godfrey had been violently done to death some days before. Obviously this was a case of murder.

Who were the assassins? In the then state of public opinion there could be no doubt that they were Roman Catholic plotters. Even before the body was found, steps had been taken to search for the offenders among the Catholic population. It seemed so obvious. For some little time before, one Israel Tongue had been suggesting a Catholic conspiracy; he had been joined by Titus Oates, and on 26th September, 1678, Oates had seen Godfrey; had lodged sworn informations with him, and the worthy magistrate was actively investigating the allegations. Besides that, he had disappeared on his way back along the Strand. But in the Strand stood Somerset House, not the present building, but its predecessor, the residence of the Queen, and a hive of Catholics. One of the men arrested was Praunce, employed in the Queen's service, and he had confessed, implicating a number of men in the actual commission of the offence. Three were seized—Robert Green, Henry Berry and Lawrence Hill; three more, of whom two, if not all, were priests, had made good their escape. And on 10th February, 1679, these men were indicted in the King's Bench for the murder. It was a trial *in banc,* before the Lord Chief Justice, Scroggs, whose reputation for vileness is second only to that of Jeffreys, and two puisne judges, Wild and Dolben. This trial was the first of a remarkable series which prove, not, indeed, the existence of a Papist Plot, but the intensity with which the people of England believed that there was such a plot, and the firmness of their intention to preserve the religious and civil liberties of England.

The Counsel for the Crown were an imposing array. The

Attorney-General (Sir William Jones), the Solicitor-General (Sir Francis Winnington), Serjeant Stringer, and the redoubtable Jeffreys, then Recorder of London. By the end of the year four of the judges and counsel had lost their places. Scroggs and Wild had resigned, the Attorney and Solicitor-General had lost their offices. Mr. Justice Dolben was dismissed in 1683. Stringer and Jeffreys had increased their prospects. Stringer was promoted in 1679, and later became a judge. As in the case of Jeffreys, the Revolution proved fatal to his career. But in February, 1679, all these men were in power, and they all believed in the Plot. So did Parliament. So did the people. With that belief in high places, with the populace howling for blood, it is not to be expected that the prisoners would have a fair trial. The times were almost the worst in our history for prisoners charged with offences coloured by a political tinge. Everyone, including the prisoners themselves, knew what the result would be unless a miracle happened.

This was the story related by the prosecution, and if it be believed, then the prisoners were guilty: On 12th October, Green went to Godfrey's house, telling the maid that he had business with her master. He and Hill were both there that morning, and their purpose, it was suggested, was to dog Sir Edmundbury's movements. Soon after midday, Godfrey went to a house near St. Clement's Danes and stayed till past seven in the evening. To reach his house he would go along the Strand, passing Somerset House. And here conspirators were waiting to do him to death. As soon as the watchers reported him to be on his way, the prearranged scheme was put into execution. A man called the justice into Somerset House on the cry that two of the Queen's servants were fighting. At first he refused, thinking that it was an ordinary scuffle, but at last yielded to importunity and went through the gateway into the courtyard. As soon as he was fairly inside, the doors were closed. He went forward to a fight then being acted by Berry and a priest named Kelly. As he approached the fight stopped abruptly. Berry, who was a porter there, went to guard the Water Gate. Praunce was already watching the back gate into the Strand. As peace was restored, Godfrey's visit had ceased to have any object. He hesitated, and decided to go away. As he began to move Green came behind him and put a cravat round his neck and twisted it, much in the same manner as the Thugs murdered their victims. As soon as he did this, Hill, Kelly and a second priest named Gerald threw themselves on to the victim, and soon they had to all appearance despatched him. Praunce came forward to satisfy himself, and noticed that his legs were twitching, and in order to make sure Green twisted the head right round. Father Gerald wanted to make even more sure. He suggested running the body through with a sword, but the others objected because the blood could not be removed and would be visible to everyone the next morning.

Then came the ordinary difficulty. How was the body to be disposed of? A temporary hiding place was easily found. The corpse was taken to Hill's rooms in Somerset House, and there kept for a short time. It was later shifted to another room, and on the Monday, two days after the murder, which was on a Saturday, it was removed to a third room, where it lay on the floor covered by a cloak. But removing the body from room to room within the limits of Somerset House was a mere temporary expedient, and soon it would become impossible to conceal its presence. Accordingly they hit upon the plan of removing it in a sedan chair. They procured one and put the body inside, forcing it into a sitting position. Berry was porter at the Strand Gate, and when a man stationed outside gave a prearranged signal that the coast was clear, Praunce and Gerald acting as chairmen carried the chair into the street. At Covent Garden they were so wearied by their unaccustomed toil that they had perforce to stop. Hill and Kelly relieved them and they went to Long Acre, where these two called a halt. Praunce and Gerald again took over, and thus they reached a spot near the Grecian Church hard by Soho. There they met a man who had brought a horse, upon which they set the body with its feet tied under the horse's belly. For greater security

Hill mounted up behind, and thus they came to the fields by Primrose Hill. At a suitable spot they deposited their burden in a ditch, having first caused it to fall on Godfrey's own sword. Near the spot they left some of the dead man's belongings, and they carefully left all his money in the clothes, so that everything he had when last seen was found upon him or near him. Having thus prepared an apparent suicide, they left in the darkness of the night.

Early next morning the constable found the body, and the coroner was summoned. Two surgeons came and found that Godfrey had been dead for days, and were convinced that the wounds were inflicted after death. Indeed it is difficult to imagine how anyone could have hoped that the jury would find a verdict of *felo-de-se*. The neck was obviously broken by violence, and not by self-inflicted violence. No one presumably would twist the neck of a man who had killed himself by falling on his own sword, and no one could do that so as to leave him in the position in which he had impaled himself. Nor could the deceased after all have thrown himself on to his own sword not once, but twice, after someone had broken his neck. Besides, a surgeon would obviously be summoned, and unless extraordinarily ignorant could not fail to see at once that the wounds were inflicted long after life was extinct. The point is material, since the priests and Praunce were men of education and standing. More startling than this act of stupidity, the offenders, so the prosecution alleged, wrote an account of the murder and called a convivial meeting of priests at the King's Head (or Queen's Head) at Bow, to rejoice over the deed, at a time when a hue and cry after the Catholics was in its earliest intensity.

The first witness was Titus Oates. This was his earliest appearance in that capacity. He merely proved that he had lodged sworn informations with the dead man. Then Godfrey's friend, Thomas Robinson, a superior officer of the Court of Common Pleas, told how Godfrey had confided to him that he feared the investigation would lead to his becoming the first martyr.

Then came Praunce. He had been early arrested and ex-

amined by the Privy Council, who committed him to prison.
While there, he made a confession, and was then released.
Once released he retracted his confession, and was at once re-
arrested. This induced him to change again, and he again
confessed. He was once more released, but apparently kept
under observation. The prisoners alleged that Praunce confessed under torture, but he denied this and said that he had
retracted his confession because his life was in danger. So
intent were the prosecution on establishing his credit that they
called a Captain Richardson to prove that Praunce had told
him that he withdrew his confession from fear, and also that
he had become a Protestant. They also called Sir Robert
Southwell to prove that Praunce had, without any hesitation,
taken him to the various places he had mentioned in his
confession. This impressed the Court immensely, though
Praunce, by reason of his position, should know his way about
Somerset House, and he would not be likely to name places
in parts which he did not know. However that may be,
Praunce gave his evidence as to the plot, the murder, the disposal of the body and the merry meeting of the priests at
Bow. Hill objected to the evidence as perjured by the witness's
own retraction, but to Scroggs it was enough that that retraction was not on oath. As might be expected, the prisoners,
deprived of counsel, made a poor show at cross-examination.
Scroggs took the opportunity of forcing each prisoner to
admit that he knew Praunce.

After him came William Bedloe, only second to Titus
Oates in the subsequent prosecutions. He, too, was making
his début. He introduced himself with a short speech about
his acquaintance with Jesuits and how they asked him to
murder some man unnamed. Then he was set to make
acquaintance with Godfrey. Soon after undertaking this
task he met Father Gerald. On the night of the murder
his Jesuit friends told him that an unnamed person was to be
put out of the way. He asked who it was and was told that
it was the man who had received the information from Oates
and Tongue. They gave him a rendezvous at Somerset
House, but the righteous Bedloe, realising that murder was

afoot, kept away. On the Monday, however, he was taken to
see the body and recognised who it was. He apparently never
met any of the prisoners, though he said that on that occasion
he had seen Green in the courtyard. Hill denied ever having
seen him, and indeed he did not claim to know either Hill
or Berry.

It is easy to form a confident opinion that Bedloe's evidence
is a vague denunciation of unknown Jesuits, trimmed to agree
with Praunce. He had to be careful, because the Crown
might not want more than one participant in the murder,
and if he had confessed to a greater share in the crime his
danger would be extreme. But he had not come forward
to risk his neck. If believed, his evidence corroborates Praunce
but is intrinsically worthless.

After him came the constable who found the body, and
the surgeons. And the prosecution concluded with witnesses
to prove that Hill and Green had been to Godfrey's house
pretending business, that the prisoners knew and consorted
with Praunce, Gerald and Kelly and as to the congratulatory
evening of the priests at Bow. During the closing stages
the Lord Chief Justice made some characteristically unjudicial
remarks as to the way the Papists committed perjury.

Then Hill called his evidence. The first was the housekeeper at his place of service. She said Hill was trustworthy
and never out after dark. Scroggs elicited from her the admission that she was a Papist and did not conceal his conclusion that she was capable of perjury. Jeffreys weighed
in with an edifying hope that she did not spend the whole
night with Hill. In the badgering that followed she by a slip
said that she and the family were out of town in October. The
prosecution and the judges were delighted. In vain she tried
to correct it, and was supported by the maid, who was clear
in her detailed statement that they were away in September.
These two women lived in the house where Praunce said the
body was first put. Their evidence that they were constantly
in the room and that no corpse could have been placed there
without their knowledge was met by a solemn statement from
the Bench that it was indeed well for the maid that she was

not indicted.   That may do for the trial, but it is the fact
that three respectable women (for a second maid gave similar
evidence) faced the ordeal of that trial to prove that the body
was never there.   If they were right, then Praunce's evidence
was untrue on a point where mistake was impossible, and
if he invented one incident what becomes of his credit?   The
first maid, too, had to admit that her brother was a priest.
A man named Gray gave evidence which told neither way.
The next witness, How, called to give evidence as to Hill's
movements during the day, tried to make the Court believe
that he was a Protestant.   He was caught out and mangled
in cross-examination.   Other witnesses were called as to Hill's
movements.   One spoke of the night when Hill was arrested.
Scroggs failed to see the relevance of this, till Hill explained
that it showed that he knew that the murder had been discovered in ample time to escape, had he been guilty.   The
judge countered this point with "And so you would, if you
had thought they would have been so nimble with you."   Hill's
last witness was as to character, and came after Green's
evidence had begun.   The judges at once attacked him as to his
religion.   He led them on, and they were sure that they had
caught another Papist, but the Attorney-General, seeing that
they were about to fall into a trap, informed them that this
man was a Protestant.

Green called his landlord and his landlord's wife and the
maid.   They were hazy about dates, and finally the wife,
by making a calculation, hit what was obviously the wrong day.

Then Berry, the porter, took up his defence.   He called
Corporal Collett, who swore that no sedan chair left by the
Strand Gate of Somerset House on the night of 16th October.
He was supported by the sentinel, one Trollop.   If this
evidence were true, then the whole story of the disposal of
the body was a lie of Praunce's.   The judges tried to get
them to admit that they were away tippling, but they denied
this.   No attempt was made to suggest that these men were
not on guard, or to call any rebutting evidence on this point.
At this stage Mrs. Hill was allowed to suggest that Praunce
had been tortured.   She was not ejected for the interruption,

but Praunce was recalled to deny it. She also complained that the Court merely laughed at the witnesses for the defence.

After these witnesses came the speeches. The Attorney-General excused himself from making a long speech on the ground that the prosecution had proved stronger and the defence weaker than he could have foreseen. The Solicitor-General followed, mainly devoting himself to vindicating Praunce.

Scroggs's summing-up was not long and need not be described. At one stage Berry interrupted to say that he had never spoken to the dead man in his life. The judge retorted: "You must say and believe what your priest would have you." It would have been more effective to have reminded Berry that no one had ever said that he had. Scroggs's conclusion was:

"But in short, there is a monstrous evidence of the whole plot itself by this fact; for we can ascribe it to none but such ends as this that such a man must be killed; for it must be either because he knew something which the priests would not have him to tell, or they must do it in defiance of justice and in terror to all that dare execute it upon them; which carries a great evidence in itself and which I leave to your consideration, having remembered as well as I could the proofs against them and all that is considerable for them. Add to this the condition that we are all in at this time and the eagerness of the pursuit that these priests make to gain the kingdom, that for my part I must put it into my Litany, 'That God would deliver me from the delusions of Popery and the tyranny of the Pope,' for it is a yoke which we who have known freedom cannot endure and a burden which none but that beast who was made for burden will bear. So I leave it to your consideration upon the whole matter, whether the evidence of the fact does not satisfy your consciences that these men are guilty. And I know that you will do like honest men on both sides."

After this plain hint the honest men retired, but soon came back with a verdict of "Guilty." Scroggs expressed his concurrence, saying, "If it were the last word I should

speak in this world I should have pronounced them 'Guilty,' "
and at this the bystanders broke out in rapturous applause.

Next day the prisoners were sentenced in due form by
Mr. Justice Wild, and ten days later they were all hanged,
protesting their innocence till the last.

After this for some months Oates, Bedloe, Dangerfield
and others were busy denouncing Papists, many of whom
were tried and executed. Oates at last got too bold. He
even attempted to accuse the Queen. Finally Scroggs himself refused to believe Oates. In 1680 came the constitutional
struggle over the Exclusion Bill. Then followed a reaction
in which James, a declared Catholic, was allowed by Charles,
a secret one, to wreak vengeance on Oates. He was cast
in £100,000 damages for libel, and, convicted of perjury,
was sentenced to lifelong imprisonment with intervals of
whipping at the cart-tail and the pillory. After the
Revolution he regained his liberty and was given a pension,
but his credit was hopelessly gone. William of Orange had
no need for a perjurer like Oates.

Were these men guilty? The trial goes for nothing. It
was a travesty of justice, but an unfair trial is no evidence
of innocence. If Praunce be believed, then they were all
implicated in the murder, but Praunce is discredited not
only by his repeated confessions and withdrawals, but also
by the contradiction of his story in two capital respects. Besides, what could be gained by murdering Godfrey? It is
true Scroggs suggested terror, but prisoners and criminals
have always realised that that weapon is potent only against
witnesses, and the witnesses remained unmolested. It is
indeed possible that investigation, if pursued, might have
revealed a plot—not that concocted by Oates and his crew,
but a real one—but even then no Government would have
stultified itself by paralysis before the murder of a mere justice
of the peace.

It is indeed doubtful whether there was a plot, but the
probability is that some conspiracy was always on foot. The
penal laws against Catholics, which could not be removed so
long as Parliament remained in its temper, and the fact that

James was an avowed Catholic, might, and probably did, lead many Catholics to plan the gaining of religious freedom by overthrowing the Government and substituting autocracy. That there was a real danger, instinctively perceived by the nation, the subsequent history of James's reign proves to the full. But an impartial observer is left with the uncomfortable feeling that Oates and his colleagues, or unscrupulous men behind them, may perhaps have committed the murder in order to rouse popular feeling against the Catholics. Whether that be so or not, can never be settled. The murder of Sir Edmundbury Godfrey must remain an insoluble mystery.

LORD MOHUN

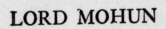

LORD MOHUN

CHARLES BARON MOHUN of Okehampton, who flourished under William of Orange and his successors, was a dissolute young man, given to tavern haunting and low society. One evening in December, 1692, a friend of his murdered Will Mountford, the actor of Drury Lane Theatre, in Lord Mohun's presence, and, as was alleged, with his lordship's countenance and support. The murderer fled, but the peer was taken and charged with the murder. Thus it was that on 31st January, 1693, the Marquis of Carmarthen sat as Lord High Steward at Westminster Hall, commissioned by their Majesties, with his peers to try the offender. This solemn assembly with all its ceremony was necessary because, as is well known, a peer of the realm who is accused of treason or felony cannot be tried by judge and jury, but must come before his fellow peers who alone can say whether he is guilty or no.

It was a disgraceful business. The man who actually killed the actor was a Captain Hill, a friend of Mohun's, who had seen and admired the beautiful Bracegirdle, one of the leading ladies at Drury Lane. He became enamoured and made advances to her, which she repelled. Probably these approaches were not matrimonial, since the Captain attributed his failure to the fact, as he alleged, that the lady was the mistress of Will Mountford. The actor alone, he believed, stood between him and the beauty's favour, and feeling insulted by this preference, he swore to be revenged. There was no proof that his suspicions were right. Mountford was a married man living with his wife, who knew Miss Bracegirdle. But the actress inflamed his desires more vividly than the actor roused his anger, and he set himself with his noble friend to gain her by force and fraud. Accordingly, on the evening of the 9th December, 1602, the two friends ordered a coach to be in readiness in Drury Lane at nine at night, with armed men adjacent in case of trouble. They then proceeded to a tavern, The Three Tuns in Chandos Street, where they dined with an unmarried lady named Elizabeth Sandys. Their conversation was loud and unrestrained. Having settled to their satisfaction the terms on which Mountford was with Mrs. Bracegirdle (the term "Mrs." was not then appropriated exclusively by married women), and thereby besmirching the lady's reputation, they talked about a plan they had of seizing her and taking her into the country. Hill said the armed men were ready, and Mohun expressed the opinion that the affair would stand Hill for £50. Apparently the idea occurred to them that Mountford would attempt to protect the lady, since Hill exclaimed, "If the villain resist I will stab him," and Mohun rejoined, "I will stand by my friend!" After this burst of melodrama, they went to the theatre, only to find that the lady was not billed to appear that night. They went from the pit on to the stage, and the man who took the money requested extra money, as they had only paid for the pit. They refused, Mohun adding that if he brought any of his masters he would slit their noses for them. The man knew them well as habitués of the theatre, and he noticed that they had exchanged coats.

There was nothing to be gained by staying at the theatre, and having learned behind the scenes that Mrs. Bracegirdle was supping with her friends the Pages in Drury Lane, the two young men went there with their retainers and waited in the road until 9 p.m. Nothing had happened, and to make sure they sent the coach to Howard Street, off the Strand, where Mrs. Bracegirdle lived. The coach returned, and, satisfied that they had chosen her resting place, they waited. At 10 o'clock the lady came out with her mother and Mr. Page, prepared to walk home. A little way down Drury Lane they saw the coach in which (though they did not know it) sat Lord Mohun with several cases of pistols. Hill and his men were lurking near, and, when the party reached the coach, the door of which stood open, they rushed forward. Hill seized the actress and tried to force her into the carriage. She struggled, Page intervened, and was knocked down for his pains, but the mother clung to her daughter and delayed the abduction so long that help came and the whole design miscarried.

What happened then is not quite clear. The henchmen were dismissed, but the two principals proceeded with the party to the house in Howard Street. Apparently they were endeavouring to explain their conduct and make their peace, but without success. On the way Hill swore that he would be revenged, but did not say on whom.

On arriving home Mrs. Bracegirdle's party went indoors, but not the two. They remained outside with drawn swords walking up and down. It seems that they insisted upon seeing the lady to demand her pardon, and would not depart until she had so far relented as to see them. She did not see them, and one may guess that they were sufficiently tipsy not to realise either their duty as titular gentlemen or their interest as foiled villains. So they paced up and down the street, importunate for pardon. It was dark and cold, and they felt they needed stimulants. They sent for wine, and drank it in the street. So two hours passed. The watch came by, and asked Lord Mohun why his sword was drawn. He deemed it sufficient answer to say that he was a peer of the land. When Hill was asked the same question, Lord Mohun answered for him, that he had lost the scabbard. The watch deemed it best to make more enquiries, and went for convenience to an alehouse near by. It was then near midnight.

The Bracegirdles were alarmed that Hill meant to do Mountford a mischief, and sent to his house in Norfolk Street, a road which crosses Howard Street, to warn his wife. He was not at home, and the messenger went to the end of Howard Street in case she would find him. It was not his direct way home, but as ill luck would have it, he came along at midnight, just as the watch was in the alehouse. The messenger tried to stop him, but he brushed past her—perhaps mistaking her motive—and went towards the waiting pair. The path there was paved; the road was not. The two were on the path, and there Mountford met them. Lord Mohun greeted him, and said, "I suppose you have heard about the lady." To which the actor replied, "I hope my wife has given your Lordship no offence."

"No," said Lord Mohun. "It's Mrs. Bracegirdle I mean." And Mountford rejoined: "Mrs. Bracegirdle is no concern of mine, but I hope your lordship does not countenance any ill action of Mr. Hill."

At these words Hill came forward, and according to the prosecution, boxed Mountford's ear, and as the assaulted man growled, "Damme, what's this for?" thrust him through and through with his sword. Mountford called out, "He has killed me," and fell in the roadway. The watchers in the windows raised the cry of "Murder." The watch came out of the tavern, and found the wounded man lying in the road and Mohun on the pavement. Another account was that Hill thrust at Mountford, calling on him to draw. Others called for the defence said that both men crossed swords and fought. All agreed that Lord Mohun remained upon the pavement and that by this time he had sheathed his sword. After the watch came the constable, but Hill made good his escape before any of them came.

What was the design of the two men in walking up and down outside the beautiful actress' house? Was it to meet and wreak vengeance upon Mountford? It is hardly probable, since they did not know that he was within, and his way home from Drury Lane would not normally be by Howard Street. Was it, as Lord Mohun alleged, to persuade Mrs. Bracegirdle to see them and receive their humble requests for pardon? It sounds improbable, but if it is assumed that they were tipsy, it is not impossible and no better explanation was given. The point is of importance. If the two men were waiting for Mountford with their swords drawn, then it is obvious that they had a common design against him, and each would be answerable for what the other did. It would in that case be no answer to say that Hill's was the hand that did the deed. If, on the other hand, they were in a maudlin state of penitence, importuning for pardon, then the meeting with Mountford was a chance affair. Hill's deed was then his own sudden act, for which Lord Mohun need not answer.

Hill's footboy had said before the coroner that when Hill drew, Mohun said that he would stand by his friend, and a witness had heard a boy in the dark implore one whom he called "My Lord" to alter his resolution. At first sight, too, it might seem that Mohun detained the man in friendly talk so that the other might the more easily run him through. But then, why did he not, like Hill, escape while yet there was time?

The watch came and he stayed. The constable arrived and he was still there. Mrs. Page called on the constable to arrest him and he made no effort to resist. As the constable arrested Lord Mohun, Bassett, one of the watch, seized him by the sleeve and said he to the prisoner, "you shook and quaked and trembled as if you would tear it to pieces." He was taken to the Round House and there enquired for Hill. On learning that he was not to be found, he said, "God damme. I am glad he is not taken, but I am sorry he had no more money about him. I wish he had some of mine. I do not care a farthing if I am hanged for him."

The constable heard that Mountford's sword was broken, and searched and found a piece of sword in the road.

Mountford lingered until one o'clock the next afternoon. His wound was mortal, but he was able to tell Bancroft, the surgeon, "My Lord Mohun offered me no violence, but whilst I was talking with my Lord Mohun, Hill struck me with his left hand, and with his right hand ran me through before I could put my hand to my sword."

When he died, the coroner sat with his jury and found a verdict of wilful murder. An indictment was preferred at Hicks' Hall, where the Grand Jury of Middlesex sat to find bills, and on their finding a true bill, the indictment was removed to the Court of the Lord High Steward.

Accordingly, on 31st January, 1693, the Lord High Steward assembled with his retinue and followed the peers to Westminster Hall. Sir John Somers, Attorney-General, Sir Thomas Trevor, Solicitor-General, and Serjeant Thompson, appeared for the Crown. The prisoner was not allowed counsel except to argue a point of law, and in case any point should arise Sir

Thomas Powys, Mr. Hawles and Mr. Price had been named to argue for him. But unless such an event happened they could neither advise him nor aid him in any way. Even Judge Jeffreys had protested against the harshness of a rule which denied to a prisoner the legal aid which the Crown freely used against him, and soon afterwards the rule was changed.

After silence was proclaimed the Royal Commission was read, and the Deputy-Governor of the Tower was commanded to produce his prisoner. Lord Mohun came to the Bar of the Court accompanied by the Gentleman Gaoler who bore the axe with its edge turned away from the prisoner. If the accused were convicted then its edge would be turned towards him. He knelt; the indictment was read and the prisoner pleaded not guilty. Serjeant Thompson explained the effect of the indictment and then Sir John Somers rose and made the opening speech for the prosecution. It was short, clear, and temperate, a great contrast to the unfair violence of the law officers in the last reign. Then one by one the witnesses came and gave evidence. Lord Mohun was entitled to cross-examine, and he availed himself of his right, not indiscriminately or injudiciously. He contented himself with cross-examination of those witnesses when he thought it might help him, and confined his questions to the point he sought to make. The skill and discretion he showed proved at least that he was a man of ability, who might if he had chosen have taken a proper place in the debates in the Lords. Thus when Elizabeth Sandys told of the wild talk at the Three Tuns he merely asked her if she were married, and was content with her answer that she was not. His main point was that he had taken no part in the scuffle. This he put to several witnesses, who all agreed. He also sought to show that he made no effort to escape, and this the witnesses again accepted, though Bassett, the watchman, by his answer already quoted plainly intimated that Lord Mohun was paralysed by fear.

When the prosecution had done, Mohun called his witnesses. The first was Thomas Lake, Hill's footboy, who was there. His story was one of a fight between Hill and Mountford, both with drawn swords. Sir John asked him whether he had not sworn before the coroner that when Hill and Mountford were pushing Mohun had said he would stand by his friend. Later on Somers produced the deposition which contained that statement. The witness also denied that he was the boy who said, "My lord, alter your resolution."

Next came Elizabeth Walker, Mrs. Bracegirdle's maid. The prosecution had been searching for her ever since she had been to Hicks' Hall. She said she went away because the players threatened her, but, reading between the lines, it is probable that she had been in Hill's interest both before and after the affair of the 9th. In any case, when she left her employment she had kept in touch with the defence. She was questioned more than once about her departure, but maintained throughout that it was because she had been threatened. It was she who took possession of Mountford's sword which several of Mohun's witnesses said was broken in the fight, but this valuable evidence was not produced. All the witnesses for the defence swore that both men fought with swords drawn, save one, who was called merely to prove that Lord Mohun had commended Mountford's acting and that very week had invited him to come and drink wine. Elizabeth Walker said that she had never "seen men naked fighting so before," at which there was a great shout of laughter. She explained that she meant men fighting with naked swords.

At the close of the evidence Sir Thomas Trevor, the Solicitor-General, summed up. The general burden of his argument was that the evidence proved a common design of the prisoner and Hill against the dead man. During this speech a lady in the gallery had a fit, and the proceedings had to be suspended until she could be removed. He concluded that Hill committed murder, while Lord Mohun stood by his friend without offering to part murderer and victim; and he submitted that it was established that Lord Mohun was privy to Hill's design. When he had done, the Lords adjourned.

The next day there was much private debate among their Lordships, and the Judges were sent for. When they arrived the Court assembled, and put a point of law to the Judges, who were headed by Chief Justices Holt and Treby. They desired to withdraw to consider their answer, but leave was refused. It then occurred to someone that prisoner had counsel for the express purpose of arguing points of law and each of the three addressed the Court. The Attorney-General in effect declined to argue on the other side. He said that before arguing the law one must know what the findings of fact were. Then the Judges declared their opinion that merely being in the company of the murderer did not of itself render his companion equally guilty of murder. Various of their Lordships were anxious to know how the law stood on various hypotheses, and these were argued by prisoner's counsel and the Judges delivered their opinions. The sitting began late, and when these discussions ended, the Court adjourned.

On the 4th February, the Lords re-assembled and voted on the indictment. The Lord High Steward called on them one by one, beginning with the junior peer. As each was named, he answered, placing his right hand on his breast, "Guilty, upon my honour," or "Not Guilty, upon my honour." Lastly the Lord High Steward gave his vote. It was early seen that the majority were for an acquittal. At the close of the vote, the Lord High Steward called Lord Mohun and informed him that he had been acquitted by 69 votes to 14 and was discharged. Silence was then proclaimed and a proclamation read dissolving the Commission. As the last words were pronounced the Lord High Steward held the White Staff above his head in both hands and broke it in two, and their Lordships proceeded in solemn state to the House of Lords.

Lord Mohun's defence had indeed involved the admission that he had been engaged in a scandalous and criminal conspiracy to abduct Mrs. Bracegirdle, but as he was not charged with any such offence, he escaped scot free. It should have been a lesson to him, but seven years later he again stood before his peers to answer a second charge of murder. On this occasion the Lord High Steward was Lord Somers, who had in the meantime became Lord Chancellor, but was on the eve of resignation. Sir Thomas Trevor, the former Solicitor-General, had succeeded Somers as Attorney-General and led for the prosecution. He was assisted by Mr. Cowper, himself one day to sit upon the Woolsack, and curiously enough, destined before then to come as a witness for his own brother on a charge of murder.

Nor on this occasion also was Lord Mohun the man who had inflicted the wound. His trial followed that of the Earl of Warwick, who was convicted of manslaughter, and pleading his clergy, was by the singular survival of the mediæval respect for ability to read, allowed to go free.

The affair having occurred in the dark in Leicester Fields, no clear account was forthcoming, but it was clear that in a threefold duel there Captain Coote had been killed and Captain French wounded.

On the evening of Saturday, 29th October, 1699, a select party were drinking at the Greyhound in the Strand kept by one Locket. At first they were five in number, the Earl of Warwick, Lord Mohun, Captains Coote and French and Mr. Dockwra. During the evening Captain James arrived. The carouse lasted until one or two on the Sunday morning. Then coaches were sent for, but none were to be had, so they sent for sedan chairs. While they were waiting a quarrel arose and swords were drawn. It seemed to the observers that the two peers and Coote were ranged against the other three. When the six chairs arrived, each man got into one, and they proceeded in the pitch dark as far as the Strand end of St. Martin's Lane. There they halted and Lord Mohun tried to persuade Coote to go home, but he insisted upon going on with the business, which was obviously a duel, and accordingly the chairmen went to the spot where Green Street runs into Leicester Square. There they were dismissed, but, scenting further employment, did not go away. Instead they proceeded along the Fields until they reached the top. In the dark they heard the sounds of fighting, and soon men approached calling out "Poor Coote," or some similar words. These men were James and Dockwra, supporting between them French, who was badly wounded. They hailed the chairmen and took French to a bagnio in Long Acre. The affair was too open and notorious to escape the notice of the watch. Coote's body was found and taken to the watch house in St. Martin's Lane. He was quite dead and had been run through twice with a sword. Lord Mohun was afterwards found to have a slight wound in the hand. He was arrested and again came before the Lords for solemn trial in the manner already described.

The evidence merely established the facts which I have stated. Lord Mohun's statement in defence threw little more light on the affair. He said in effect that he had not wanted to fight and had only gone after exhausting all efforts to induce the others to abandon the affair. Certainly if he had drawn back then, he would, according to the code of honour of his day, have shewn himself a poltroon. The Lords, eighty-seven in number, unanimously pronounced him to be Not Guilty. When informed of the verdict Lord Mohun promised reform, and he kept his word. Although he lived for many years he never again offended against the law, but lived a quiet, steady life.

Was he guilty? After a careful study of the evidence on both sides, I think that with regard to Mountford the acquittal was right. It is true that reading the record is no sufficient substitute for hearing the witnesses give their evidence, but, making all allowances for that defect, the impression left upon my mind is that it was a case of suspicion, indeed of grave suspicion, but the prosecution does not satisfy me beyond all reasonable doubt. It is highly probable that there was no design against Mountford, that the meeting was by chance and that Hill acted without premeditation. It was an affair of seconds, and, unless Lord Mohun realised what was toward, and aided and abetted the murderer, then whatever crime he had committed that night he was guiltless of murder. In the matter of Coote, I do not agree with the verdict. Although he went reluctantly and after dissuading the others, yet he went to a murderous fight voluntarily and took part in it. According to our modern ideas, such acts on his part would undoubtedly lead to his conviction. One may note with moderate satisfaction that he learned a lesson and profited thereby.

THE TRIAL OF
SPENCER COWPER

THE TRIAL OF SPENCER COWPER

In the days of William of Orange the judges still rode circuit attended by their officers and accompanied by the barristers of the circuit. It was on a Monday (the 13th March, 1699) that the Lord Chief Justice, Sir John Holt, rode with his train into Hertford to hold the assizes. With him came a numerous company, of whom three were in consequence doomed to come to the next assizes—not to see the prisoners stand their trial, but in their own persons to experience the ordeal of standing at the bar charged with murder. These three were William Cowper, a member of the circuit attending in the ordinary course of his practice; Stephens, an attorney who held the office of Clerk of the Paper in the Court of King's Bench; and Rogers, another attorney, who was Steward of the same Court. At Hertford they separated to engage their lodgings.

Spencer Cowper was then a young man of thirty, recently married, and not long called to the Bar. His elder brother (William) was a leading member of the circuit, and represented Hertford in Parliament. On this occasion the elder Cowper was detained in town, being "in the money chair" at the House of Commons. He had a standing arrangement to take the best lodgings in the town with a Mr. Barefoot. On this occasion he had forgotten to inform his landlord that he would not be coming, and in consequence his rooms were ready and he would have to pay. The two brothers were on very affectionate terms, and when Spencer learned that the lodgings were prepared he decided, money being an object with him, to make use of them, and accordingly did not occupy his usual rooms at the house of a Quaker widow, Mrs. Stout, who lived there with her two children, John and Sarah. The daughter was a handsome young woman of a romantic disposition, little inclined to the quiet, uneventful existence of a Quaker family in a country town.

Spencer Cowper knew Hertford well. His wife usually lived there, and he spent most of his vacations with her. They were both on friendly terms with Mrs. Stout, and thus it was that when William did not go on circuit and had remembered to cancel his lodgings, Spencer stayed with the Stouts, who on this occasion were expecting him. He did, indeed, send his horse, with a message that he was lodging elsewhere. Mrs. Stout invited him to dine and spend the evening. He accepted, and eventually went away at eleven at night. After his leave-taking Sarah was missed. Her mother and the maid stayed up to await her, but she did not come. She was never seen alive again.

After the Judge had arrived, Stephens and Rogers secured lodgings with a Mr. Gurrey. To them in the late evening came another attorney named Marson. He was an attorney in the Southwark Borough Court, where he had been detained by a case. Gurrey repelled him, though he pleaded that he had just arrived. It was about eleven, and he had been in Hertford since eight. The other two were friends and overruled Gurrey, and the three sat down to three quarts of wine. They discussed the business that had detained Marson, and how much he had made out of it, and in the course of their talk Sarah Stout's name came up. One of them wanted to see her and rallied Marson for having been her sweetheart. He had a bundle with him and made curious observations about the girl. At length the wine being finished they went to bed.

Next day the assizes had to compete with another sensation. Early that morning Sarah Stout's body had been found floating in a milldam some two miles from home. There was an inquest, at which Spencer Cowper gave evidence, and before it was over he sent for his horse, though he was not travelling that day. The jury found a verdict of suicide while insane. Later in the day Cowper and the three attorneys made a country excursion together.

Assizes at Hertford do not seem to have lasted much longer than they do to-day. By Wednesday the business was concluded, and Sir John Holt and the others took horse for Chelmsford. Among the train of the learned judge was Spencer Cowper.

The whole affair had so far run the normal course of these pitiful cases. A girl had disappeared, her body was discovered in the water, and the coroner's quest had found that she had drowned herself. But though she lay buried, her story was not all told. Hertford was torn with faction, and the opposition had not any advantage from this occurrence. The Quakers were incredulous, since suicide among them was unknown. Soon people began to ask whether the matter was quite so simple. Did a body float so soon after death? Sarah Walker, the maid, began to whisper that all had not been well, and like wildfire there ran through the town a rumour as baseless as it was cruel: that Cowper had taken advantage of her, and then had murdered her to avoid the consequences of their illicit affection. Then there were some strange marks on the body—soon they became clear marks of strangling. The Gurreys added their quota. One of their guests of the assize had said that a friend would be "even with her by this time." He had said that he had £50 for his share. Besides, not only did he have a bundle unlike one of an honest man, but he had said he had just arrived, though he had been seen openly in the streets by others just three hours before. On the day the body was found, too, they had acted more strangely. Not only did they go to see the body, but on the way Rogers had told Gurrey to take up Marson for his words of the night before. And then, to crown all, had not Cowper joined these three men on a jaunt to Hoddesdon on the Tuesday evening?

It was decided to exhume the body, and accordingly six weeks after her death the poor girl was taken from the grave. Examination showed that the rumours against her virtue were slanderous inventions, but as she had little or no water in her stomach the local physicians concluded that she had not been drowned, an opinion aided, so some suggested, by their political antagonism to William Cowper. No sooner was this opinion made known than the populace concluded that Sarah had been cruelly murdered, and by no other than these four men.

Naturally the authorities could not ignore so public and pointed an accusation. The Lord Chief Justice himself examined the witnesses, and committed Spencer Cowper and the three others for trial. Accordingly, in July, 1699, when Baron Hatsell attended to hold the next assizes, these four were in the town, not as in March, attending on the Lord Chief Justice, but as prisoners, awaiting trial. It is a curious circumstance that Hatsell was sent to this assize. He was so incompetent that when Queen Anne ascended the throne he was superseded. He gave a finished exhibition of his incompetence on this occasion. He certainly was not chosen because of his leaning towards the prisoners, for during the hearing on several occasions he hindered Cowper from developing the defence properly.

On the 16th July, 1699, the crowded court saw the unusual spectacle of four lawyers being arraigned for murder. In those days counsel were not allowed to prisoners charged with felony, but here that was the case only in name. Spencer Cowper was an advocate of ability, and it may be conceded that he had every motive to throw himself whole-heartedly into his case.

The prosecuting counsel was one Jones, who, though unknown to fame, knew his work. He undertook to prove that Sarah Stout was murdered, and laid stress on the fact that Spencer Cowper was the last person with whom she was seen alive, and dwelled on the incidents connecting him with the other three, and on their dark sayings on the first night of the last Assizes.

He then called Sarah Walker, Mrs. Stout's maid. She was a confident, but lying witness. Mr. Cowper was lodging at Mrs. Stout's. There was no doubt about it. At eleven she was sent up to warm his bed, and while she was upstairs the door slammed. When she came down, Cowper had gone, and so too had Sarah. It was 11.15 when she came down. In cross-examination she admitted that she had said 10.30, but explained that the clock was half an hour fast. This would make her return downstairs 10.45. Sarah Stout had been ill and moping. The maid was then asked about buying poison. Yes, she had done so twice. It was white mercury to kill a dog. The other maid administered it. That was why she told the Lord Chief Justice that she had given it herself, because she was there. What dog it was she did not make clear, and she certainly did not know what had become of it. Nor could she explain why she had gone to Barefoot's to invite Mr. Cowper to dine with Mrs. Stout.

The next witness, James Berry, had found the body. The water was thick and only some clothes showed on the surface. The body was five or six inches under water, and one arm was through some stakes. The eyes were open, no marks or wounds to be seen. Others who helped to take her from the water were called. One said that froth came from the nostrils and mouth.

Then came the medical witnesses. Medical jurisprudence in England was hardly yet born, and this trial is noteworthy not only for the number of expert witnesses called but also by reason of some of them having performed experiments to qualify them. The doctors retained for the defence were allowed to come into Court to hear this evidence. The first was Dr. Dimsdale, a local practitioner, whose son was created Baron Dimsdale in 1728, as a reward for inoculating Catherine of Russia against smallpox. The witness described the marks on the body but could give no reason for them, save that those on the neck were the "settling of blood." He definitely denied that there was the circle round the neck that Mr. Jones had undertaken to prove. After him, Sarah Kimpton who had seen the body, "lank and thin." She had seen a child who had been drowned at the same place ten weeks before. He was found on the river bed, with eyes shut and body swollen. A midwife then proved that the dead girl was not pregnant.

Then Dr. Coatsworth. He had attended the exhumation. He was of opinion that the girl had not been drowned, because there was no water in the body. His examination seems to have been very superficial. After he had given evidence, Cowper objected because the exhumation was unauthorised and illegal. The judge overruled the objection, rightly saying that, even if the exhumation were illegal, the evidence was admissible. After Dr. Coatsworth came two more medical Dimsdales who confirmed his opinion for the same reason. The second of them had seen the boy, already mentioned, in whom he found abundance of water.

Now the first Dr. Dimsdale was recalled to admit in cross-examination that Dr. Camblin had disagreed about the drowning, and that high words had passed between them on the matter. Coatsworth, too, was recalled. He said drowning was caused by suffocation through drawing water into the lungs. Much water would naturally be swallowed. He knew this because when he was nearly drowned, he had swallowed a lot. If the body were recovered at once after drowning then, he conceded, there might be little water in the stomach. If the body lay in water several hours the belly must get full. He could not say that the reverse was impossible. Cowper did not follow this up, but his object will be seen later on. Finally Dr. Coatsworth said that he had known several cases of drowning, but none where the body floated so soon.

At this stage the Judge said that Sir Thomas Browne had a chapter on this subject in "Vulgar Errors," but that he, the Judge, did not understand it. He afterwards proved that he really did not, and this gives us a standard by which to measure him. The chapter should be understood by anyone of mediocre intelligence.

Dr. Nailor's evidence was chiefly remarkable in that he was cross-examined as to his political opposition to William Cowper. Spencer said that he had meant to ask the same questions of the Dimsdales, but the Judge seemed to think that it did not matter at all.

After a surgeon named Babington had spoken of a woman who had lived for some hours after having been submerged and had vomited much water, the Judge contributed another remark. Bodies buried at sea, he said, had shot tied to them. This served to introduce two sailors. Edward Clement had served in H.M.S. *Cambridge* at the battle of Beachy Head.

The men who were shot and fell overboard floated. Those who were drowned sank at once. He had watched the wreck of the *Coronation* in September, 1691, from H.M.S. *Duchess.* The crew of the wrecked ship were swept off by twenties and they all sank at once. The other sailor was Richard Gin, who said that bodies buried at sea always had weights tied to them. He was asked as to his war experience, but would only say that he had been in two sea fights against his will.

This, said Mr. Jones, was the evidence that Sarah Stout had not committed suicide. He then called evidence to fasten guilt on to the prisoners. After proving that Spencer Cowper had left Hertford on the Wednesday, he called Gurrey. This witness said that Stephens and Rogers had hired a room from him. Late in the evening, about eleven o'clock, Marson came in, heated and muddy, saying that he had just arrived from London. It is a curious fact that Marson did say this. He had arrived about eight and did not go to Gurrey's for at least two hours, but he explained that he said he had just come so as to get a lodging. It would have been far simpler to have set about that task on his arrival. Gurrey then detailed their conversation. Rogers and the others had asked if they could see Sarah Stout and had rallied Marson about her. On the Tuesday they went to see the body, and on the way Rogers, pointing at Marson, said to him: "Landlord, you may take up that rogue for what he said last night." Later in the day he saw Cowper talking to Marson and Stephens. In cross-examination he was forced to admit that he had expressed doubts about Sarah Walker's truthfulness. Mrs. Gurrey then detailed her doubts about Marson's bundle and how she found a cord by it. Elizabeth Gurrey came forward to say that she had heard Marson say that his share was £50. Then, after putting in Marson's deposition before the Lord Chief Justice to prove that he had admitted being in Hertford at eight on the Monday evening, Jones closed his case. There might have been some evidence against Cowper, but it is incredible that the Judge did not stop the case against the others.

No prisoner charged with a criminal offence could then give evidence, though they might make statements. Cowper was allowed to open the defence by a speech in which he commented on the evidence given and explained his movements. It only differed in name from a speech for the defence. He then called his witnesses. The first two were Dew the beadle, and Young the constable, who helped to take the body from the water. Dew explained how the arm was entangled in the stakes. The Judge here complained of Cowper's many questions, but they were all relevant and he was on trial for his life. After these two Cowper tendered the coroner's depositions, but the Judge ruled that they could only be used to contradict witnesses for the crown. Mr. Jones, however, admitted that the verdict was suicide while insane.

Now was the turn of the defence to call expert evidence. First came Sir Hans Sloane, the celebrated physician, who said that much liquid could be swallowed without suffocation, instancing drunkards and persons subjected to torture by water. On the other hand, a small quantity could suffocate, as had happened when patients took medicine down the wrong way. In his opinion the evidence was consistent with drowning. Dr. Garth expressed the view that it was as natural for a body to float sideways, as Sarah Stout had done, as for a shilling to stand on edge. It was, in fact, an odd thing that she had floated some inches under water, and, though it is not clearly stated, the point was obviously made that the body was supported by the arm which had got between the stakes. When Dr. Garth said that dead bodies usually sank, the Judge called his attention to the seamen's evidence about burial, but the witness explained that the weight used for a body buried at sea was sixty to seventy pounds, wholly excessive to sink it, but necessary to prevent the body rising after decomposition. He added that seamen had many strange notions; they even whistled for a wind. Dr. Morley gave evidence as to two dogs he had drowned the day before. One floated and had no water in its stomach. The other sank. The next witness was William Cowper, the discoverer of Cowper's glands, but, as the prisoner regretfully remarked, not related to him. His evidence was that when the head was under water the first breath drew in water, and the quantity that could be inhaled was but three ounces. This would cause suffocation and after that no water could be swallowed. This evidence showed that Coatsworth was ignorant. The swallowing of water precedes and does not follow drowning. Dr. Cowper had experimented on dogs. A smooth-haired dog, being put dead into water, sank at once. He had drowned three dogs, all had water in the lungs, but none in the stomach.

The prisoner then observed that the prosecution had made no suggestion of the cause of death if not by drowning, and the Judge agreed. But there was no legal point in this, since the prosecution has never been obliged to prove the exact cause of death. The judge was getting impatient, and told Dr. Crell, who came next, to confine himself to his own experience. The witness promptly quoted Ambroise Paré, the celebrated French surgeon of the sixteenth century. Two Fleet surgeons then contradicted the seamen and the procession of experts was closed by Dr. Camblin who swore that at the post-mortem examination Dr. Dimsdale had agreed that the marks which were found were those of drowning.

It might have been safe to have closed the defence at this stage, but further and more dramatic evidence was to come. Cowper apologised for calling it, but the necessity of defending himself from a charge of murder had formed his excuse. Sarah Stout had long been secretly in love with him and at last had been unable to restrain herself from confessing it to him. He had gently but decidedly repelled her. After that he had carefully avoided meeting her, though she wrote to him and made attempts to come his way. After that she had been melancholy and ailing, discontented with her lot, and threatened suicide. Evidence was also given to explain his movements and to show that it was impossible for him after leaving Mrs. Stout's to have gone to the milldam and back to Barefoot's in the time.

After this the other prisoners made their statements. They contained nothing new, except that Elizabeth Gurrey, the listener, had twisted the £50 share out of a remark by Marson

that he had had 50s. for his case at Southwark, and that the
mysterious bundle merely contained spare clothing, as might
be guessed.   They were cross-examined on their statements, a
practice then usual but afterwards discontinued as a result of
Lord Chief Justice Holt's objection to it.   They called one
witness, Mrs. Davis, Gurrey's sister.   She proved that the
three men came in about ten on the Monday evening and went
to bed after drinking a quart of wine each.   So they could not
have gone to the milldam.   Mr. Jones then made a final effort.
He proved that at the inquest Spencer Cowper had sworn
that he knew of no reason for the girl's death.   Baron Hatsell
then summed up.   The case had gone on continuously since it
began and he was plainly exhausted.   He made a lame attempt to sum up, lamented his inability to follow the scientific
evidence, and finally abandoned the attempt to guide the jury.
They promptly acquitted all four, and there can be no doubt
that they were right.   They were discharged.

Nowadays that verdict would be final, but then there was a
means of challenging a verdict on a Crown prosecution.   The
dead person's heir could "appeal" the accused, and if he did
then the prisoner would have to stand his trial again just as
though he had never been before a jury.   This "appeal" was
not in any sense the kind of appeal that we know now.   It was
then becoming so rare that Judges usually directed a prisoner
to be discharged on acquittal.   If he did not, then it was taken
that he disagreed with the verdict, since it was technically much
easier to "appeal" a person in custody than one who had been
set free.

Sarah Stout's mother had brooded over the tragedy so long
that she had convinced herself, contrary to the evidence, that
the prisoners were really guilty.   It has been stated that only
her scruples against taking an oath prevented her from giving
evidence which would have conclusively proved Spencer Cowper's guilt.   But the maid who was with her at the time gave
evidence, and was an obvious partizan.   We may assume that
the suggestion is not well founded.   She had also convinced
herself that her cause was so righteous that she might stoop
to deceit to gain her ends.   The proper person to "appeal" was

the heir, who was a mere child; his next friend was his widowed mother, and she was not willing to prosecute the accused. Mrs. Stout tricked the widow into signing an authority to prosecute by inducing her to believe that it was a document necessary to get Sarah's belongings for her child.

On the production of this authority the Court ordered an "appeal" to be tried. Mr. Toler, the Under Sheriff for Hertford, received the writ and he not only showed it to the widow but let her handle it. The woman was horrified and promptly put the writ on the fire. Mrs. Stout applied for a fresh writ, but the only result was that Mr. Toler went to prison for contempt of court. The King's Bench judges would grant no further process, seeing that, as Holt, L.C.J., pointed out, the proper party had repudiated the authority to apply and no evidence existed to show that the accused had procured that repudiation. The prosecution then finally dropped.

The affair had at last convinced all thinking people that it was a case of suicide. Neither the Cowper family nor any of the other prisoners lost any reputation or esteem as a result of the trial. William Cowper became a law officer and eventually under Queen Anne attained the Woolsack. Spencer, after an honourable and successful career at the Bar, was made a Judge of the Court of Common Pleas in 1728. He who had once been arraigned on a capital charge was now entrusted with the duty of trying others so accused. He did not live long to fill his exalted office, dying later in the same year in the sixtieth year of his age. He has another title to remembrance. One of his grandsons was Cowper the poet, and it is interesting to note that impartial justice saved not only these innocent lives but also enabled us to enjoy those poems in which the world has so long delighted.

THE TRIAL OF
CAPTAIN KIDD

THE TRIAL OF CAPTAIN KIDD

To arive at real pre-eminence as a pirate must always in any age have required a rare combination of force of character, recklessness and luck. To command a miscellaneous crew of desperadoes gathered together by chance, all of whom had forfeited their lives and had renounced obedience to law and order, must have been an ordeal which none but the strongest could survive. The exploits of the most famous of their leaders prove that under happier auspices they might have risen to fame in the legitimate service of their country. But it must be confessed that William Kidd, judged solely by his piratical career, did not display any marked ability, and cannot be ranked as a really great pirate. His claim to the notice of posterity rests upon two facts. First, that he, almost alone among their number, was sent out to catch, not to lead, pirates, but unmindful of his duty, turned from gamekeeper to poacher. The second remarkable circumstance of his career is that he nearly involved in his misdeeds no less a person than the Lord High Chancellor of Great Britain.

Before his one long cruise as a pirate he had a career of which no one need be ashamed. Born at Greenock, he was bred to the sea, and in the wars had commanded a privateer, fighting with courage and success. In one encounter in the West Indies his ship and its consort had emerged victoriously from a bloody combat with no fewer than six French privateers. Eventually he settled at New York, and traded in his own ship along the coasts of North America.

At the end of the seventeenth century pirates infested these coasts and caused great losses to the merchants of New England. A trading vessel which continually passed along the Atlantic shores of North America must needs fall in with them.

Kidd, in fact, knew many of them and their haunts, which excites suspicion that he was of assistance to them; else how did he escape their marauding propensities? But at the time no suspicion attached to him, and he was accustomed when in port to interest his merchant friends by outlining plans whereby the pirates could easily be suppressed. He was known as a skilful seaman, he was privy to the pirates' habits, he was experienced in the ways of sea warfare and had proved himself to be a courageous fighter. It was natural, when the authorities determined to tackle the problem of piracy seriously, that his claims for employment should receive early and favourable consideration. And so it fell out. In 1695 Lord Bellamont was appointed Governor of Massachusetts Bay, and he was instructed to take effective measures to suppress piracy. Before he sailed for America, Colonel Livingston, a prominent member of the New England community, had brought Captain Kidd to him in London and suggested his employment. Lord Bellamont agreed, and approached the Admiralty with the proposal that Kidd should receive a commission, and be given command of a man-of-war. The Admiralty vetoed the proposal, probably because all the available warships were needed for the war with France, which was then raging. After much discussion it was agreed that Kidd should sail as a privateer under letters of marque with a special commission under the Great Seal, authorising him to cruise against pirates. A small syndicate was formed to finance the scheme. The agreement is dated 10th October, 1695, and thereby a fund of £6,000 was to be raised. Livingston and Kidd agreed to find one-fifth, and the remainder was found by Lord Orford (First Lord of the Admiralty), Lord Somers (Lord High Chancellor), Lord Rodney (one of the Secretaries of State), and Lord Shrewsbury, who was one of the Lords Justices entrusted with the administration of the country during King William's absence at the war.

A small ship of 150 tons, named *The Adventure,* was purchased and fitted out at Plymouth. She sailed on 1st May, 1696, with a crew of 80, and carried 30 guns. Her destination was New York, where she arrived in July, with a French ship which she had captured as a prize on the voyage. At New York, Kidd gave out that he was bound for Madagascar, which was then a noted haunt of pirates, and called for volunteers. He made up his complement to 155, and set sail. For three years no authentic news of him reached England or America, but ugly rumours came that he had turned pirate, and friendly States began to protest that their ships were being seized. In December, 1698, the Government issued a Proclamation offering to pardon all pirates who surrendered to four named Commissioners and took service in the Navy, but Kidd was excepted by name. Orders were issued that he should be captured.

At last in 1699, he arrived at Boston in a small sloop. He was seized and protested that he had come to clear his name. All the ships he had taken were, he said, lawful prize. But he had been betrayed. Early in the year he had reached the West Indies in a ship called *The Quedagh Merchant*. His fame had preceded him, and he was refused supplies, but eventually, through an Englishman named Button, he managed to revictual at a small Spanish island. He there made his plans. He buried the bulk of his hoard on Gardner's Island, where probably it still remains, as the Government failed to find it. He then bought from Button a small sloop, in which he and some of his crew embarked, taking some of the treasure with them. *The Quedagh Merchant* he left in Button's charge, but no sooner had he sailed than that worthy sold the vessel to the Spaniards and set off for Boston to give information. He arrived before Kidd, who thereby lost the advantage that he had planned. Lord Bellamont realised that he had an important prisoner, and sent to England for instructions, and when they arrived Kidd was sent home for trial.

The news of his capture had caused great excitement. It was known that he had been sent out by Somers and his friends, who were now the object of fierce attacks in Parliament, and it was now certain that he had turned pirate. What an opportunity if only he would implicate them in his misdeeds! The Junto was on the eve of its fall, but the trial must take place in England, since Lord Bellamont might, if

Kidd were tried in America, burke all the evidence reflecting on the syndicate. The first move was a frontal attack. A motion was proposed in the Commons that the Commission granted to Kidd was "dishonourable to the King, against the law of nations, contrary to the laws and statutes of the realm, an invasion of property and destructive to commerce." This motion failed, but a more reasonable one was carried, namely, that Kidd should not be tried until the next session of Parliament, and that all the depositions and papers should be sent home. On his arrival on 8th April, 1700, no time was lost in bringing him before the Bar of the House of Commons. It was a sad disappointment. He was half drunk and made a poor show. He would not admit that he was a pirate, and then and throughout never said a word that would implicate his employers. One of the most eager of the Members to have him examined angrily exclaimed: "I thought the fellow had only been a knave, but unfortunately he happens to be a fool likewise!" Perhaps Kidd was not such a fool. There would only have been his bare word. They were powerful Lords, even after their fall from power, and to seek to involve them necessarily deprived him of his only defence, as no doubt he clearly perceived.

In the meantime, the King's Proclamation had become known, and a number of the crew had gradually been collected. What they had not realised was that the surrender could only be made to four named persons, and then certain conditions had to be fulfilled. The poor men thought it meant that surrender to the authorities would ensure their pardon, and only too late realised that their confession stood and that the pardon was not to be had.

The Crown was now ready for trial, and Kidd and his nine associates were brought up at the Old Bailey on the 8th May, 1701. At that date criminal jurisdiction was exercised by the Court of Admiralty when the offence was alleged to be committed on the high seas. The trials were held at the Admiralty Sessions at the Old Bailey, and the main differences between them and the ordinery Sessions was that the Judge of the Court of Admiralty presided and charged the Grand Jury and sentenced those found guilty.

After Dr. Oxenden, the Admiralty Judge, had charged the Grand Jury, the latter found true bills against Kidd for murder and piracy, and against the others for piracy. Two of the nine were also indicted with Culliford, another notorious pirate, who was tried at the same Sessions for other piracies.

The trials began at once. On the Bench were Lord Chief Baron Ward, Mr. Justice Turton, Mr. Justice Powell, Mr. Baron Hatsell, and the Recorder (Sir Salathiel Lovell), all of whom sat with Dr. Oxenden.

Kidd refused to plead and asked for Counsel, who were then only allowed to argue points of law for the defence. When asked why, he explained that he wanted to put off the trial as long as possible in order to get his evidence. His papers had been seized, including the French passes, which showed that the captured vessels were lawful prize. A wrangle ensued, during which Kidd repeated that he "wasn't ready," and the Recorder very unjudicially retorted, "Nor never will, if you can help it." But he still refused and the Court proceeded to take the pleas of the others. More difficulty. Churchill, the first of them, wanted to raise the plea that he came in under the King's Proclamation, but he was told that he must first plead. So he pleaded Not Guilty, and so did all the others, of whom Owens and Mullins also claimed to have come in under the Proclamation. Then again Kidd was called on. He again refused, and repeated his protest about his papers, but eventually being informed that, if he refused to plead, the penalty was condemnation without trial, he gave way and pleaded not guilty.

Then came the turn of prisoners' counsel. Dr. Oldish and Mr. Lemmon had been assigned to them. The first point was that a necessary witness named Davis was indicted with Culliford, and that the trial must be put off until Davis had been tried. He was in Newgate awaiting trial. The Court held that the fact that he was committed on another charge did not prevent him giving evidence, and sent for him. Then counsel pressed for an adjournment to obtain the French passes that, as Kidd alleged, Lord Bellamont had seized. Besides, they said, they had not had time to get ready. Though a fortnight's notice had been given, the £50 granted for expenses had been paid to a person who had gone away, and they had only got the money the night before. Dr. Oxenden queried this. He had ordered the money to be paid to Kidd, and the Registrar said that he had paid it to Kidd. At this stage the Solicitor-General said that none of the reasons for adjournment applied to the murder charge, and consequently no reason existed why this should not be gone into, and so this course was adopted.

The murder charge spoils the story. It was an incident of the whole voyage, but most of the facts of that voyage were quite irrelevant to this charge. For that reason, probably, the opening speeches were short, probably the shortest on record, for the opening of the indictment by Mr. Knapp and the speeches by the Solicitor-General and Mr. Conyers could not have taken five minutes in all.

The charge was that Kidd had in October, 1697, murdered his gunner, William Moore, by striking him on the head with a bucket. *The Adventure* was then cruising off the coast of Malabar. About a fortnight before they had fallen in with a Dutch vessel, *The Loyal Captain,* of which one Hoar was master. There had been some talk of taking her, but she was allowed to part company, and apparently this had caused some discontent. The chief witness for the prosecution was Joseph Palmer, one of Kidd's men, who said that as Moore was grinding a chisel, Kidd came to him and questioned him about a safe plan which Moore had for taking the Dutch ship. Moore denied it, and in the altercation Kidd called him a "lousy dog." Moore replied: "If I am a lousy dog, you have made me so. You have brought me to ruin, and many more." Kidd took several turns up and down the deck, muttering, "Have I ruined you, you dog?" and then, seizing a bucket bound with iron hoops, he struck Moore on the right side of the head. Bradinham, the surgeon, was called, and proved that the gunner was a healthy man and died of the wound the next day. Kidd's defence was that there was a mutiny because he would not take the Dutchman, and in this mutiny, Moore was a ringleader. "So," said Kidd, "I took up a bucket, and just throwed it at him, and said, 'you are a rogue to make such a motion.'" Unfortunately, the witnesses for Kidd did not agree, except that the altercation was days after the Dutchman had sailed her way. One witness agreed with Palmer that Kidd did not throw the bucket, but held it by the strap. There was no evidence of a mutiny on the day of the murder. The only difference was as to the language used. Apparently Kidd got enraged when called a "sawney." An attempt was made to prove that Moore was a sickly man, and that Bradinham had said that he had not died of the wound. Bradinham promptly denied this. Moore had never been under his care except for the wound. The Lord Chief Baron summed up. He put Kidd's version to the jury, and asked them to consider whether the words alleged were a provocation. He also put to them Palmer's version, and directed them that if those were the words used they were too slight to be a provocation. Kidd then asked to call witnesses to his past services. It was too late then, and, as he was reminded, they would not help him on a murder charge. The jury convicted him.

The trial has been criticised on the ground that the only witnesses were two of his own men, and that the summing-up was unfair. Neither criticism is well founded. There was never the slightest suggestion that either witness took any part in the altercation, and, indeed, Bradinham was not there when the wound was given. He was merely the surgeon who proved the cause of death. The summing-up, if unfair, was unfair only to the prosecution. It is undoubted law that mere words are no provocation, and the defence had proved that any discontent about the Dutch vessel had occurred days before, and that at the worst the only provocation was that Moore was grossly impertinent.

The conviction of Kidd on a capital charge took all the interest out of the main trial. The first indictment for piracy charged Kidd, and the nine men, Nicholas Churchill, James Howe, Robert Lamley, William Jenkins, Gabriel Loff, Hugh Parrot, Richard Barlicorn, Abel Owens, and Darby Mullins, with the piratical capture of *The Quedagh Merchant* on 30th January, 1697-8. In the course of this trial the story of Kidd's voyage was told in full.

After leaving New York in July, 1696, *The Adventure* reached Madagascar in July, 1697. The adventurer could have found ample employment at that nest of pirates, but instead he went off to the Red Sea and lay off a small island in the entrance called "Bab's Key," waiting for the Mocha fleet, consisting of Indian vessels trading between the Red Sea and India. He declared that he would ballast his ship with gold and silver. Three times he sent out boats to reconnoitre, and at last, on 14th August, 1697, the fleet came by. Kidd sailed into her midst and opened fire, but he was answered by a convoy, which he had not expected, and made a hurried flight.

Having thus miscarried in his first attempt, he cruised about off Arabia and India, capturing Arab and Indian vessels. The first ship taken hailed from Bombay. Her master was an Englishman, and there was a Portuguese on board. The rest were natives. The two Europeans were taken on board, and soon after the ship arrived at a factory, where Kidd was asked to surrender them. They were hidden in the hold, and he denied that he had any such persons on board. At one place the cooper went ashore and was murdered by the natives. In revenge, Kidd landed and plundered and burned some houses, and tied a native to a tree and shot him. The plundering of these ships led to the sending of two Portuguese men-of-war against him. One fell in with him and maintained a running fight for several hours, but he got away with a loss of only ten wounded. In October, Moore was murdered. In November they took a ship from Surat. Kidd hoisted French colours and went in chase of her, but she also hoisted French colours, and apparently had a French pass. She was taken to Madagascar. In December they took a ketch, and sent her adrift after plundering her. In January, 1697-8, they fell in with *The Quedagh Merchant*. The pirate hoisted French colours and overtook her. She was owned by some Armenians, who were on board. After that they boarded several vessels, and plundered them. Finally they decided to make for Madagascar, taking a native ship on the way. They arrived in May, 1698, and proceeded to a complete share out. The money and goods were divided separately, each into 160 shares. Kidd took 40 of each, and each seaman had one complete share of each, and each landsman one half share; but for equality of division some men had half a share in the money and a whole share in the goods.

At Madagascar they fell in with Captain Culliford on the pirate ship *Resolution,* which, before her capture, had been a merchantman named *The Mocha Frigate.* Culliford was a notorious freebooter, and Kidd's advent filled him and his band with alarm. They had heard of his commission, but not of his dereliction of duty. Their fears, however, were soon allayed, and the two bands fraternised. Their new friend swore that his soul would fry in hell before he harmed them, and he gave practical proof of his pacific intentions by supplying Culliford with two guns and ammunition and stores.

By this time *The Adventure* was foul and leaky, so she was destroyed. Kidd transferred to *The Quedagh Merchant,* but with the share out the cruise had come to an end. Several, including Bradinham, left him, and some of these joined Culliford. The rest sailed with him for the West Indies, where many rich prizes could be picked up. At this point the story ended, as the Crown had no evidence to show what had become of *The Quedagh Merchant* or how Kidd had managed to reach Boston in the sloop.

Palmer and Bradinham were the only witnesses for the prosecution. It is not easy to say why, since it came out that one of the Armenian owners of *The Quedagh Merchant* was actually in court.

During the murder trial, Kidd's defence suggested that in these piracies he was the unwilling follower of his own men, but he did not take that line on the actual charge of piracy. Possibly the presence of the owner warned him that there was evidence available as to what he had done at the capture. His defence now was that the ship had a French pass and was, therefore, lawful prize. Davis was called, and swore that, at Amboyna, Kidd had shown some papers in his presence to another captain, who said they were French passes, and offered to turn them into Latin. Davis did not explain what he or Kidd were doing at Amboyna, and certainly gave no evidence that the papers related to this vessel or that he had read them himself. Bradinham was interrogated, but all he knew was that Kidd had always said that the ships had French passes, but he had never seen them himself.

At this stage Churchill made his defence. It was limited to a claim to pardon under the Proclamation. In fact, none of the nine men ever made the slightest attempt to deny piracy. He called Jeremiah Bass, the former Governor of New Jersey, who said that Churchill and Howe had surrendered to him, but he had not accepted the surrender, and had left them in custody when he came home. Lamley said he was Owens' servant. Jenkins that he was Bullen's servant. Loff declared that he joined at New York, and had obeyed Kidd's orders. He had gone to serve the King. He was asked how he came to share the proceeds, and answered that he only took what the others chose to give him. Parrot said that he was at Madagascar when Kidd first arrived. Hearing that Kidd had the King's commission he joined him. He thought he was safe where the King's commission was, and had obeyed Kidd in all things. Barlicorn called witnesses as to his character, and said that he was Kidd's servant. Owens relied on the Proclamation. He had a certificate from the Justice of the Peace that he had surrendered and had joined the Navy. He was serving when arrested. Mullins also relied on the Proclamation. He and Churchill had joined Culliford at Madagascar, and had afterwards reached America. As Bradinham was asked about Mullins' health on the voyage it seems probable that he joined Culliford. He had quitted Kidd at Madagascar, and was on the same ship with Churchill and Mullins when they surrendered. He confirmed Mullins' statement that he was ill of a "bloody flux" on that voyage.

Kidd called witnesses to impeach Bradinham's veracity and also as to his meritorious services in the former wars. He again called for the French passes, which he alleged Lord Bellamont had taken from him. They were never produced, nor did the prosecution ever attempt to prove that no such passes were found among Kidd's papers. It is indeed highly probable that some at least of the captured vessels had provided themselves with French passes. It was a time of war, for the news of the peace had not reached Indian waters, the seas swarmed with French privateers, and many mariners in such times took the precaution to procure passes from both sides. On the other hand, none of the nine men charged with Kidd ever said that the documents existed. Palmer said nothing about them, and Bradinham had only heard Kidd say that they existed. The nearest to proof was Davis' statement that Kidd had some papers which someone else examined and said were French passes. Perhaps the prosecution desired not to confuse the issue by a false point. Although Kidd, as a privateer, could lawfully seize such ships, yet it was his duty in such a case to bring them in for adjudication by a Court of Prize, and, with the captured ship, all her papers, not merely the pass. He had never attempted to do this, but by dividing the spoils at Madagascar had clearly shown that he had abandoned his letters of marque and was a mere filibuster. Kidd knew the procedure required. He had been a privateer before, and had actually brought in for adjudication the lawful prize made by *The Adventure* on her voyage to New York. The Lord Chief Baron summed up. He ruled that the defence that the ships were lawful prize could only be sustained by evidence that the ships were French or were sailing under French passes. He was strikingly lenient to the three servants, for he contented himself by directing the jury to consider whether they went voluntarily, and, if not, then to acquit them. The jury took the hint and promptly acquitted Lamley, Jenkins, and Barlicorn but convicted Kidd and the others.

The prosecution then went on with a third indictment for the piratical seizure of an unknown native-owned ship in 16th September, 1697. The defences were the same. Mr. Justice Turton summed up, and the jury convicted the same seven.

Then came three more indictments, and the same verdicts followed.

After this Churchill and Mullins had still to meet two other charges.   Captain Culliford and some of his crew were arraigned on a number of indictments charging them with piracy in seizing several ships, and they pleaded guilty.   On two of these indictments Churchill and Mullins were also accused. They pleaded not guilty to raise the point of their surrender under the Proclamation, but eventually confessed guilt.   The sentence for piracy is death by hanging, and this was pronounced upon all those who were convicted by Dr. Oxenden. Kidd had the last word.   "It is a very hard sentence," he complained.   "I am the innocentest person of them all.   Only I have been sworn against by perjured persons."

On the 23rd May, 1701, he was taken to Execution Dock, and there hanged in the sight of all vessels using the Port of London.

There can be no doubt of his guilt.   The facts alleged were hardly disputed.   It is idle to say that the evidence was only that of two of the gang.   In such cases the evidence of accomplices must be taken.   Nowadays the court requires corroboration, but the necessary corroboration was certainly available. Besides, Kidd did not deny the facts.   He merely said that the ships were lawfully captured, and the other men either made no defence on the merits, or claimed that they had obeyed his orders.   What his motive was it is impossible to say, but it is not improbable that the Heaven-sent opportunity of a good ship, well armed, and manned with an adventurous and manageable crew, was a temptation too strong for him; opportunity makes the thief.   He thoroughly earned the hangman's rope.

THE WARDENS OF
THE FLEET

THE WARDENS OF THE FLEET

THE term "office of profit" has been relegated to the vocabulary of lawyers, and with them it is rarely used except when arguing the provisions of the taxing Statutes which have preserved those magic words. There was, however, a time when a salaried civil servant was a very rare creature. Most Government employees held "offices of profit," and by reason of that position enjoyed the right or were able to assert with effect a claim to receive various customary payments and dues which would recompense them for their labours. Pepys has preserved for us the practice and principles of one of the most upright officials of his time. He would nowadays be ignominiously dismissed for gross corruption. Opinion conceded that there was a limit at which perquisites became bribes, but the line was hard to draw. Bacon had suffered because his precepts excluded the legality of his practices. Macclesfield at the time of this trial was on the brink of impeachment by reason of his failure to draw the line.

It was, to our modern notions, a curious corollary to the existence of an "office of profit" that it should be regarded as a kind of property vested in the holder. Though he held by grant, sometimes revocable and sometimes not, there was a custom which enabled a holder to surrender his grant in favour of a nominee, who paid a consideration to the former holder, and the nominee obtained a fresh grant. This was so in the case of the Masters in Chancery who had the care of suitors' money (and, according to the principles of the day, could use it for their own benefit provided it was ready when needed). The South Sea Bubble had provided precedents where the money was not ready but was hopelessly lost. A master would have borrowed money to pay his predecessor and then repaid the lender out of suitors' money, trusting to be in office long enough to replace it.

This system was in 1728 in full force in the case of prison Wardens. They were almost all men who had paid large sums for their positions, and looked to the prisoners for their income and the means to replace the capital they had sunk. They need not necessarily act in person. They need have no education, standing, or capacity. In view of their position and the source of their earnings it is not surprising that the history of prison administration in England is unpleasant reading.

At this period not only was the community of the county, hundred, parish, or other local unit responsible for the safe custody of prisoners awaiting trial or sentenced to imprisonment, but creditors, too, were entitled to seize their defaulting debtors, either on mesne process (that is, after the issue of a writ, but before judgment) or under a judgment. Debtors arrested on mesne process could obtain their release by giving security, but once a judgment was obtained they could only escape by payment. It was not until long after a trader could be made bankrupt and obtain discharge from his debts that the unfortunate non-trader could obtain similar relief. The universal speculation and widespread ruin caused by the South Sea Bubble led to an Insolvent Debtors Act, 1725, giving non-traders relief. Once a man was arrested for debt, other creditors could take steps to protect their interests by lodging "detainers" so that the debtor could not go free until all had been satisfied, the attorney's costs paid, and the fees of the prison-keeper satisfied.

The root idea was that the man or woman should be held. There was little or no idea that there was any duty towards the unfortunate.

There seems to have been no proper supervision. Although the Judges and Justices had the oversight of prisons, effective reform would cost money and involved ideas of policy which were foreign to all but a few speculative thinkers. Inside a debtors' prison there was a mob of people, swindlers and swindled, without proper separation or segregation of the sexes, often, in the country, mingled with malefactors, without any regard to order or morality. Money was the sole means of obtaining seclusion or decency. By money, if in the first instance any escaped the sponging houses, the debtor could obtain separate accommodation furnished to his taste, entertain himself and his friends with the luxuries of the season, and could even, on giving security that he would not escape, live out of prison in certain defined areas known as the Liberty of the Rules. Every day and in every way the keeper and his satellites were on the look-out for gain, and woe betide the unfortunate debtor who was without means to satisfy their greed, the more so if it were known that he had means and contumaciously refused to submit to the rapacity of his keepers. He could look forward to insult and injury, and if he had sufficient spirit to appeal to the Court, might even find himself a condemned felon upon a false accusation, supported by the evidence of professional perjurers.

Prisoners had only one redress—death. The lack of elementary decency led to a strange disease, jail fever. Often at Assizes the prisoners diffused a strange and dreadful odour which brought death to the Judge on the Bench and to the Counsel and spectators at the Bar. In 1730, at the Somerset Assizes, jail fever destroyed the Lord Chief Baron and his servants, the High Sheriff and his attendants and many learned Serjeants and Counsel with their clerks. So common was this disease, that it was regarded as unavoidable, and to account for a prisoner who had been done to death was easy, if it were even whispered that he had caught the fever. Death by a filthy, loathsome disease was often the penalty inflicted upon an innocent person who was suspected of crime and upon an unfortunate who was alleged to have failed in payment of debt.

In 1728 public opinion was greatly stirred by rumours of strange happenings in the Fleet and the Marshalsea Prisons. The Act of 1725 had caused the release of many who otherwise would have suffered life imprisonment for debt, and their tales of prison caused a widespread belief that wholesale breaches of the law formed part of the ordinary routine of prison administration. One of the prisoners who had died was Robert Castell, a merchant whose tastes lay in the study of antiquity and architecture. He was a quiet, peaceable man, a great friend of General Oglethorpe, then an M.P. Oglethorpe brought the scandal to the notice of the House. A Select Committee was chosen to make an enquiry. The reports led to the immediate arrest of the Wardens of the Fleet and of the Marshalsea, charged with murder and robbery with violence.

The Fleet was an ancient prison to which prisoners had been committed by the Star Chamber. When that Court was abolished in 1641 it became a prison in which the Courts of Chancery, Exchequer, and Common Pleas confined persons in debt or found guilty of contempt. By an Act of Charles II, prisons had been put under the supervision of the Judges and the local Justices of the Peace, and the Warden was subject to them. A table of fees had been framed in Queen Elizabeth's days, and this table was confirmed under Charles II. That monarch had granted the Wardenship as a freehold to Sir Jeremy Whichcoat, together with the lands going with that office. Sir Jeremy in return bound himself to rebuild the prison. From him others acquired the office, but their conduct was so scandalous that the grant was revoked. A fresh grant was obtained by John Huggins for his own and his son's life. He gave £5,000 to Lord Clarendon for the right, and held the office for many years. He seems to have been a man held in esteem by his friends and neighbours, who cared or knew little of the methods by which he obtained his ample means. He went but seldom to the Fleet, leaving the charge to subordinates to whom he sold their places at exorbitant rates. He had no real authority to appoint tipstaffs, but assumed the right. There were five of these officers, and in November, 1724, he appointed Richard Corbett as one of them. Huggins' deputy was one Thomas Bambridge. In 1727 Huggins found himself stricken in years, with a son who absolutely declined to take over his office. Accordingly he agreed with Bambridge and a man named Dougal Cuthbert to surrender his patent on payment of £5,000, and a new grant was accordingly made.

Bambridge had reduced the task of extracting fees to a fine art. He did not keep proper books or note the reception and discharge of prisoners, so that there was little evidence to show who was or who was not in his custody. He made a private door in the wall of a yard where dogs were kept, and out of the door he was accustomed to grant exit to prisoners who paid him well for the privilege. Of course they did not complain; but the surprise caused at Islington may easily be imagined when men saw at large a smuggler named Boyce who was known to be in the Fleet for Exchequer penalties amounting to £30,000.

A debtor could if he so desired go in the first instance to one of the Fleet inns. These were called "sponging houses," but by law no one could be forced to go there. The intention was that a debtor might lodge there while seeking to discharge his debt. They were let by the Warden to creatures of his, who, in return for exorbitant rents, were allowed full licence to plunder. Bambridge forced debtors with means to go there whether they liked it or not, and even went so far as to refuse to let them in the prison. The charges were enormous. Inside the prison there were two sides or departments. The Master's Side, where debtors with means could hire accommodation, and the Common or Poor Side, where in theory the debtors obtained adequate shelter for nominal fees. All the prisoners were of course subject to the necessity of buying food and drink in the prison, and the Warden drew profit from this source, and also from those who paid him not to see practices forbidden in prison. A debtor who gave security might leave the prison for the Rules, but this would to a great extent cause him to be less profitable to the Warden, who accordingly saw to it that departure from the Rules, unless obtained by substantial payment, was ruthlessly obstructed by requiring exorbitant security.

A graver abuse of authority was actual violence. Men who complained of exactions were assaulted, ironed and placed in the Strong Room. Each side had a room of this kind. On the Master's Side it was a building 8 ft. by 11 ft. and 9 ft. high. It was over the common sewer and next to the place where the prison ordure was deposited. It was damp, foul and noisome. The ostensible purpose of the place was the confinement of refractory prisoners. There they were flung, fettered,

without fire or bedding, lying on the damp ground and surrounded by walls streaming with moisture. Its other use was
as a mortuary for dead prisoners awaiting inquest. The only
ventilation was by a hole over the door and one by the side
big enough to pass a quart pot. These dungeons had been
built contrary to the orders of Lord King, when Chief Justice
of the Common Pleas, who ordered that there should be no
prison within a prison. One man placed there was somewhat
unstable in his mind. He had only a feather mattress and
crept inside for warmth. One day the door was left open
and he rushed out into the hall, almost naked, covered with
filth and feathers, more like some strange fowl than a human
being. It is said, however, that there was a worse place than
the Strong Room, a hole called Julius Cæsar's Ward.

It may be added that there was a scale of fees, a right to
claim redress from the Judges, and in any case where men
were confined without being separated, a right to organise
opposition. The law required that the scale should be ex-
hibited. The Warden had it hidden away, so that only guesses
could be made as to the right fees. Objectors went to the
Judges. Before anything could be done they found themselves
at the Old Bailey charged with assault on clear evidence, all
suborned. Organisation did exist. The prisoners elected a
Court of Inspectors who were allowed to exercise jurisdiction
within the prison. It was alleged during the trial that they
were all-powerful and that the Warden did not dare go inside.
He was caught out in this lie because it was admitted that he had
been to the Chapel, which could only be entered by going inside
the prison. Probably he could not venture alone within the
walls for fear that his victims would avenge their wrongs.

One case illustrates many of the malpractices. John Houlder,
a Spanish merchant, had a room which he furnished himself.
Bambridge turned him out into the Common Side. Finding
that the man was dying he had him carried back to the room
and he died there. Trustees had been appointed by will, and
they came to take an inventory. They found that Bambridge
had broken into the room and seized the effects. He shut one
executor out of the prison and locked the other in the Strong

Room, in order to prevent them carrying out their duties. The Commons directed the prosecution of Huggins, Bambridge and several others. They also investigated cases at the Marshalsea, and ordered the prosecution of William Acton, the Deputy-Warden there.

The prosecutions were set on foot, but delays occurred. Application after application was made for bail; in the meantime public indignation subsided, and the prisoners' friends worked hard in their interests. It is not always to the interest of a prisoner that he should have a speedy trial. At last, on 21st May, 1729, Huggins came up at the Old Bailey before Mr. Justice Page, Mr. Baron Carter and Serjeant Raby, the Deputy-Recorder, to stand his trial for the murder of Edward Arne on 7th December, 1725.

Arne was a quiet, inoffensive man who had been arrested for debt on mesne process on 12th May, 1725. Barnes, a prisoner promoted to be watchman, had seized him and placed him in the Strong Room. He was the man who had crept into a feather bed. The evidence to connect Huggins with the offence was that he had twice been up from the country and had seen Arne in the Strong Room and left him there after being appealed to for mercy. Indeed, it was said that when a plea was made for Arne to Huggins, Barnes had said, "Let him die and be damned."

Yorke, the Attorney-General, Talbot, the Solicitor-General, Sergt. Cheshire and Mr. Holland, M.P. for Chippenham, were for the Crown. The prisoner was represented by a strong team, headed by Sir John Darnell, Judge of the Marshalsea Court, but their function was limited to arguing points of law for the prisoner.

The defence was that if anybody was guilty it was Gibbon, the deputy, who was dead. He had paid £400 a year to Huggins for his office. Bygrave, the clerk, had paid a lump sum of £750 10s. for his place. It was suggested, and with apparent reason, that Arne was not right in his head. Witness after witness was called to prove that he was a quiet, healthy man when put in the Strong Room, and a dying wreck when he came out just before his death. Evidence was given in great details showing that Huggins saw him there; that he must have known that the place was a death-trap, but left him there to die.   On the other hand, much testimony was given to prove that Huggins was never there at that period; that the Court of Inspectors had sole control of the prison, because Gibbon did not dare to enter, and that Huggins, as he declared, never even knew of Arne's existence.

The summing-up was by Mr. Justice Page, who confessed, and with justice, that there never was a case with so much conflict of evidence.   He directed the jury that a prison for debt must be kept in a becoming way, and that if Arne's death was caused by his confinement in an improper place, it was murder.   To convict Huggins they must, however, find that he was privy and consenting to the confinement.   The jury retired and came back.   They had agreed on the facts but desired to state them in their verdict, so that the Court could say whether Huggins was guilty or not.   This is what is known as a special verdict.   In effect they found that Huggins knew that the Strong Room was unhealthy, and that Arne had died through being confined there, but that he did not know from the first that Arne was put there, though he saw him there at least fifteen days before his death.

The effect of this verdict was twice argued; once in the Court of King's Bench, and once before all the Judges and Serjeants Inn, sitting as a tribunal, now replaced by the Court of Criminal Appeal.   Eventually it was held that in the absence of an express finding that Huggins knew the room to be dangerous to life (which presumably was what the jury meant), the prisoner must be acquitted, and he was discharged.   The case is reported in 2 Strange 883; and 2 Lord Raymond 1574.

Next came Thomas Bambridge who, on the 20th May, 1729, pleaded not guilty and came up for trial on the 22nd of that month.   The charge against him was that of murdering Robert Castell, Oglethorpe's friend, on 12th December, 1728.   The trial was a fiasco.   The witnesses for the prosecution merely proved that Castell was mortally afraid of smallpox, which had broken out at his lodgings.   He asked to leave the Rules and go into the prison, where he caught smallpox and died.   An acquittal was inevitable, and the prisoner was found not guilty. From the subsequent proceedings, it is beyond doubt that the witnesses had been suborned and were deliberately lying. At that date an acquittal was not decisive. Certain of the dead man's relatives were entitled to have a second trial, by proceedings known as "Appeal," and Castell's widow appealed Bambridge for the murder. This was tried on 26th January, 1730, before Lord Chief Justice Raymond at the Guildhall. The case for the prosecution was that Castell, who was detained for debts amounting to less than £400, was not allowed the Liberty of the Rules until he had found a security on five different occasions for sums totalling £5,200. At one stage in his detention he received £125 and Bambridge, hearing of this, had him taken to his sponging house which was rented from him by Corbett, who was also included in the appeal. There was a case of smallpox at Corbett's, and Castell, who feared the disease, repeatedly asked to be allowed to go to his lodgings in the Rules. It was quite illegal to send a debtor to a sponging house without his consent, but in spite of that and of his statement that he had not had smallpox he was forced into the house, where he caught the disease and died. There were at least two empty rooms in the prison.

The defence was a complete denial. Bambridge was actuated by the most benevolent motives, and let Castell go to the sponging house to suit himself. White, the smallpox patient, was well, so the witnesses averred, at least a week before Castell went there.

Lord Chief Justice Raymond directed the jury that a man lawfully taken must be lawfully confined. There was no evidence that Corbett knew of the smallpox (in his own house), and he must be acquitted. As for Bambridge, if he knew that Castell had not yet had smallpox and nevertheless obliged him to go to a house where it was, whereby he caught the disease and died, then they must convict. The jury acquitted. They, of course, had seen and heard the witnesses, but it is safe to say that Castell's movements are incomprehensible unless he went against his will. That he, being nervous of smallpox, should leave his lodgings and go to a place where he would

be overcharged for everything, and where smallpox had just
occurred, in order to avoid the peril he was running into is
beyond belief.   Men do strange things, but Castell was a merchant of experience, and was expecting his release.   He was
a truthful man, and died denouncing Bambridge as his murderer.

This ended the proceedings regarding the Fleet.   Bambridge had in the meantime survived a charge of stealing.
This trial was at the Old Bailey on 5th and 6th December,
1729.   He was accused of stealing the goods of Elizabeth
Berkeley on 3rd October, 1727.   She was a prisoner who lived
in a room on the Master's Side.   Bambridge turned her over
to the Common Side, and broke open her boxes and took her
jewellery and property.   Afterwards he made an inventory,
alleging that she owed him rent.   The judges on this occasion
were Eyre, the Lord Chief Baron, Mr. Justice Reynolds, Mr.
Baron Carter, and Serjeant Raby.   After the witnesses on
both sides had given wholly incompatible evidence, Eyre,
L.C.B., summed up.   He told the jury the whole question was
whether there was a real or a pretended distress.   It was no
defence to the charge if Bambridge had used a legal process
with felonious intent.   The jury acquitted.

There was a curious sequel.   Rumours went round that Eyre
had visited Bambridge while in prison and had sent him a
hundred guineas to help his defence.   The House of Commons
investigated the matter, and decided that it was a conspiracy
to defame Eyre, who had done nothing of the kind.

The four charges of murder against Thomas Acton concern
the Marshalsea.   The prison was used by the Court of King's
Bench and the Court of Admiralty.   Sir John Darnell had
supervisory jurisdiction over the prison as Judge of the Marshalsea Court.   He could not therefore appear as counsel for
Acton, as he had done for Huggins, but he came as a witness to
character, which in the circumstances reflects greatly upon his
own credit.   Acton was head turnkey and deputy warden.   Before taking up this responsible work he had been a journeyman
butcher.

The trials were held at Surrey Assizes in August, 1729, where Mr. Barton Carter sat at Kingston. The first case related to the murder of Thomas Bliss, who died on 21st October, 1727. This man was confined in the Strong Room, a kind of lean-to near the sewer, in which pirates were confined while awaiting trial. He was put there in irons, and without bed or straw. It was damp, dark, and unventilated. Before then he had been beaten so cruelly as to cut his clothes off. While so confined, Acton one day had company and sent for Bliss. To make sport, he fitted on the prisoner various instruments of torture he had found in the prison, an iron skull cap, an iron collar and thumbscrews. The man was healthy when first confined, and weak and ailing when released. Indeed, one woman said that his mouth was so sore while in the Strong Room that he asked her to chew his meat for him, as he could not. He had been discharged from prison on 25th March, 1727, and evidence was given of his attempts to work and of his collapse. The weak point of the case was that the man lived for seven months after his discharge. The defence was that the man was hurt in trying to escape, having fallen twenty-four feet in the attempt. The attempt to escape, the prosecution alleged, led to his beating and confinement. He had, according to the defence, been sent to the sick ward and only confined to prevent a further escape. After release he spent several days drinking and thereby caught cold. Many witnesses were called to substantiate the defence and an imposing array of witnesses to character came, headed by Sir John Darnell. One of these, a J.P. for Surrey, indeed said that he thought Acton was unfit for his position, because he was too compassionate!

Mr. Baron Carter summed up by going through the evidence. He directed the jury that if they believed the evidence for the Crown they should convict. They acquitted.

On 2nd August, Acton came up on the charge of murdering John Bromfield. The dead man had been a captain in the Army. He was received in prison for debt on 1st March, 1725. He had at first been on the Master's Side, but in May had been taken to the Common Side, so he was apparently without means. He incurred Acton's displeasure and was beaten, placed in irons, and put in a hole under the stairs. This was a place too small for him to stand upright or to repose at full length. One witness said that the place was about as big as a large coffin. The floor was bare earth and too damp to lie on. After several days in this place he fell ill and died early in June. Acton's defence was that the prisoner was put in irons because he stabbed another man named Perkins. He was well when released, but afterwards caught jaundice of which he died. The jury again acquitted.

On the same day came the third trial, for the murder of Robert Newton. This man was described as a fat, jolly man. He shared a room with a man named Hartness. The prosecution called witnesses to prove that one of them attempted to escape. Newton was seized, fettered and placed in the Strong Room. He fell ill in consequence, and was removed to the sick ward, where he died. Sir John Darnell had been applied to in this case, and had ordered Newton's release, but Acton paid no heed. In this case one of the witnesses said that the Strong Room was verminous and infested with rats. He had seen a man's face which had been eaten by rats while he was lying there for a few hours awaiting burial. In none of these cases had an inquest been held, although the death of every prisoner should have been the subject of a coroner's inquest. The defence merely said that inquests were not customary in the Marshalsea. Acton's defence was that both men tried to escape, and were put in irons for some days. They merely slept in the Strong Room and were about during the daytime. Newton fell ill after his release. A third time the jury found Acton "Not Guilty."

The fourth and last trial followed immediately. This concerned an unfortunate man named James Thompson, who died in 1726. He suffered from diabetes and his complaint caused him to stink. The Ward Company, as the prisoners' committee was called at the Marshalsea, had complained of him in consequence. Acton had him taken to the Strong Room and he lay there for ten days, during which time his left side mortified. One witness said that after his death a clenched fist could be put in the hole in his side. He was taken out but put back again and died there. It was stated that when representations were made to Acton that the man would die, he exclaimed, "Damn him, let him lie there and perish." Again there was no inquest. The defence was that Thompson was living in a ward called the Pump Room. The other prisoners there complained of his offensive smell, fined him, taking away his coat as he had no money, and ejected him from their room. He applied to Acton for somewhere where he might be in peace. He declined to go to the Sick Ward lest he be fined and have more clothing taken, and elected to go to the Strong Room, where he had a bed and was alone. The jury acquitted.

Then followed a curious scene. The prisoner's counsel applied that he be discharged, but the Judge peremptorily refused to order it. Such a refusal indicated then that the Judge disagreed with the verdict. A prisoner at that date was not entitled to discharge as of right until it was clear that no "appeal of murder" would be brought. Mr. Paxton was appealed to, but he walked out of Court. General Oglethorpe was then asked to intercede. He expressed resentment at being approached. He was, he said, a member of the Commons Committee that had ordered the prosecution, and therefore deemed it his duty to be present, but he was not responsible for the prosecution, and could not imagine why any application should be made to him. He, however, gave his views. He desired the prisoner to be released, not because he thought him innocent, but because every Englishman who had been acquitted had a right to be discharged. "Nor can any subornation of perjury or management of the jury prevent it." These last words give a clear indication of his opinion as to the means whereby the prisoner had escaped sentence of death. The latter was, in fact, afterwards discharged. Another attempt was made to bring him to book, but failed. A Justice of the Peace was found willing to commit him on a fifth charge of murder in the prison. He applied for bail, but was remanded to the next assizes, where the Grand Jury threw out the bill. Sir John Strange, who appeared for the defence in all these cases, in relating his last failure comments that Acton was acquitted to the satisfaction of almost everyone. His sympathy went out to the harpies who had battened on the misfortunes of those whom the law had entrusted in their unworthy hands; not a word for the dead, who had died and were forgotten.

The cases caused a great sensation. A Committee of the House of Commons had, after careful investigation, reported that grave crimes had been committed under the cloak of the law, and had ordered the offenders to be prosecuted. All of them were acquitted. This series of trials shows that the scenes of the "Beggar's Opera" were not the invention of the dramatist, but were taken from life and appreciated as such by the audiences, more easily moved by the humour of the situation than by the misery and degradation of those who were condemned to a living death in prisons that were a disgrace to the country and kept by men unworthy of their trust.

Nevertheless the revelations effected some good. Parliament by Statute removed some of the grosser evils thus disclosed. Others still remained, and public opinion was not sufficiently enlightened to insist upon root and branch reform until the work of John Howard and his followers in later years had borne fruit.

Moreover, from the miserable death of these guiltless prisoners has sprung the great and prosperous State of Georgia. Oglethorpe was not a man to be content with an investigation of prison life and an attempt to avenge his friend. He meditated upon a remedy, and after mature thought decided that men who had no chance in England might in another land, and with renewed hopes, regain prosperity. In June, 1732, he obtained a charter establishing the Colony of Georgia, and thereafter devoted his life to promoting its prosperity. Georgia reveres Oglethorpe as its founder; but it may be doubted whether if the gentle Castell had not died at the hands of the brute Bamfield, that State would have come to such happy birth.

THE TRIAL OF
EUGENE ARAM

THE TRIAL OF EUGENE ARAM

THE real story of the murder for which Aram was hanged, fifteen years after the crime, will never be known. There are three versions: that of Aram himself when examined; next the greatly different one which he told in the few days of waiting after his condemnation; and, thirdly, that of Houseman, who turned King's evidence. Houseman may have been right as to the main fact, but he had much to conceal. Aram's first account is almost certainly not true; and of the second the probability is that only the fact of the murder may be accepted. There seems to have been too many people interested in concealing their share in the crime, but enough is known to conjecture that, as in so many other crimes, committed by several in concert, there was a criminal conspiracy the members of which were not loyal to one another. Perhaps, indeed, the murder was only a casual consequence of thieves falling out.

There are two other circumstances besides the mystery of the murder which have combined to make the trial of Eugene Aram so noteworthy. One was that the interval between the crime and the punishment was so long. Justice is leaden-footed, but rarely, in this world at least, do the mills of God grind so slowly as in this case. It was not until Daniel Clark had been in his grave for thirteen years that steps were taken to charge his murderers, and then a year elapsed before the one who was eventually condemned paid the forfeit. The other circumstance was the intellectual superiority of Eugene Aram. True it is that he was a struggling schoolmaster in a remote town and that the world did not know of his marked ability as a scholar, but that such a man, given to hard study in his scanty leisure, should join in a vulgar fraud or a sudden crime in the company of men of no great education is remarkable. Intellect is no guarantee against crime; but of all men the earnest solitary student seems most exempt from temptations which to others appeal so strongly. One may add to these reasons, also, the singular chance which added a new instance to the old saw that "murder will out." It is not surprising, therefore, that Thomas Hood found in the story the inspiration for a moving poem, or that Bulwer Lytton built upon it a narrative embellished by his fecund imagination. Few years have elapsed since Aram suffered on the gallows without some account of his crime being published for the amusement or instruction of the public.

Let us first examine the kind of man he was. He was born at Ramsgill in the West Riding. The date of his birth is nearly indicated by the fact that he was baptised on 2nd October, 1704. His father was a gardener, respected for his integrity and natural ability. Eugene was educated at small country schools, where he profited by the meagre instruction then afforded, and learned, what is most important, how to learn for himself. From his earliest days he was a student, for ever teaching himself some fresh branch of knowledge, with a strong bias for languages and what is now termed philology. After a short experience of office life he commenced schoolmaster, as the saying goes, at his native village, where he taught with success but with rigid severity. A number of the boys who at various times and places came under his instruction afterwards made their way in the world.

On 4th May, 1731, he married Anne Spence. Little is known about her. She seems to have been of an inferior station in life, and to have gained small affection or esteem from him. While they lived together she bore him many children, but her society was not otherwise congenial. When he deserted her, she seems to have accepted her lot with resignation and made no attempt to recall him to his duty. Apparently she knew of the murder, but until the discovery she kept her peace.

What was the attraction or motive which led to this ill-assorted and ill-starred union it is idle to speculate. But the support of a wife and a large and increasing family must have been a severe tax upon Aram's limited resources. It was in 1734 that he went to Knaresborough, attracted by the post of steward to a small estate, which he combined with that of a private schoolmaster. He had by this time acquired a knowledge of Latin and Greek, and there began to tackle Hebrew and subsequently the Celtic languages. Study and his garden were his only relaxations; but how he could find the opportunity for pursuing knowledge in his small house with his scanty means and leisure it is difficult to imagine, the more so as his neighbours were not such as to afford him much chance of intellectual companionship. It was in these circumstances and amid these surroundings that he perceived that Latin and Greek were cousin languages, and not daughter and mother as scholars then believed; and so he claimed that the Celtic languages belonged to the European family, a circumstance which remained unperceived by other scholars for many years. The notes on the subject which he prepared prove that with better opportunities he would have become a scholar of world-wide reputation. Such was this solitary severe student, hampered by poverty, an uncongenial wife, and the routine of a small school.

Near the schoolhouse lived Robert Houseman, a sturdy broad-shouldered man, who followed the calling of a linen weaver. In the same town also lived Henry Terry, a publican. Houseman, Terry and Aram, were destined to be charged with the same murder, but their fates were widely differing.

The victim was Daniel Clark, who, though only twenty-three, had a thriving business as a shoemaker in which he had succeeded his father. He was pale, and pock-marked and stammered, but these defects had not prevented him from attaining the hand of a young lady of means, large for their station of life. In February, 1745, he was anxiously awaiting the birth of a child.

He had been engaged in some curious transactions which must have caused comment in so small a town. Though his wife had brought him several hundred pounds, he had been buying goods on credit and the goods were of such a kind as to be easily portable. He still owed for the goods when at

nine o'clock on the night of 7th February, 1745, he left home
for the last time. He said he was going to visit his wife, who
was then staying with relatives at a neighbouring village.
Whether that was an excuse or not is uncertain, but he could
hardly have meditated departure since he made an appointment for the next morning. The fact that he did not keep
this appointment led to enquiries which revealed the disquieting
circumstance that he had not seen his wife at all. Nor was he
alone missing. His money and goods had gone. The only
curious feature was that he had not taken his horse.

Now during the night he had been seen by a number of
people. At one time he had been with Houseman; at others
with Houseman and Aram. At two or three o'clock in the
morning he had called up a man who noticed that the other
two were with him. Next morning the man missed a pick,
which was recovered two or three days later from Aram's
house.

After a day or two Clark's absence alarmed his creditors.
They drew the most uncharitable inference and advertised for
him. Reward £15 "and no questions asked." His association with Aram and Houseman led people to think that all
three were in the fraud, and these two men had to submit to a
search. Both had many of the things missing from Clark's
house. The plate had disappeared. Terry was not suspected, but,
with the recovery of part of the goods, the creditors were satisfied and the population settled down to its drab existence. If
Clark had bolted, the absence of the property was explained.
If the other two had aided him, a division of the spoil would
account for what they had. Therefore, as it was generally
believed that Clark had defrauded his creditors, his absence
only troubled his family and those creditors. One cannot dismiss the belief in such a fraud as mere wicked inference from
his disappearance. The circumstances are not entirely inconsistent with a criminal design.

But there were other suspicious matters. Only a few days
later Aram was arrested for debt. The officer, who knew his
means, was astounded when the needy schoolmaster produced
quantities of guineas and paid the debt on the spot. It is true

that this led to Aram's arrest on a charge of stealing Clark's things, but the evidence was not strong enough and he was discharged. About this time he also paid off a mortgage, so that his means had suddenly increased for no obvious reason. It was only after many years that people remembered that Mrs. Clark's dowry was missing, and associated the two facts. At the time they believed that Clark had the money.

Soon after this Aram left Knaresborough. Why he should do so is a matter for conjecture. He left ostensibly on a visit to some relatives, but the neighbours asserted that they still saw him creeping about at night. Mrs. Aram flatly denied this. However that may be, by April, 1745, he had found his way to London and henceforth, so far as is known, his family knew him no more.

There is a curious story that, posing as a man of means, with an estate in Essex, he visited a lady who was under the protection of a man from Leeds. The latter found him at her house, and recognising him, armed the lady with a few pertinent questions by which she could test his bona fides. When next he came she found an opportunity to ask him about Knaresborough. In some confusion of manner he admitted that he had been there on business. When this question was followed by the enquiry whether he knew Daniel Clark he was visibly confounded. He faltered out that he believed that he had read about a man of that name in the newspapers, but why should she ask him about a shoemaker, hastily adding that such was he believed the occupation mentioned in the papers. Then he began to ask questions about her interrogatory. The lady replied that the gentleman he had seen came from Leeds and thought he recognised an acquaintance, but as it was all a mistake it was no great matter. But it was a great matter to Aram, who came no more.

Though for a time he lived on his means, he soon had to find an occupation. He became Latin and writing master at a private school in Piccadilly, where, as part of his remuneration, his employer taught him French. After that he became writing master at a school at Hayes, in Middlesex. He may, though it is not certain, have visited France. His last employment was as a law copyist, a steady, but unremunerative and essentially unexciting occupation. Eventually, during the latter part of 1757, he was engaged as usher (or assistant-master) at King's Lynn, his appointment being duly confirmed by the Town Council. Among his pupils there was James Burney, afterwards an Admiral, brother of Fanny Burney. In addition to his post, he earned money by taking private pupils. There was a lady with him, his niece he said she was, and he found her lodgings at a baker's. His own quarters were a room in the master's house. Some afterwards said that she was his mistress. Others that she was a daughter. A few indeed have been obscene enough to combine the hypotheses. Whatever the relationship, there is a plausible reason for the deceit. An usher's salary and quarters were designed for a bachelor. A mistress must be disguised as a relative. A daughter would lead to enquiries about the rest of the family. Whoever the lady was, there she was, but what became of her is unknown. There is a similar conflict about his life at Lynn. According to some he was a learned, cultured gentleman whose society was much sought after by the local clergy and professional men. According to others he was a solitary, moody, moping individual averse from all social life. Probably the truth lies between the two. An elderly unknown assistant-master would hardly be chosen as an equal companion, but he must have had to meet men who could recognise ability and respect it.

One thing is certain, that he was recognised and the news that he was living there soon reached Knaresborough. As soon as a warrant was issued, the parish constables went as straight to Lynn as a homing pigeon makes for its loft. The current story is that a groom travelling with a stallion who had lived at Knaresborough saw him at Lynn and took the news back. It is at least probable: for somebody saw him.

Meanwhile the disappearance of Clark remained a mystery, though none thought it to be one. No one, not even his family, believed him to be dead. Indeed, his brother-in-law even went so far as to sue him, and when he did not appear to answer the claim, had him outlawed, as was then the practice. The outlawry was declared on 20th October, 1746, and remained on the records until 1832, when someone with a glimmering of sense, thought that a man who had been murdered eighty-seven years ago did not deserve to have the entry renewed, and omitted it. Houseman alone gave a hint of uneasiness. Though it escaped comment at the time, his townsfolk noticed that whenever the Lidd overflowed its banks, he wandered along the stream as far as St. Robert's Cave, the reputed home of a mediæval hermit. He had reason. The mystery of Clark's disappearance might be solved by the swollen stream.

At last on 1st August, 1758, a labourer named Thompson, while digging at Thistle Hill, near Knaresborough, brought to light some human bones. Two days later he uncovered the rest of the skeleton. The news caused great excitement in the town and for some reason the popular imagination jumped to the conclusion that the bones were Clark's and that he had been murdered. Why the mere unearthing of a skeleton should cause this *volte-face* it is too late to enquire. The coroner was informed. Surgeons were called to examine the remains and on the 14th August the coroner and his jury "sat upon" them. Witnesses deposed that about fourteen years before they had noticed, at the spot where the bones were found, the earth recently disturbed. Mrs. Aram gave evidence that she believed Clark to have been murdered, and one witness swore that, as Clark was the only person missing thence in his time, the skeleton must be that of Clark. The surgeons were sure of it. The bones were those of a young man of Clark's age and size and had lain on the ground for the right period. The jury were convinced. The verdict was that the body was Clark's, and that he had been murdered by a person or persons unknown.

The local worthies then proceeded to apply what they considered an infallible test. They brought up Houseman to see the bones. He responded beautifully. The summons caused him alarm and confusion. He came with reluctance and, with visible repugnance, took up one of the bones when ordered so to do. But all these signs of guilt did not evoke any response from the dead. In fact the contrary occurred. Houseman said, "This is no more Dan Clark's bone than mine."

Asked his reason he said that he had a witness who saw Clark after his disappearance, and sure enough the man was produced and declared that such was the case. For some reason this was thought conclusive, though why Daniel Clark could only have been murdered on 7th February, 1745, is not obvious. The coroner was still in the town. He summoned a fresh jury whose verdict was an unknown person murdered by someone unknown. Incidentally, as all the evidence of murder related to Daniel Clark, these events do not reflect much credit on the coroner's intelligence. It was about equal to his law, for he should have known that only the Court of King's Bench could authorise a second inquest on the same body. It is just possible that Houseman's signs of guilt were not misplaced. There is a story about a Jew pedlar, a young man who had been in Knaresborough, but no one had seen him go. But that may be mere idle gossip.

The jury having decided that the remains were not Daniel Clark's, the local justice of the peace decided to issue a warrant to arrest Houseman and Aram for murdering Clark. The evidence available was the same as when he had disappeared. The only charge was that men had jumped to the right conclusion, but had found the wrong body. Now came the turn of Houseman. He was examined, and like most other criminals he said too much and too little. He would only admit that he was with Clark and had left him at Aram's house, but indicated that there was more to tell. He was committed to prison and on the way convinced his custodians that he was conscious of guilt. When they reached York, the justice, by a coincidence hardly fortuitous, happened to be there, and to him Houseman then confessed that he had seen Aram strike Clark several blows when they were near St. Robert's Cave, but he knew nothing more, as he ran away. Afterwards Aram came back alone. After that he described where the body lay —which he could not have known had his story been literally true—and at the precise spot he mentioned inside the cave men dug up a body. At the inquest many witnesses deposed to what they had heard. The evidence was mostly hearsay, but a coroner is not bound by the laws of evidence as at a trial.

What was certain was that this dead man had been murdered by a crushing blow on the base of the skull. The jury found that this body was Clark's and that he had been murdered by Houseman and Aram. The former was in custody. The next day, 19th August, Aram was arrested at Lynn. He reached Knaresborough in custody on the 21st.

The return of Aram was greeted by a crowd. His wife and daughters went to see him, but they had to wait until he had finished conversation with the local notabilities. The wife met with an off-hand recognition. Naturally he did not know his daughters whom he had left as little children. His examination by the justice was inconclusive. He knew nothing about Clark's disappearance. For the most part he said he did not remember when facts were put to him. He was ordered to prison, but like Houseman, manifested a desire to say more, and was brought back. Then he admitted that he with Houseman and Terry had aided Clark to remove goods from the latter's house. Eventually all four went to St. Robert's Cave, where they beat most of the plate flat. By then it was nearly four o'clock, much too late for Clark to set off, and it was arranged that he should remain in the cave until the next nightfall. Terry undertook to bring food. Next night all three went to visit Clark, but he (Aram) remained on watch outside. He heard a noise which he put down to beating out the rest of the plate. After an hour the two came out and told him that Clark had gone. Then they went back to Houseman's. Afterwards Terry told him that he had disposed of the plate in Scotland. That, declared Aram, was all he knew.

Terry was at once taken and examined. He met Aram's allegations with a flat denial, but was also committed. The three had a long wait for trial. The next Assizes were not until March, 1759, and then the only event was a successful application to postpone the trial. The prosecution were in a difficulty. Apart from the confessions, the evidence, so far as it was admissible, merely established a case of grave suspicion. The question had to be faced whether one of the prisoners should be admitted to give evidence. Houseman's story was the most direct, but there were inconsistencies; and to use him would

mean that Mrs. Aram could not give evidence. On the other
hand, Aram's statement was consistent with Clark not having
been murdered, but, if believed, he would implicate both the
others. Terry declared he knew nothing and his evidence would
of course be useless. Aram got an inkling that Houseman
would rat and enquired about the admissibility of his evidence.
In the meantime he was preparing his defence and occupying his
spare time in writing and study. On 28th July, 1759, the
Summer Assize began. Mr. Justice Noel took the pleas of the
Crown. True bills were returned and on 3rd August the three
men came up for trial. Houseman had counsel. Aram had not.
The former's trial was a mere form. No evidence was offered
and he was accordingly acquitted. Then came Aram's turn.
Mr. Fletcher Norton, K.C., a celebrated hectoring leader, with
three juniors, was charged with the prosecution. The opening
speeches have not been preserved. The first witness was
Houseman, who in the main repeated his confession. If believed, the jury could convict on that alone, but it is a rule
of practice, almost a rule of law, that the evidence of an
accomplice must be corroborated. There are too many reasons
against relying solely upon such evidence, and accordingly
witnesses were called to prove the events of the fatal night,
the prisoner's unexplained possession of sudden means, what
happened at his arrest, the finding of the body and the medical
evidence that the deceased had been killed by violence. The
case for the prosecution had been thoroughly and competently
revised and followed the familiar course of such trials. Aram
was then called on to make his defence. He read his celebrated speech. After introductory remarks concerning his
ignorance and inexperience in the ways of the law, and a
protest against being charged with a crime of which he was
incapable, he made his points. His whole life, he declared,
refuted the charge. "I concerted not schemes of fraud, projected no violence, injured no man's person or property. My
days were honestly laborious, my nights intensely studious,"
and he remarked that no man was "ever corrupted at once.
Villainy is ever progressive." At the time of the murder he
had just risen from a sick bed and indeed had never fully

recovered. Nor had he any motive to murder Clark. Secondly, he averred, there was no evidence that Clark was dead. The inference from his disappearance was too fallible. He cited the case of a manacled criminal who had escaped from York Castle in 1757, and never been heard of since (his remains were found in 1780). The skeleton proved nothing, as was shown by numerous instances which he cited. Indeed another skeleton had been identified as Clark's. Moreover, there were authentic cases of men reappearing after others had been convicted of murdering them. His first example was that of the Perrys for the murder of William Harrison in 1661, a celebrated case, though modern research has tended to prove that it never occurred. Then with a general denial of guilt he concluded with these words: "I, at the last, after a year's confinement, equal to either fortune, put myself upon the candour, the justice, the humanity of Your Lordship, and upon yours, my countrymen, gentlemen of the jury." It was a remarkable speech, but its merits are purely academic. No lawyer would have been content with such an appeal. Prepared as it was in advance, it ignored the proof advanced against him. There was no comment upon Houseman's evidence or upon his credibility; nor was there any attempt to answer or evade the corroborative evidence. It is useless to declare "I did not do it" when the evidence is that you did. It is idle to say "I had no motive" when proof shows both motive and attainment of the desired gain. Such evidence must be dealt with to convince the jury that it should not be accepted or does not prove the fact. Nor is it of any advantage to cite other instances to discredit evidence which points definitely to murder at a particular place, and a definite place of burial, and when a body has been found at the designated place, obviously murdered in the way described. Mere reasoning has never weighed much against definite, positive evidence, and as a defence the speech was futile. Even an alibi would have stood more chance. The whole prosecution rested upon Houseman. If the jury could be brought to believe that the turncoat was the murderer, an acquittal was possible, for, if he were wholly discredited, the rest of the evidence might be explained away. The fact that contemporary attention was directed to the defence shows that Aram's cross-examination could not have had any point, if indeed he did cross-examine at all. To question witnesses is an art which demands both practice and natural ability, and there is nothing in Aram's speech which suggests that he had any aptitude for the task. Consequently the case must have been "dead," and the judge would not spend much time upon the summing-up. The jury certainly had no hesitation in pronouncing Aram guilty. He received both verdict and sentence with composure.

Then came the trial of Terry. The only evidence against him was Aram's confession, which was not admissible and accordingly he was acquitted without trial. That day, he rode rejoicing out of York into oblivion.

The execution was fixed for the 6th August, and in the few remaining days of his life Aram set to work to compose a justification and to see his visitors. To a clergyman he admitted the murder, but attributed it to his belief in an intrigue between his wife and Clark, a most unlikely story. He assented to the suggestion that the murder was not at the Cave and to another that Houseman had urged him to murder his wife in order to close her mouth. Indeed, the most reasonable hypothesis on the known facts is that Clark was murdered in or near Aram's house. In spite of his assured air, Aram was profoundly moved by the disgrace, and on the night before his execution attempted suicide. Although this left him weak, the sentence was duly carried out on the Knavesmire, in the presence of an immense multitude. The sentence went further and directed his body to be hanged in chains at Knaresborough, and this was done. There it remained for many years, and tradition asserts that, as it disintegrated, his widow gathered up and buried the fragments that fell. A local physician, Dr. Hutchinson, one night stole the skull and this is now placed in the Museum of the Royal College of Surgeons.

Houseman incurred the full force of public dislike of an informer. A mob, thirsting for his blood, chased him through Knaresborough on his return. He never afterwards was seen in the day-time, and soon removed from the town. He is said to have attempted several times to hang himself. At last he returned to die in 1777, and his body was secretly removed to Marton for burial, lest scandalous tumults should break out at Knaresborough.

A subsidiary mystery is why one Francis Iles of York was able to suppress such part of the examinations as reflected upon him. It would seem that he had received some of the goods and his reputation was that of a "fence." But that part of the case was never mentioned.

Thus died Eugene Aram, a man of natural, even of brilliant, ability, who in happier circumstances might have lived to earn a scholar's reputation, and to gain credit for his country. Falling, one knows not how, into temptation, he brought himself to a shameful end and involved with him an innocent family.

"Murder will out."

THE TRIAL OF
DR. DODD

THE TRIAL OF DR. DODD

On 27th June, 1777, the streets and houses on the route from Newgate to Tyburn were thronged by an immense multitude who came to see a parson die on the gallows. It was the famous preacher, Dr. Dodd, who had secured as a special favour that he might make this last journey in a coach. Though he tried to conceal himself, he was seen by many, who remembered to their last moments the dreadful despair of his ghastly face. At Tyburn the crowd had waited for hours, and before the coach arrived it had swelled to such dimensions that the memory of man could not recall so large an assembly. At last the coach came, followed by the cart in which rode his fellow victim, a young man attended only by his father. As the procession moved on, all hats were removed and the long-threatened rain fell in torrents. But the crowd had come to see a memorable execution. They stayed, and in their turn were startled at the agony depicted on the face of the sufferer. He had been attended by fellow-clergymen and friends, but when he saw the friendless state of his companion he forgot his own doom and devoted himself to ministering to the wretched youth. Dr. Dodd had committed forgery, and therefore had to die. The other had attempted to commit suicide, and the law, in its horror at such an act, was now to punish the attempt by completing it. To-day neither could be sentenced to death. After comforting the other, Dr. Dodd turned to his companions and accepted their religious ministrations. All this took place in deathly silence. The last words were soon said; but the public heard none of them. Dr. Dodd had indeed prepared a speech from the gallows, as was then customary, but so great was the multitude that few could have heard, and he judged it best to go silent to his doom. The hangman then made ready. His more famous victim whispered earnestly to him before the nooses were adjusted. When all was ready, the cart was driven away, leaving the two men hanging. The executioner at once ran to Dodd and steadied his legs. There he hung until the prescribed period was over. Then the bodies were cut down and handed to their friends. Dr. Dodd's party at once set out in a coach for Goodge Street, where a hot bath and a surgeon were waiting to make an attempt to revive him if life were not quite extinct. But whatever chance may have existed was defeated by the throngs which encumbered the streets. The coach took an interminable time to travel the distance, and, in spite of all that human skill could do, the body remained inert.

Dr. Dodd had been a notable figure in London.

Without birth or influence, he had made a rapid advance. At an early age he was a fashionable preacher, an accepted author and a man to whom the aristocracy entrusted their sons. Having achieved all this by the age of thirty, there was no position in the Church to which he might not legitimately aspire. But a lack of balance, which led him to a life of display beyond his ample income, and to commit follies fatal to the reputation of a clergyman, at last resulted in the forging of a bond in order to raise money owing to pressing creditors. The forgery was discovered, and from that moment his doom was sealed.

He was the son of the Vicar of Bourne, in Lincolnshire, and was born there on 29th May, 1729. A promising scholar, he gained in 1745 a sizarship at Clare Hall, Cambridge. His undergraduate career was noteworthy. His application to his studies pleased his tutor and gained for him the position of 15th Wrangler. Apart from that he was a social success. His manner was pleasing, he was apt in conversation, and shone in undergraduate circles. His love for dress and dancing and his sprightly wit made him an equal favourite with women. And he earned money for his pleasures by his pen, succeeding in that venture when he was but eighteen. It was his success in speaking and in writing that led him on taking his degree in 1749 to descend upon London, instead of waiting to see whether he could gain preferment at the University. He had no defined plans. He thought that he could make a name in literature. He had some thought of the Bar, but took no steps to join an Inn. Instead he took to writing poetry, and for amusement he took to debating and to other and grosser pleasures. Thus nearly two years passed, and then he took a step which in the end involved him in responsibilities which he was unable to bear. He married. The bride was Mary Perkins, a lady with charm and beauty, but of no family. Not content with undertaking the support of a wife when he was barely able to support himself, he took a house in Wardour Street, which he furnished exquisitely. There could be only one end to this extravagance—long years dragged out in a debtor's prison. His friends were alarmed. They informed his father, who came to London to advise his wayward son. The situation was too plain to misunderstand; and young Dodd was easily persuaded to give up his house and to adopt a profession. There was only one which could yield him an immediate income, and so on 19th October, 1751, he was ordained at Caius College, Cambridge, by the Bishop of Ely, and took up his duties (how sharp a downward social curve!) as curate to the Rector of West Ham.

In the same year he published his book on "The Beauties of Shakespeare," which earned him an immediate reputation and is still sometimes to be met with on the bookstalls. He settled down to his work and became an immediate success. His sermons attracted large congregations, and though some complained that they betrayed the fervour of a Methodist, all agreed that they were eloquent and touching. By 1752 he had been elected to a lectureship at St. James's, Garlick Hill, in the City; this, in 1754, he changed for a similar position at St. Olave's, Hart Street (Pepys's church), where he remained for some years, holding also the appointment of Lady Moyer's lecturer at St. Paul's. His reputation as a preacher was growing, and this gained for him in 1758 the position of chaplain at Magdalen House, a newly-established refuge for fallen women. The chapel there was opened to the public, and it was crowded to the doors by hosts of fashionable ladies.   But he did not confine himself to his duties as a chaplain.   He threw himself into philanthropic work and helped to found the society for the Relief of Poor Debtors, and the Association now known as the Royal Humane Society.

He had from ordination supplemented his income by receiving into his house at West Ham a few boys of family. He was thus enabled to proceed M.A. in 1759, and his reputation gained him the support of men of influence.   In 1763 the young King George III, made him a chaplain-in-ordinary and seriously considered appointing him tutor to the Duke of York.   The Bishop of St. David's presented him to the Prebend of Brecon.   The Bishop also recommended him to the Earl of Chesterfield as tutor to Philip Stanhope, his godson and heir.   In an evil hour for himself Dodd was fortunate enough to obtain the position.   In 1766 he obtained the degree of Doctor of Laws of Cambridge.

Up to this period, Dr. Dodd had increased in reputation and fortune; but he now changed his mode of life.   He had retained his house at West Ham in the hope of obtaining the rectory, but being disappointed he broke up his establishment there and took a house in Southampton Row.   He resigned his lectureships in the City, and embarked on a life of ostentation and luxury far beyond his very considerable means. He acquired a country house at Ealing and he and his pupils could frequently be seen driving through the streets of London in a sumptuous coach.   Having won a lottery prize of £1,000, he invested the money in a partnership with a builder, who built him a proprietary chapel.   The income so obtained was large, but not large enough to meet his increasing expenditure. In 1772 he obtained two benefices, Hockliffe and Chalgrove, in Bedfordshire.   These were the first livings he enjoyed.

It was at this period that he made his first acquaintance with the criminal courts.   One day, when he and his wife were driving home from Barnet, their coach was stopped near St. Pancras by a highwayman who fired a bullet which fortunately only broke the glass.   He was arrested, convicted and hanged.

Next year, in 1773, his pupil, Philip Stanhope, succeeded

as Earl of Chesterfield, and at once appointed Dodd as his chaplain. If he had kept himself within reasonable limits he would have been firmly established. But his rapid advance and his ostentation had gained him detractors, who whispered to one another stories of his early life of dissipation, and soon, had more interesting and recent stories to retail. His brother clergymen were shocked at his publishing a novel in the style of Smollett, called "The Sisters," the tone of which they thought unworthy of the cloth. In March, 1773, paragraphs began to appear commenting on a pretty serving-maid at his house, and others made merry about his friendship with Polly Kennedy, a noted woman of the town of those days. In December of that year another public attack on his morals appeared. These might have been ignored as mere slanders, but he took a foolish step which involved him in open and notorious disgrace. It came about in this way. In February, 1774, the vicar of a well-endowed parish in London was made Bishop of Bath and Wells. This created a vacancy, and the patronage was in the Lord Chancellor's hands. Lord Apsley was then on the Woolsack. A few days after the announcement of the vicar's promotion Lady Apsley was astonished and angered at receiving an anonymous letter offering her £3,000 if she would procure the presentation for a person who would be named later. She at once showed the letter to her husband, who caused an investigation to be made. The letter was traced to Dr. Dodd's household. He denied responsibility, but in such a shuffling manner that none doubted that he was the instigator. Lord Apsley reported the matter to the King, who at once struck Dr. Dodd off the list of Royal chaplains. The affair having become public, he was lampooned in the public Press, and Foote staged at his theatre in the Haymarket a diverting and successful extravaganza based on the incident. Dodd found it convenient to take refuge on the Continent. The scandal had resulted in loss of reputation and means and had increased the pressure of creditors upon him. At Geneva he met Lord Chesterfield, who came to his aid by presenting him to the living of Wing, in Buckinghamshire. He came back to London to find that his character was gone, and he was imprudent enough on returning to France to appear on a racecourse with low companions, where he was seen. The incident was duly commented on in London. The notoriety he had gained forced the resignation of his chaplaincy, and shortly afterwards he sold his chapel to meet pressing debts. But he abated none of his ostentation, and on the brink of ruin entertained sumptuously all who would accept his discredited hospitality. At one such dinner in January, 1777, John Wilkes was a guest. Whatever may be thought of Wilkes, he was by his life and conversation the last person with whom a scrupulous clergyman would have been on intimate terms, and the fact of the intimacy weighed heavily against him when his fate was in debate.

This dinner was the last act of his prosperity. The catastrophe was at hand. On 2nd February, 1777, he preached his farewell sermon at Magdalen to an audience who were deeply moved by his eloquence and fervour. They little thought that they were listening to his last sermon in public.

On the 4th February, he went to a broker named Robertson to entrust him with a secret and delicate negotiation. He had been asked, so he said, to arrange a loan on bond for a nobleman who had just come of age. He brought the bond, which was for £4,200 but had no date or signature, nor were the lenders to be present when it was signed. Robertson tried in the usual quarters, but most refused to entertain such a mysterious transaction. At last Messrs. Fletcher and Peach were found, and they agreed to lend the £4,200. Robertson informed Dodd, who then gave him the bond, bearing the signature of Lord Chesterfield, with Dodd as witness. The broker was aware that two witnesses were necessary, and so as not to delay the advance, he added his own name as the second witness. He then received the money, which he handed to Dodd, who gave him £100 as his commission.

The lenders handed their bond to their solicitor. He, for some reason, felt suspicious, and went to Lord Chesterfield, who at once repudiated the signature. The solicitor thereupon went to the Lord Mayor, who by great ill-luck happened to be an active member of the Court party opposed to Wilkes, and warrants were at once issued against Dodd and Robertson.

After arresting Robertson, the officers went with Chesterfield's agent to take Dodd. The news overwhelmed him, and he offered to make what reparation he could. The agent, Mr. Manley, told him that the only way to save himself was to restore the money, and Dodd at once produced £3,000 in notes, and gave two cheques for £700 altogether, and suffered judgment for £400 on the security of his furniture. The remaining £100 was obtained by Robertson giving up his commission. Dodd expected to obtain the bond back, but the Lord Mayor insisted upon the charge being pressed, and so he was brought up at the Guildhall. He protested his innocence, not that he denied the forgery but on the ground that he had no intent to defraud. Tradesmen were pressing him and he needed £300. The only reason for the large sum raised was that the actual amount needed was too small for a peer to seek to borrow. He could have made the money good. "My Lord Chesterfield," he pleaded, "cannot but have some tenderness for me as my pupil. I love him, and he knows it. There is nobody wishes to prosecute. I am sure Lord Chesterfield don't want my life. I hope he will show clemency to me. Mercy should always triumph over justice." The Lord Mayor insisted on committing both men for trial. Dodd was taken on foot through the streets to Wood Street Comptor, thus giving the populace the unusual experience of hooting and jeering at a clergyman in the hands of authority on a capital charge.

Little time was lost. On 19th February he was brought up at the Old Bailey to plead to the indictment. Mr. Mansfield and Mr. Davenport appeared to prosecute, Mr. Howarth, Mr. Cooper and Mr. Buller represented the prisoner. Though two men had been committed, the indictment was against one only. The other's name appeared on the back as a witness. Robertson had succeeded in convincing the prosecution that he was a mere dupe and the charge against him was dropped. Before pleading, Dodd objected to the indictment. His point was that he had been committed with another and the indictment had been found on that other's evidence. His counsel moved to quash the indictment, and after all the legal gentlemen had

had their say, the Court persuaded them to agree to the trial proceeding, promising to reserve for the opinion of the judges at Serjeants Inn the question whether Robertson was an admissible witness. Thereupon Dr. Dodd pleaded not guilty. Three judges attended: Mr. Baron Perryn, Mr. Justice Willes and Mr. Justice Gould. The trial was soon over, since there could be no dispute as to the facts. Lord Chesterfield and the other witnesses gave evidence and then the prisoner was called upon for his defence. It was a mere repetition of the too familiar plea of the detected defrauder, that he never meant to defraud. He added that he had been prosecuted after the most solemn engagement to the contrary given him by Lord Chesterfield's agent. Then he referred to the evil consequences which would ensue to his wife and creditors if he were convicted, and ended: "If, upon the most impartial survey of matters, not the slightest intention of injury can appear to anyone . . . and if no injury was done to any man upon earth, I then hope, I trust, I fully confide myself in the tenderness, humanity and protection of my country."

The summing-up was short and the jury retired, but returned almost at once with a verdict of Guilty, but added a recommendation to mercy. Dr. Dodd could have had no illusions as to the verdict, and he probably made his appeal with the object of obtaining such a recommendation. There was, indeed, much to be said in favour of mercy. The offence was an isolated one, there had been complete restitution on what certainly looks like a promise of immunity, and the consequences to the prisoner were terrible, even if he escaped all judicial punishment. For the time being sentence was deferred until the judges had given their opinion whether Robertson's evidence was admissible. Dodd went back to Newgate, where he stayed for a long period of waiting. He occupied himself in writing a book, published under the title of "Thoughts in Prison," and in ministering to his fellow-prisoners. On 26th May, 1777, the judges, having decided that the trial and conviction were good in law, Dodd appeared at the Old Bailey for sentence. It was, and still is, the practice to ask a convicted felon whether he has anything to say why sentence should not be passed upon him. The wretched man read out a moving appeal, composed for him by Dr. Johnson, who, though only having the slightest acquaintance with him, had been moved by compassion to alleviate his sufferings. The reading of the speech was an agony to the prisoner, but he struggled through to the end, and then was so overcome that it was some time before the Recorder could pass sentence. He had no discretion, for the only penalty was death, but he took occasion to warn the prisoner not to expect a reprieve.

Now came the great effort on Dodd's behalf. There had been a revulsion in his favour. The promise made and broken, and the fact that Lord Chesterfield had given evidence—though he could not refuse—caused men to think that the prisoner had been ill-used. The newspapers were filled with paragraphs and letters all advocating a reprieve. Nearly 30,000 signed a petition. Others exerted influence more privately. Even the City presented a petition, composed by Dr. Johnson, who worked manfully. He wrote to the Lord Chancellor and to the Lord Chief Justice. He petitioned both the King and the Queen, and even composed Dodd's last sermon which he preached to the prisoners at Newgate on the Sunday before his execution. But all efforts were in vain. As Dodd had been unfortunate in his Lord Mayor, so he was unfortunate in having his ultimate fate decided by the young King, advised by the aged Lord Mansfield.

It was then the custom for the King to consider death sentences at a meeting of the Privy Council, and Dodd's case came up at a meeting on 13th June, 1777. Lord Mansfield had the chief voice. He was moved by the fact that there had been some notable cases of forgery recently, and on this occasion the crime was committed in abuse of a position of great trust. The current ideas on punishment then favoured the notion that severity was the best deterrent, and Lord Mansfield was not disposed to make an exception which might render it difficult to execute the supreme penalty against less prominent offenders. The King was frankly prejudiced. He was a young man who abhorred vice, and Dodd had already excited his disgust. His past life had not been creditable to a clergyman, especially to one who had been a royal chaplain. They decided that Dodd was to die. The execution was fixed for the 27th of the same month.

Even now there was a faint hope. Friends renewed their supplications, but all in vain. On the 26th Dodd saw his wife and friends and bade farewell to the world. His remaining hours were devoted to preparation for the next world, and his dread and horror at his shameful end drove him to penitence and prayer. Those around him were shocked at the corpse-like pallor and the agony of his expression as on the fatal day he prepared to mount a coach once more to drive along those streets where formerly he had been driven in splendour, but now was destined for Tyburn. His end has been described.

Thus died William Dodd, who by his eloquence and brains had overcome the disabilities of poverty and the lack of influence, and was established in a career at an age when the fortunate who begin with all advantages have barely put their feet upon the ladder. But he was a weak man, without morals or discretion, and when temptation came his way he fell at once. Fortunately his parents had not lived to see his disgrace, but his poor wife, faithful to him in his misfortunes, dragged on a wretched existence, insane and poor, for ten more years. When she died, the family came to an end. There are none who trace their descent from that gifted, drifting, versatile and wretched man.

THE TRIAL OF
WARREN HASTINGS

THE TRIAL OF WARREN HASTINGS

WARREN HASTINGS was the first Governor-General of British India. The East India Company had begun as a trading enterprise but by degrees had added to its commercial pursuits the attributes of sovereignty. Supremacy in India had been won by the triumphs of Clive, and common expectation had settled down to an enjoyment of the fabled wealth of the East. The British Government exacted tribute, the shareholders demanded increased dividends, with the result that the local administrators, faced with the task of re-organising a land recently ravaged by war and with the necessity of remitting vast sums to England, found their position impossible. In a few years the Company was reduced to hopeless insolvency, and was forced to come to the State for assistance. That assistance was given, but at the price of a measure of control. Two Acts were passed in 1773, one to provide finance and the other to regulate administration. The latter Act was imperfect. The Government of British India was vested in a Governor-General and a Council of which he and four others were members, and a Court was set up for the administration of justice. The Governor-General was seated at Calcutta with control over the Governors of Bombay and Madras. The Act was couched in vague terms and did not afford effective and definite rules for the vital matters upon which good government alone could be based. The relations between the Governor-General and the Council were left uncertain, and as he was only one of five, with a casting vote in case of equal division, he might and did find himself in a minority, though bearing all the responsibility for failure. His control over the other Presidencies was not effective and he might and did find himself committed to measures which he would never have sanctioned. The spheres in which the Council and the Court were to exercise their respective functions were not marked out, nor was any care taken to state or define the system of jurisprudence which the Court was to adopt.

As if these problems were not enough, the Company's position was dual in two respects. It was at once the Government and a trading concern. As Government, its powers were derived from the British Parliament, and from grants and appointments from native rulers, whose position as sovereigns or as subordinates of the Grand Mogul would have defied any lawyer to state with precision. Moreover the new régime was almost at once tested by a war which threatened its very existence.

Warren Hastings owed his selection to a long and honourable career. He had been educated at Westminster, where he formed a life-long friendship with the poet Cowper, and was a fellow-pupil with Elijah Impey, the new Chief Justice.

As a youth he had been left an orphan and thereby deprived of the hopes of an Oxford career by his guardian, who had procured him a writership under the East India Company. In India he had pursued the normal career of a subordinate official, but when troubles came he rose rapidly. He escaped by good fortune the horrors of the Black Hole, and after acting for the Governor of Calcutta at the Court of Surajah Dowlah, he shouldered a musket under Clive. That genius very soon recognised Hastings' merits and appointed him as Resident at the Court of Meer Jaffier, the successor of Sarajah Dowlah in the rule of Bengal. In the period of misrule that followed, Hastings kept free from the prevailing scramble for quickly but doubtfully-earned wealth, and on reaching England in 1764 he was not, according to the standard of the "Nabob," a man of any great means. For several years he lived here in retirement, but in 1768 he was appointed one of the Council of Madras, where his reform of the Company's business and finances earned him promotion to be Governor of Calcutta, an office conferred upon him in 1772, which he held when appointed to be Governor-General.

His Council consisted of four members: Barwell, a man of

great experience in India, General Clavering, Colonel Monson, and Philip Francis, the last named being the reputed author of "The Letters of Junius." These three owed their places to their Parliamentary connections in England, and knew nothing of India. Yet at once, headed by Francis, they set up in opposition to the Governor-General, who found himself in a permanent minority.

His position was the more remarkable in that it passed the wit of man to say what constitutional position he occupied. The great Empire of the Moguls still existed and most of the native rulers owed at least a nominal allegiance to the Grand Mogul. The Company by its servants exercised functions delegated to them by the Nawab of Bengal, who was in fact their nominee. Over some princes the Company claimed dominion, with others the tie was the bond of treaties. In some matters the Governor-General was exercising sovereign powers, in others he was the delegate, while at the same time his authority was limited by the control of the Company, which was in turn bound by statutes and charters, many of the provisions of which were so loosely drawn as to encourage doubt and disobedience. The other Presidencies had separate administrations. They could and did ignore Calcutta, but their security was of vital importance in India. Hastings found himself administering provinces lately ravaged by war, he was forced to reconstruct the methods of administration, compelled to raise and remit moneys to England, and faced with persistent opposition from an irremovable majority. And in spite of all, with brilliant persistency and resource, he vindicated the interests of Great Britain in India.

The majority endeavoured to force him to resign. He did authorise his agent in England to proffer his resignation in certain events, but withdrew that power in 1775. The first important step of policy that Hastings adopted was to come to an arrangement in 1774 with the Nawab of Oude, with a view to using Oude as a bulwark against the Mahrattas. This policy had been suggested by Clive. The Nawab demanded the assistance of English troops to overcome the Rohillas. These were lent him, and the victory was followed by more than the usual atrocities on the part of the ruler and his followers. Soon afterwards an accusation was made by Nuncomar against Hastings. Nuncomar had been a candidate for the post of deputy for the ruler of Bengal, but another was preferred. Hastings had in former years fallen out with him. He now said that Hastings had accepted bribes. The Council voted for an enquiry. Soon afterwards Nuncomar was charged with conspiracy and then with forgery. He was tried by Sir Elijah Impey, the Chief Justice, with a European jury, convicted and hanged. I will not stay to consider the difficult legal and Constitutional questions that arise concerning this trial. Though the conviction was welcome, Hastings swore an oath that he did not promote the prosecution, and it was not charged against him at his trial. In 1777 Hastings' agent, alarmed at the attitude of the Home Government and the Directors, placed his resignation in the Company's hands. In July Mr. Wheler arrived to fill the vacant place. The usual dispute arose with the Council, for Hastings relied upon the withdrawal of his agent's authority, and eventually the High Court of Calcutta pronounced the resignation invalid, and Wheler became a member of the Council. Monson had gone and in November General Clavering died. Henceforth Hastings was in general supported by the Council.

The American Revolution was by this time absorbing the energies of this country. France was about to declare war and French agents were stirring the princes, who were watching their chances. In 1777 the Bombay Government became embroiled with the Mahrattas. Hastings planned to crush them, but Hyder Ali, the ruler of Mysore, began hostilities against Madras. Once again his forces swept over the Carnatic, the British forces were defeated and it seemed with the advent of French forces that the work of Clive would be destroyed. Hastings threw himself into the struggle. He realised that Hyder Ali was the main danger and strained every nerve to oppose him. Eventually, despite the arrival of French troops in 1781, Sir Eyre Coote won the Battle of Porto Novo in 1782. Soon afterwards the Mahrattas made peace, the French withdrew after the Treaty of Paris, Hyder Ali died and his son made his peace. The struggle was over, and British rule remained. One of the main problems had been to raise money, and this led to two celebrated incidents. The Rajah of Benares was a dependent of the Company and was asked for a contribution. He refused and was fined £500,000. Hastings went in person to arrest the Rajah and was besieged in Benares with a small force by the subjects of the Rajah who rose in his defence. The Governor-General was equal to the occasion. The Rajah's forces were defeated and he was deposed.

The position was not clear. As in the case of the Rohillas, the demand on the Rajah related to matters outside the Presidency territory and it was doubtful how far Hastings had or had not power to act. The Council had condemned the Rohilla arrangement, but, as the Rajah of Benares had paid, though reluctantly, in 1778, 1779 and 1780, this trouble arose when the Council acted with him. Unfortunately the administrators appointed to govern the country after the Rajah was deposed behaved with great oppression and were removed. After Benares came Oude. The Nawab had died and was succeeded by his son. The new ruler's mother and grandmother, called the Begums of Oude, had retained the late Nawab's treasures and lands. In the disputes that arose the Council had decided, against Hastings, that the Begums were to be left undisturbed. Naturally a demand for contributions was not welcome and when, in September, 1781, Hastings met the Nawab an arrangement was come to. The published terms did not mention the treasure, but it is clear that some understanding existed. The Nawab seized the eunuchs who administered the Begums' estates and forced them to sign bonds. By February, 1782, £500,000 had been extracted. To get more the unfortunates were tortured, but nothing was gained and they were released in December. Rightly or no it was believed that the treasure amounted to £3,000,000. The Nawab presented Hastings with £100,000. He asked leave to retain this money. Leave was refused and he paid it into the Company's funds. It had been the custom for the Company's servants to accept large presents. The Act of 1773 forbade the practice, but Hastings appears to have found it more convenient to take the moneys in order to pay them over to the Company than to refuse.

A third incident was the appointment of Deby Singh to administer Dinagepore in 1780, when the Rajah of that place died, leaving a disputed succession. It was alleged that Deby Singh was guilty of fraud and oppression. There was undoubtedly unrest. The Company's resident reported adversely of Deby Singh, who was summoned to Calcutta. There a new enquiry was held and he was absolved.

The course of events in England must now be described. In December, 1775, the Directors had approved the action of the Council, and Lord North, the Prime Minister, had also declared against Hastings. It was in consequence of this news that Hastings had authorised his resignation. After that the country became absorbed in the American troubles, but in 1781 the Company's charter was about to expire and Indian affairs became important. The Commons appointed two Committees in 1781, a Select Committee of which Burke was a member, and a Secret Committee over which Dundas presided. The reports were adverse to Hastings. In March, 1782, the Marquis of Rockingham, an old patron of his, became Prime Minister. Burke was now in the Government and he threatened to resign if nothing were done. Accordingly in a Committee of the whole House, Dundas carried a resolution condemning Hastings' schemes of conquest. On 30th May, 1782, the Commons resolved that Hastings should be recalled. The Directors obeyed, but their decision was overruled by the Court of Proprietors. Next year Dundas again demanded his recall, and Burke denounced him as "the grand delinquent of all India." The Coalition proposed Fox's India Bill of 1783, but its defeat in the Lords caused George III to dismiss the Ministry and make Pitt Prime Minister. Dundas joined Pitt.

On 30th July, 1784, Burke moved for papers relating to the case of the Begums, but Pitt opposed in a speech which eulogised Hastings. In 1785 Hastings finally retired, and arrived in England, where he was enthusiastically received. On 25th June, 1785, Burke gave notice of motion to discuss his conduct, but the session ended too soon to pursue the matter.

Next year, with singular imprudence, Major Scott, who looked after Hastings' interests in the Commons, recalled the fact that the motion had not been proposed. Burke at once took up the challenge. On 4th April he tabled nine articles of accusation and produced twenty-two more. Hastings petitioned for leave to reply, and was called to the Bar of the House. He was not skilled as an orator, and he bored the members with an extremely long statement read from a document. On 1st June, 1786, Burke's motion as to the First Article condemning the loan of troops against the Rohillas was negatived. On 13th June came the motion of the Second Article concerning Benares. The Government Whips were out against the motion but, to everyone's surprise, Pitt supported, and the motion was carried. This change of attitude is attributed to Dundas, who had, in the former debate, been faced with the fact that he had reported against Hastings and could make no adequate reply. Next year the matter was revived, when Sheridan made a speech, celebrated in the annals of Parliament. In April, 1787, a Committee was appointed to draw up Articles of Impeachment. An attempt was made then and later to find room for Francis, now an M.P., but the House would never allow him to appear against a personal enemy, who had in 1780 wounded him in a duel. On 10th May, 1787, impeachment was voted and the Commons appointed their managers, of whom the leaders were Burke, Fox and Sheridan. Their counsel was headed by Dr. Scott (afterwards Lord Stowell). Hastings retained Law (afterwards Lord Ellenborough), Plumer (afterwards Master of the Rolls), and Dallas (afterwards Chief Justice of the Court of Common Pleas).

The trial opened in Westminster Hall, on 13th February, 1788. The Lord Chancellor (Lord Thurlow) presided over 170 peers. The trial lasted till April, 1795, coming on at irregular intervals on 148 days. Ultimately, after many changes, the Lord Chancellor having resigned and no less than sixty peers having died, Hastings was acquitted. He left the Court absolved but well nigh ruined.

It was a stately scene in Westminster Hall, when the Lords arrived in a long procession, headed by the junior peers and

"I impeach him in the name and by virtue of those eternal laws of justice which he has violated.

"I impeach him in the name of human nature itself which he has cruelly outraged, injured and oppressed in both sexes, in every age, rank, situation and condition of life."

The tremendous speech was often interrupted by the applause even of the Lords themselves. But it is one thing to deliver a philippic, another to manage a prosecution. It was an error to choose as Managers Members who were not trained lawyers. Even the advising lawyers were headed by two civilians unused to the forms and rules of evidence adopted by the common law. A dispute immediately arose as to procedure. Burke wanted each article to be taken separately, but the defence said, "No. Prove all your allegations and then we will defend them." Lord Thurlow was not in favour of the impeachment and needed no encouragement to hamper the Commons. The Lords decided that the plan suggested by the defence was best.

Then Fox spoke on the charge relating to the Rajah of Benares. He was followed by Grey (afterwards Earl Grey). Then came the edifying spectacle of trained lawyers preventing inadmissible evidence being given. Objection followed objection, and the Managers were overruled time and time again. They showed an inability to understand the rules of relevance and admissibility, and from time to time they made angry protests. Each objection was considered by the Lords. They rose, went in procession to the House of Lords and returned to announce their decision. "The Lords proceed, and the trial stands still," said one of their number. Sometimes the further hearing was postponed to consult the judges, and when they were away on Circuit weeks might and did slip by.

On the fourteenth day Mr. Adam opened the second charge and eventually Sheridan summed up. This closed the Session. By that time the expense of the trial and the length to which it was running excited much discussion.

When the session re-opened on 3rd February, 1789, there was a petition from Hastings as to delay and expense, claiming that the trial should proceed more quickly. The dispute over the Regency Bill absorbed attention, and it was not until 21st April, 1789, that Burke resumed, to open the Sixth Article, detailing hundreds and hundreds of lakhs of rupees which were alleged to have been presented to Hastings. On 7th May, in the course of his speech he said of Nuncomar that Hastings "murdered this man by the hand of Sir Elijah Impey." The matter was raised in the Commons, who resolved that they had given no direction to make such a charge and ordered that it be withdrawn. Hastings' supporters had hoped that a public humiliation would induce Burke to withdraw, but he submitted, and made it clear when doing so, that he intended to pursue the trial to the end. So June came. On the 10th Burke declared that a ruling of the Lords was preposterous, but explained that he merely used the word as meaning putting the cart before the horse. Next day, Law was reprimanded. On 7th July, Burke was stopped from impeaching the credit of his own witness, which made him indignant. On 8th July, when the Session ended, Hastings made another protest. Not one tenth part of one Article had been proved. His life would not be long enough nor his fortune sufficient to enable him to complete such a trial. Had he pleaded guilty his punishment could not have been heavier.

In 1790 proceedings resumed in February. Burke, surprised at a ruling that he could give no evidence to prove allegations not charged in the Articles, protested that the Commons of Great Britain were not bound by any rules of pleading. As laymen they were ignorant of them. The evidence as to bribes proceeded slowly. Objection after objection was taken, for in truth the managers had taken a wrong view of what would be admissible evidence. On 7th, 8th, and 9th June, 1790, Fox summed up the case on the Sixth Article, parts of the Seventh and the Fourteenth which together constituted the thirteen charges of bribery. Before then the Managers had become alarmed at the inordinate length of the case and obtained the authority of the House of Commons to abandon charges. The session ended in June and the case went for the usual long rest for the remainder of the year.

This time there was a real hitch. In December, 1790,

Parliament was dissolved, and when the new Parliament met the question arose whether the impeachment had ended with the old Parliament. It was a difficult question, on which opinions differed. Eminent judges and lawyers took opposite sides. Sir John Scot (the Solicitor-General) thought that the old charges were ended and proceedings must be begun again. So high was feeling that the fact that such was his opinion was deemed by some partisans sufficient proof that he had been bribed. At last it was settled that dissolution does not end an impeachment, and so on 23rd May, 1791, Mr. St. John opened the Fourth Article, charging Hastings with making corrupt contracts and agencies and illegal allowances. By 30th May, the case was closed, and on 2nd June, the prisoner made his general statement in defence. No more was done that year.

On 14th February, 1792, Mr. Law spoke for the prisoner, and was followed by Mr. Plumer. Altogether they occupied eight days, and then on 1st May, 1792, the evidence for the defence began. Now was the turn of the Managers to make objections and they did, but not with much success. The case was beginning to bore people. There was often a difficulty in forming a Court. Often no more than thirty or forty Peers were there, and Burke alone of the Managers was constant in attendance. The war which began in 1792 completed the divergence of views begun by the French Revolution, and they were no longer a united body. Besides, many impartial observers had come to see the hardships of the protracted trial. A petition by Hastings for continuous sittings produced no relief, but often the course of the case was interrupted thereafter by counter-allegations that the other side were causing delays. By 7th June, 1792, the evidence for the defence on the First Article was closed and Dallas summed up in a speech of great power.

When on 15th February, 1793, Mr. Law opened the defendant's case on the Second Article, 121 changes in the peerage had occurred. On 2nd May, the Lord Chancellor warned both sides against unnecessary interruptions. Mr. Burke was most in trouble. On 20th April, in objecting to a report by Sir J. Shore (who was then Governor-General) he said it was the production of one of the persons concerned in fabricating the defence. The other side promptly pointed out that Burke had in a previous year actually called Shore for the prosecution. The defence were making great headway. They were able to call witness after witness who had been in India, for Anglo-Indian opinion was almost wholly in Hastings' favour. Residents there knew the risks that had been run and the perils that Hastings had overcome. Propaganda outside was ceaseless and a stream of returned officials and soldiers added their voices to the turn in the tide. On 26th April, Plumer summed up the defence on the Second Article and on 9th May, Dallas opened the defence on the charges of bribery. On 25th May the Archbishop of York was moved to protest at the tone of Burke's cross-examination. He treated, so the Archbishop averred, the witness as a pickpocket. If Robespierre or Marat had appeared they could not have said things more inhuman or more against all sentiments of honour and morality. This incident nearly caused a conflict between the two Houses, but it passed over. To speed up matters the defence made no speeches on the Fourth Article as to contracts and allowances and their evidence closed on 28th May. Burke succeeded in postponing further proceedings for the rest of the year.

Next February counter-evidence was called. An attempt was made to call Francis, but objection to him was upheld. The tide of objection continued. Once Burke declared that Hastings had published a libel on the Directors. Hastings rose and said, "I beg leave most solemnly to deny it, and to affirm that that declaration is a libel and is of a piece with all the declarations I have heard from the authorised and licensed" —He paused and looked straight at Burke and then added, "Manager." At last the new evidence was concluded and then Mr. Law spoke, dealing with the evidence. Finally came a flood of eloquence for the Commons. Grey spoke on Benares, Sheridan on the Begums, Fox on the bribes, Taylor on contracts and allowances, and finally came Burke's speech summing up the whole case. On 16th June, 1794, he concluded.

Four days later Pitt proposed and carried a vote of thanks to the Managers. Next day Burke applied for the Chiltern Hundreds and left Parliament for ever.

The Lords then discussed the question who was entitled to vote, and finally decided to leave it to the conscience of each Peer whether he should vote. A committee was appointed to consider and report. Next year the report was considered. The charges were all negatived in it, and the debate of 1795 on the report concluded proceedings. On three of the bribery charges no Peer voted for conviction. The greatest vote for an acquittal was 26, the highest for guilty was six. Each charge was voted on separately and on each Hastings was pronounced Not Guilty, and on 23rd April, 1795, after eight years' trial, he was formally discharged.

The solicitor for the Commons put in a bill for £61,695, of which £16,996 was disallowed. The defence cost £71,080. A discussion arose as to the payment, and eventually the East India Company granted Hastings an annuity of £4,000 a year, paying the first ten years immediately. He retired into the country, making one essay in politics in 1806. In 1813, when a renewal of the Charter was under discussion, Warren Hastings, then in his 81st year, came to the bar of the Commons to give evidence. The House rose and uncovered in his honour. Next year he was sworn of the Privy Council, the only and belated reward for his services. He died in 1818.

What was the truth of the accusation? That Burke and his associates believed it is undeniable. They were moved by generous feelings of warmth for the suffering natives of India, whose misfortunes they laid at Hastings' door. But that he was guilty of corruption cannot be truly alleged. That he strained his powers cannot be fairly denied. His acquittal was just and justified. This is true: hampered in every way, thwarted and disobeyed, he saved the Empire in India by sheer force of character and he holds an honoured place among those who have deserved well of their country.

Names which will always be illustrious in English history were employed in the attempt to disparage and destroy a most distinguished Englishman. Those names will be the poorer by reason of their exertions. Burke and Sheridan would have been greater men had they observed a truer perspective: and the bombastic orations of the Commons' spokesmen were in the event defeated, and even rendered ludicrous by the cooler but more telling exertions of trained lawyers.

THE TRIAL OF
DEACON BRODIE

THE TRIAL OF DEACON BRODIE

WILLIAM BRODIE's trial is interesting for its own sake. Rarely does a determined burglar who by his nightly exploits fills the townfolk with nervous dread double that part with the career of a leading tradesman and member of the town council.

In this case the interest is heightened by the circumstances. He was arraigned in Edinburgh in the days preceding the French Revolution, and tried before Lord Braxfield, that legendary figure who lives again as Weir of Hermiston in Stevenson's unfinished masterpiece, according to the procedure so interesting to Southerners because its appearance differs so much from English criminal procedure. The judges, who not only are addressed as "My Lord," but assume the titles of the peerage, though they remain commoners, wear judicial raiment which seems strange to those who know only the Judges of Assize. The prisoners are called the panel. The jurors number fifteen, including a chancellor who is the English foreman. The counsel too hold offices with designations unknown to the southern realm, and all the speeches come at the end of the trial. The case, too, was marked by a sensational incident, when the formidable Lord Justice Clerk, whose frown daunted the boldest advocate, was defied, and with success, by a young barrister of but three years' standing. And the chief figure in the drama when he came to die was hanged on a scaffold, which but for mere chance, he himself would have made and which was, in all probability, designed by him.

The prisoner had always lived a double life. His parents were born of respectable families. Both his grandparents were writers to the signet (or solicitors as they would be called in England). His father was a wright, in substantial business, a freeman of the city, deacon (or head) of his trade guild, and a valued member of the City Council. William was the eldest of eleven children, of whom only three survived to any age. He was born on 28th September, 1741, and his father proudly recorded the momentous event in the family Bible, from which another member cut the entry, when through this child shame and disgrace made them bow their heads.

William was brought up to his father's trade and became a freeman of Edinburgh on 9th February, 1763. He lived at home and conducted himself in business as a model young man, but his evenings were given to frivolity and debauchery. Like so many of his age he was addicted to gaming and frequenting of cockpits, and his habits must have involved him in more expense than even the son of a leading tradesman could afford. In addition to those expensive amusements he assumed obligations of a more permanent nature. He never married, but he was often absent from his home in the society of one of his two mistresses, both of whom he maintained in separate dwellings where they reared the children they bore him. By one of them, Anne Grant, he had three, two girls and a boy, and by the other, Jean Watt, two boys. A curious fact is that neither did his family know of these liaisons nor did either mistress suspect a rival. It was by writing to Anne Grant that he was traced. It was by the evidence of Jean Watt that he hoped to escape the gallows.

When and how he began his career of crime has never been discovered. In August, 1768, a bank was entered by a false key, and the thief escaped with his booty. Years afterwards, when he had been unmasked, people remembered that Brodie had been employed by the bank to do repairs there shortly before the theft. They called to mind that his occupation called him into many houses and that he had abused confidence by taking impressions of keys; and drew the conclusion that this undiscovered crime must be laid to Brodie's account. Others, too, remembered that they had seen him in suspicious circumstances. These stories may be discounted. Wisdom after the event is easy and none of the gossips had breathed a word before the trial.

Meanwhile he followed his worthy father's career. In

1781 he entered the City Council as Deacon of the Guild of Wrights, and held that office in 1781 and 1782. Next year he was a Trades Councillor. In 1786 and 1787 he was again Deacon. His father had died in 1782 at a ripe old age, and left him an ample fortune, but it was soon dissipated. In 1788 he was in embarrassed circumstances though he claimed to be solvent.

During the latter years Edinburgh was the scene of a number of mysterious burglaries, daring and successful. No arrests were made, but this is not surprising since the watch was composed of aged and inefficient men who could never at any time have been an adequate police force. It does not follow that Brodie was the offender. There were many living in the lands of Edinburgh both able and willing to commit such crimes. The impunity with which they were committed permits the inference that the criminal, whoever he was, knew intimately the habits of the victims. Perhaps the very ease and impunity with which the early burglaries were committed led him to reflect whether he too might not repair his falling fortunes, the more so because the victims often called on him to devise more secure methods of baffling marauders.

It is not till 1786 that definite information of his crimes is forthcoming. In July, 1786, an Englishman named George Smith, employed as a travelling hawker, came to Edinburgh. He lodged at a tavern in the Grassmarket kept by Micheal Henderson, and there met two doubtful characters, Ainslie and Brown *alias* Moore. The last-mentioned was an Englishman who had escaped while under a sentence of transportation inflicted upon him at the Old Bailey in 1784 and was concealing himself in Scotland. Brodie was a frequenter of the tavern, and according to Smith proposed to the latter that he should join in a series of burglaries. This proposal was apparently put forward because Smith had worked as a locksmith and seemed not disinclined to a nefarious life. In November, 1786, they began, so Smith said, but in October an important robbery had taken place which was afterwards believed to be Brodie's work. To cover Smith, Brodie found him a small grocer's shop. Thereafter the two worthies committed regular inroads

on tradesmen who kept goods of a kind coveted by thieves—
of great value in a small bulk. Of course a receiver was essential,
and, since from the commencement they went, apparently as a
matter of course, to an exiled Scot in England, it is a reasonable
inference that Brodie was well established and was only increasing his operations by the aid of the locksmith. In the
course of 1787 the two were aided by Ainslie and Brown and
the partnership was complete. In October they caused a great
sensation by stealing the silver mace of the University.

In January, 1788, the shop of some silk mercers at Edinburgh Cross was raided. As in the case of the mace a reward
was offered, and this time it was announced that any accomplice
who could procure the arrest of the guilty parties would receive
a pardon. For some time the offer seemed to be as useless as
the rewards, but it had not escaped Brown's attention. He did
not avail himself of it at the time, but he stored it in his memory. The offer had peculiar attractions to him. He alone
could, if recognised, be seized and sent away without trial, being
an escaped convict. At this time, Brodie's credit with his townfolk received a blow. The four whiled away their time one
evening with a stranger. Dice were produced and the stranger
lost heavily. He did not like this and seized the dice, which
proved to be "loaded." He at once lodged an imformation,
but after wordy warfare the dispute seems to have been
adjusted and no more was heard of it.

In March, 1788, the gang conceived a more daring exploit.
They planned to rob the Excise Office in the Canongate. Brodie
knew the buildings well, because he was often called in to
effect repairs; besides, a distant relation was in the excise and
had come to Edinburgh at times to the office. Brodie was most
kind and hospitable on these occasions. He even went so far
as to accompany his relative to the office and there was able
to glean more information. Like most Government offices, it
was deserted after office hours, only a watchman being on duty.

The plan being pronounced feasible, the preliminaries began.
Brodie and Smith called to make enquiry for his relative.
While Brodie was thus attracting attention to himself, Smith
took an impression of the key of the outer door. He was then

easily able to make the necessary duplicate. Ainslie meanwhile was watching the watchman to learn his habits, and he found that every night from eight to ten the office was left unguarded.

On 4th March they met to make their final preparations and the attempt was fixed for the next evening. On that day Brodie had a dinner party. He was dressed in his usual day attire, a suit of white, and presided over the party from three till eight o'clock, when the last guest departed. This rather upset the plan, as the four had fixed to meet at Smith's house at seven o'clock. As soon as he was free Brodie changed into black and hurried off to the rendezvous. In spite of the cold and snowy weather he was in high spirits, and burst in on the apprehensive three, singing "Let us take the road," a song from the "Beggar's Opera," the play which seems to have been his favourite. They then seized their tools and weapons, and, furnished with masks, set forth to the Excise Office. Ainslie was to watch outside the building, and if alarmed was to blow a whistle. Brodie was to go inside but lurk in the hall, also charged with the duty of watching. Brown and Smith undertook the forcing of the doors and desks. Accordingly Ainslie went first. Then Smith, who at once got to work and was inside when Brodie arrived. Brown was still on his way, so Brodie went to find him.

He soon came, explaining that he had followed home the office-keeper who locked up, so as to avoid a surprise. Brodie then took up his post and Brown joined Smith. The two made a poor haul, not more than £17 in all, and, as so often happens, overlooked the place where a much greater sum was kept. As they were searching they heard the front door open, but paid no attention, and completed their task. As they were about to go, someone ran downstairs and hurried out, closing the front door with a crash. The two became alarmed, especially when they found that Brodie was not at his post. Ainslie, too, had disappeared. He had been watched by a servant girl, though he did not know it. His absence was due to the fact that someone hurried past him into the building and then at once someone else ran out and fled into the street. After a minute another came and slammed the door. He whistled and fled. It was Brodie, whose nerve had given. Mr. Bonar, the Solicitor of Excise, was the mysterious stranger. He was hurrying to get a paper which he had left in his room. As he went in, Brodie bolted. Mr. Bonar thought he was a clerk, and went on, and finding the paper, went away.

Ainslie, Brown and Smith met again at the appointed place, but Brodie did not turn up. He was busy establishing an alibi. He had rushed home, changed, and then went to Jean Watt's house, where he spent the night. Next day he met his associates, who made no secret of their annoyance. On the second day they shared the swag and sent Mrs. Smith off with the booty preciously garnered, which had to be disposed of through their fence. The town was by then ringing with the news, and Brown had been thinking hard. That night he saw the Procurator-Fiscal and told his story. For some reason he only mentioned Smith and Ainslie, who were arrested the next day. It was not long before the news reached Brodie that arrests had been made. He could not know how much information was available, and with a courage which contrasts strangely with his flight on the occasion of the crime, he went round to the Tolbooth as a disinterested citizen curious to see the notorious criminals. He failed, because strict orders were given that no one should see them. This failure induced him to flee. He did not know that no one as yet had mentioned his name but, knowing his associates, he must have concluded that nothing but a miracle would prevent them doing so. So on the Sunday he went. As soon as Smith heard of his flight he made a confession implicating Brodie. Ainslie followed suit, and a hue and cry ensued. The officials traced him to London but lost him there. Brodie declared afterwards that he saw his pursuer several times in London, but, be that as it may, the search was abandoned. He had made his way to Holland, but entrusted letters to his fellow-voyagers who, on arriving in Scotland, at once connected him, who was known to them as Dixon, with the missing Deacon. After some hesitation they opened the letters, which left no doubt of his identity. These letters were eventually delivered to the authorities, who at once sent after him. The imprudence in sending the letters was matched by the folly of their contents, some words leaving little doubt as to his guilt. He was traced to Amsterdam, where he was taking lessons in the art of forgery preparatory to commencing life anew in America. He was seized, extradited and taken to London, where the magistrate at Bow Street committed him to prison pending removal to Scotland. He reached there on 17th July, 1788, after a remarkably quick journey of fifty-four hours from London.

Smith had relieved the monotony of gaol by a daring and almost successful attempt to escape, which Ainslie shared. Brown had been unfortunate enough to be arrested for murder, and so all four were in prison.

The authorities could not easily obtain the conviction of all four. Brown had earned a pardon, but could not give evidence, since a convicted felon was not then a competent witness. To render him available he was given a pardon for all his crimes, and so he became available. Smith endeavoured to obtain liberty by confessions, not only of crimes committed but of crimes in contemplation, of which he gave a remarkably detailed programme. It was in vain, but Ainslie did find favour, and so the two chief culprits were charged, while their meaner-spirited associates purchased life at their expense.

The trial commenced early on 27th August and proceeded continuously until the jury retired after a sitting of twenty-one hours. In the afternoon of the 28th August, the Court reassembled after a short adjournment to receive the verdict. There was in those days a general idea that a trial for felony should not be adjourned, and protracted sitting frequently wearied judge and jury and counsel, and inflicted mental torture on the accused.

There were five judges. Lord Braxfield, the Lord Justice Clerk, presided, and was accompanied by Lord Hailes, Lord Eskgrove, Lord Stonefield and Lord Swinton. A distinguished Bar had been retained: the Lord Advocate, the Solicitor-General, Mr. Tait and Mr. Murray for the prosecution; the Dean of Faculty (Erskine), Mr. Wight, and Mr. Hay for Brodie; and Mr. Clerk and Mr. Hamilton, two unknown young advocates, for Smith, whose case was hopeless. Both prisoners pleaded "not guilty." Proceedings started with a technical objection by Mr. Wight, but after argument the judges brushed it on one side. After they had given their decision, Mr. Clerk rose to object, but Braxfield ruled him out. This time he subsided. A long string of witnesses then entered the witness box one after the other to prove the links in the evidence. Disputes broke out when the eighteenth witness was called. She was Smith's wife. Clerk at once objected. The Lord Advocate said that she was only called against Brodie, but as Clerk promptly pointed out, if her evidence implicated one it must necessarily implicate the other. The judges over-ruled him. He began again. Braxfield denounced his conduct as indecent and intolerable, but the Dean of Faculty asked for indulgence for a young gentleman, and he was allowed to proceed without avail. When all this pother was over the witness was brought in and Mr. Wight objected on the ground that she was Mary Hibbutt and the indictment revealed only a "Mary Hubbart or Hubburt, wife of George Smith." The Court did not like the objection, but it turned out to be a fact, and reluctantly the judges decided that she was not competent, and the Lord Advocate withdrew her. Thus justice was done on a technicality. The file of witnesses continued. Number twenty-six was Andrew Ainslie, and objection was at once taken that he was an accessory who had been promised freedom if he would give evidence. The prosecution denied the agreement, and alleged that an accomplice was by Scottish law a competent witness. The objection was over-ruled and Ainslie detailed the story of the crime. At one stage he was asked about a £5 note, but the defence objected. The indictment had mentioned a bank note, but the document was issued by a private bank, and was therefore in law not a bank note. The Solicitor-General denounced the objection as frivolous, but it was upheld. The cross-examination was slight, principally directed to times with a view to Brodie's alibi. Next came John Brown, *alias* Humphrey Moore. He was promptly objected to as infamous. The Solicitor-General countered by producing a pardon under the

Great Seal. The defence persisted. The pardon might save him from the penal consequences, but the infamy attaching to his conviction remained. Much was said concerning the authority of Sir George Mackenzie, an old writer on criminal law, but the judges were not disposed to worship at his shrine. Indeed, they said he was inaccurate. Lord Eskgrove, indeed, would have upheld the objection, but he said this was an English pardon for an English offence, and the law of England had made the witness competent by the grant of the pardon. So Brown was allowed to give evidence, but not until Braxfield had solemnly warned him of the consequences of perjury. He was closely, but not unfairly cross-examined, and got very heated. He went so far as to protest at being teased by impertinent questions, for which he was severely reprimanded by the Court. Mr. Clerk fastened on the making of the key, and on receiving an answer objected that it was no answer to the question. Braxfield observing that it was enough to satisfy any sensible man, Clerk retorted that it was for the jury to judge that. After this, Smith's and Brodie's statements were read and the letters Brodie sent and various papers found in his possession. The prosecution had produced evidence which established the prisoner's guilt unless a vast amount of deliberate perjury had been committed, but their case really rested on Ainslie and Brown and the documents.

Then came Brodie's witnesses, introduced by the remark that they were called to prove an alibi. The first was his brother-in-law, and the Lord Advocate objected. The objection to such a relative was so unsubstantial that no formal ruling was given. He merely proved that he was with Brodie until just before eight. Then came Jean Watt. It had been rumoured that Brodie had married her in prison, and if true the fact would have disqualified her. Accordingly the Lord Advocate asked her if she were married. She denied it and was allowed to give evidence. She said Brodie came to her a little after eight and stayed all night. The maid also said it was eight. She told the time by the bell of the Tron Church, a manifest impossibility; but when asked where it was she said it stood in Parliament Close, a quarter of a mile from its actual site. Other witnesses proved that he left Jean Watt's house the next morning. Then came a witness for proving the information for cheating at dice, to enable counsel to suggest that that suit had induced Brodie to flee; and a final witness proved that the implements found at Brodie's house were usual implements kept by a wright. By this time it was one in the morning, and the Lord Advocate began his speech. It was an adequate summing-up of his case.

At its close Clerk rose. He had refreshed himself with a bottle of claret. He was a cross-grained young man defending a hopeless case, but determined at least to make a name. At such an hour and with such a Court and Counsel, scenes were only to be expected. His rotund opening was interrupted by a request that he would be short and concise, and he proceeded to state what in his view were the main points against his client, and the answers to them. For a time he went on without interruption, but when he came to deal with the evidence of Ainslie and Brown uproar began. He mentioned the objections made and over-ruled, but expressed his adherence to the objections. "Gentlemen," he said, "I think a great deal of most improper evidence has been received in this case for the Crown." The judges admonished him, and he continued: "I beg to assail at the outset the evidence of these two corbies, or infernal scoundrels." "Take care, sir, what you say," growled Braxfield. Clerk went on. As he was saying that Brown ought not to be received as a witness in any case, the bystanders broke out into applause. Braxfield reminded him that the Court had ruled. Clerk replied, "But your Lordships should not have admitted him, and of that the jury will now judge." At this the judges protested that he was attacking them, but he answered: "I am attacking the villain of a witness, who, I tell your lordships, is not worth his weight in hemp." At this stage the Dean of Faculty tried to soothe the angry man, but Clerk was not to be held in. Braxfield reminded him that the jury were to take the law from the judges. "That I deny," retorted Clerk, and amid interruptions he continued. The Lord Advocate referred to the pardon, but Clerk replied: "Can His Majesty make a tainted scoundrel an honest man?" and the bystanders again applauded. The Lord Advocate said to Clerk that the prerogative of mercy was "the brightest jewel in His Majesty's crown," which gave the latter the opening for the pointed and discourteous retort: "I hope His Majesty's Crown will never be contaminated by any villain round it." He again repeated that the jury were judges of the law, and on being reproved declined to continue. He was ordered to go on, and repeated the obnoxious remark. Again the judges warned him and he sat down. Braxfield asked if he had done, and he replied "No," but refused to go on unless he could speak in his own way. The Court then called on Erskine, but the Dean of Faculty shook his head. Braxfield then turned to charge the jury, but before he could say a word Clerk leapt to his feet. Shaking his fist at the Bench, he shouted, "Hang my client if you dare, my Lord, without hearing me in his defence." Consternation reigned in the Court. The judges rose and departed to consider what they should do. Eventually they returned and merely requested Clerk to continue. This time he did finish, mainly because he had exhausted his provocative material. It was an able argument, though impossible of success. What he did achieve was the making of a reputation.

This storm preceded the Dean of Faculty's eloquent but temperate plea for Brodie. He also attacked the accomplices but on the safer ground that, though their evidence was admissible, it could not be believed. "Is it possible," he asked, "that a King's pardon can restore purity of heart, rectitude and integrity? Can a piece of parchment with a seal dangling at it . . . turn wickedness into honour? The King has no such prerogative. This is the prerogative of the King of Kings alone, exerted only towards repentant sinners." But his main theme was the alibi. If his evidence was accepted, Brodie could not have been present at the crime. At half-past four Braxfield commenced the summing-up. The only question was, Who committed the offence?—for that the offence was committed was not in dispute. It was short and to the point. The alibi turned on the ringing of a bell, but a bell rang at ten as well as at eight. He had directed attention to the corroboration of Ainslie and Brown, and ended by expressing his opinion that both prisoners were guilty. If they agreed, then they would convict both. He mentioned a possibility that they might acquit Brodie, but never allowed that Smith might go free. It was six o'clock when he had done, and the jury retired. The Court then adjourned until one p.m.

When it again met, the jury were ready with their verdict, which was delivered in a writing sealed with block wax. The Chancellor of the jury handed it to the Court. In deep silence it was read by the judges, who then ordered it to be read aloud. In formal language they pronounced both Brodie and Smith to be guilty.

The trial seemed over, but a last attempt was yet to be made. The indictment had mentioned the house in which the Excise Office was kept, but there were two houses. Consequently, urged Mr. Wight, the indictment was bad. A lengthy argument ensued, but it failed, and the judges then proceeded to consider their sentence. It was a short deliberation, for the law allowed but one punishment—death by hanging. Lord Braxfield delivered sentence. His short but earnest exhortation was prefaced by a tribute to the counsel for the defence, whom he eulogised as though no storm had raged round one of them but a few hours before. When he had pronounced the last dread words, Brodie seemed to wish to speak, but was restrained by his counsel. The trial was over, and the prisoners were removed to await execution.

Smith broke down, and attended with apparent sincerity to the ministrations of the clergyman who attended him. Brodie, though at times serious, complained of their well-meant endeavours. He spent his time in settling his affairs and endeavouring to secure a reprieve. It was all in vain, and on the appointed day, 1st October, 1788, he was brought out to die with Smith. The latter was resigned and penitent, but Brodie showed courage and coolness. He examined the drop with a professional air, and even tested the rope. The ropes were too short, and a delay ensued while they were being lengthened. Then again the ropes were found not right and a further delay ensued, which Brodie occupied in denouncing the executioner as a bungler. At last all was ready, and at a given signal the 40,000 spectators had the gruesome satisfaction of seeing Smith and Brodie die together. The incident of the rope had been, so people said, due to an attempt to defeat justice. A short drop was to be given so that when the body was handed over it could be revived, but the trick was overdone and defeated by the lengthening of the rope. The technique of hanging was then faulty, and a few instances were known of persons reviving. It was therefore sought to revive Brodie in the hope that he, too, would be an exception. It was in vain. The executioner had not bungled. Brodie had paid the penalty of his crime.

THE TRIAL OF
LORD COCHRANE

THE TRIAL OF LORD COCHRANE

THE de Beranger fraud of 1814 was one of the most noteworthy of the many attempts that have been made to exploit the public credulity. But its chief interest lies in the fact that one of the persons charged and convicted was Lord Cochrane, who had established a reputation for gallant daring second to none among the many who held the seas for England during the great wars which were then drawing to a close.

The eldest son of the 9th Earl of Dundonald, Cochrane was in 1814, though only 39, a Knight of the Bath, a Member of Parliament and a post captain. He owed little of his position to his birth. Ardent and impetuous, he had a knack of arousing the dislike of his superiors and his politics were throughout distasteful to the authorities. His promotion was forced upon them by his daring exploits. His first command was a 14-gun brig, the *Speedy*, in which for several exciting months he harried the coasts of Spain, capturing 50 ships. On one occasion he was confronted by a Spanish frigate disguised as a merchantman. His own ship was disguised as a Danish trading ship. Escape seemed impossible, but an adroit use of the plague flag scared the Spaniards from making a close examination, and he escaped. Later, he met another frigate, *El Gamo,* and carried her by boarding—54 men against 600. Naturally he was specially promoted. He pressed for the promotion of his second in command, which was refused on the absurd ground that the loss of life did not warrant it.

This roused Cochrane's indignation, and he replied in a letter which earned him a permanent black mark at the admiralty. The First Lord, Jervis, had been created Earl St. Vincent as a reward for his own victory, and Cochrane pointed out that not only had the Admiral won an earldom but that all his ship's officers had been given promotion for their services in that battle, though the flagship had lost only one man killed. The comment, though true, was worse than tactless—it was useless. The *Speedy's* commission ended in glorious disaster when she was captured by Desaix's squadron of three ships of the line. The resentful Admiralty professed itself unable to find Cochrane another ship when he was exchanged. He employed his energies by entering as a student at Edinburgh University, attending the lectures of Dugald Stewart at the same time as the future Lord Palmerston.

When war broke out again Cochrane was banished to fishery defence off Scotland in an old converted collier. Not until 1805, when a Scot came to the Admiralty, did he obtain a chance of real work. He then was posted to the *Pallas,* a new frigate, and harried the coasts of France and Spain with great success. Once he came home with a gold candlestick five feet high at each masthead. He did not confine himself to war. In 1805 he stood as a radical for Honiton, but, refusing to bribe, was defeated. He rewarded his supporters by a gift of 10 guineas each, with the result that at the election of 1806 he headed the poll; but this time there were no guineas for his expectant majority.

His frequent cruises continued, and at one time or another he met and destroyed four French frigates and captured many prizes. In 1807 he stood for Westminster with Sir Francis Burdett and headed the poll. His efforts in Parliament to discuss and redress naval abuses did not increase his favour at the Admiralty, but he held his commands. In 1808 he threw himself into the fort of Trinidad in Spain, and for a fortnight defied a whole French army. When further defence became impossible he re-embarked his men without a casualty. In 1809, when under Lord Gambier, he organised an attack on the French fleet in the Basque roads. The attempt was successful in that several vessels were destroyed, but Gambier was averse to the attack, did not support it with vigour, and (as Cochrane averred) thereby missed the certainty of destroying the whole French fleet. Cochrane himself was made a Knight of the Bath, but in consequence of his unsuccessful attacks on Gambier in and out of Parliament was placed on half-pay and remained unemployed during the critical years of the Peninsular War. Remembering Wellington's bitter complaints that the French were permitted to carry troops and supplies by sea to Spain almost unhindered, it is impossible to resist the conclusion that a man of Cochrane's audacity and experience might easily have shortened the war in Spain and with it the career of Napoleon.

At last, at the end of 1813, he obtained a post in spite of the Admiralty. His uncle, Sir Alexander Cochrane, had been appointed to command in North American waters and named his nephew as his flag captain. As we were then at war with the United States, Cochrane could look forward to active work, especially as single ship combats, in which he excelled, were numerous. The Admiral sailed, leaving Cochrane to fit up and follow in the flagship *The Tonnant,* and he was actually engaged on this task when he was arrested for fraud.

At this time, the Allies were hoping for a speedy end to the war. Napoleon, defeated abroad, was forced to defend France against an impending invasion. Rumours were current, mostly favourable. As each gained credence stocks rose, and when confirmation failed stocks fell. Newspapers were then not proof against the temptation to invent news with a view to promoting circulation. Some men, seeing that the stock markets were sensitive, used the nefarious plan of inventing rumours in order to raise or depress prices as suited their operations. Cochrane had made a fortune under the prize system. He had, as so many others had done, bought stocks with a view to a rise. His broker had orders to sell on a rise of one point. His uncle, Andrew Cochrane-Johnstone, had purchased to an enormous extent for those days, and his friends were also largely involved in speculation. Good news would earn them large profits.

On the morning of February 21st, 1814, a man arrived at Winchester in a post chaise. He had posted from Dover, scattering French gold among the postillions; had written to the Admiral at Deal and had let out on the way that he bore glorious news.   Napoleon was killed and the Allies were at Paris.   The man was dressed in a military uniform and was traced to Cochrane's house at Green Street, Grosvenor Square. Shortly afterwards two other men dressed as French officers arrived, giving similar tidings.   They disappeared after reaching Westminster.   The effect on the market was immediate. Stocks rose, and Cochrane, Mr. Cochrane-Johnstone and others sold their holdings and thereby made large profits.   After a time the public looked for confirmation.   None was forthcoming, and the boom collapsed.

This was not the first time that the Stock Exchange had suffered.   On previous occasions the fraud was clear, but evidence was lacking to convict the perpetrators.   This time the Stock Exchange investigated with success, and on March 5th they had traced the man who called himself du Bourg and, travelling from Dover, had alighted at Cochrane's house.   No sooner had they advertised rewards for the discovery and conviction of du Bourg than Cochrane, seeing that his house was mentioned, obtained leave of absence to clear himself.   The report of the Committee was ready on March 8th, and by an indiscretion an incorrect version appeared next day in the *Morning Chronicle.*   On March 11th Cochrane sent to the Committee an affidavit, settled by Mr. Gurney, one of the most eminent leaders at the Bar, in which he set forth his knowledge of the affair, and clearly indicated that he believed du Bourg was a man called de Beranger.   At this time no one had any reason to connect the two.   It is perhaps necessary to explain who de Beranger was.   He was a Prussian subject, adjutant of Lord Yarmouth's Volunteer Rifles, who, having fallen into debt, was living in the King's Bench Rules, as prisoners for debt could then do on complying with certain conditions.   He was a skilled instructor and had asked Admiral Cochrane for employment.   Knowing his ability, the Admiral had favoured the project, but had sailed before anything could be arranged. Apparently, not only had Admiralty sanction to be obtained but it was necessary to devise some scheme to evade his imprisonment for debt.   In this way de Beranger became acquainted with the Cochranes.   He does not seem to have been very familiar with Lord Cochrane, but there is no doubt that he constantly met Mr. Cochrane-Johnstone. He wore on the journey a great coat, and the evidence was that he wore a red uniform coat underneath. Lord Yarmouth's men wore green uniforms with scarlet collars and capes.

On February 21st, according to Lord Cochrane's affidavit, de Beranger called. Cochrane was out at a tinsmith's looking after some models of a lamp which he had invented. A letter was brought to him signed in a name which he could not read. He went home and found de Beranger. The latter told him a pitiful story of financial distress, implored employment as instructor of sharpshooters on the flagship, and asked to be allowed to go on board at once. Cochrane represented that the ship was not ready, nor could he allow an alien on board without leave from the Admiralty. De Beranger expressed distress and said that he had come in his uniform of a rifle volunteer officer thinking there could be no obstacle, and he could not go about in it as it would excite suspicion, inasmuch as a prisoner for debt could not appear like that in the Rules. Cochrane therefore lent him a hat and coat and the uniform was wrapped in a towel. De Beranger then left.

During the day Cochrane's holding in Government stock was sold, but he gave no special order, and consequently it was disposed of immediately the one point was gained. The others, who had given similar orders, were in the City and, getting in touch with the broker, sold at much higher prices.

In consequence of Cochrane's information de Beranger was traced to Sunderland and then to Leith, where he was arrested.

In the meantime the other men who had come to London as French Loyalist officers had been traced and later confessed, but no connection with Cochrane was ever proved. If, as seems to be the case, they were concerned in the same scheme as de Beranger's, the failure to implicate Cochrane with them has some significance.

The Stock Exchange were determined to prosecute all those whom they thought to be implicated, and accordingly at an early date they approached the First Lord of the Admiralty,

Lord Melville, and were told that they could consult the
Attorney-General.   This was equivalent to saying that the
Government would prosecute.   It does not appear that the Law
Officers were, in fact, consulted, and the Stock Exchange bore
the expense, but one result of the interview was that their
solicitor was changed and in the prosecution they were represented by the Solicitor for the Admiralty.   Cochrane always
maintained that the prosecution was fomented by Croker,
then Secretary to the Admiralty.   It was not established, but
the two men hated one another and were political opponents.

Accordingly on April 20th, 1814, the Grand Jury of London
found a true bill against de Beranger, Cochrane, Cochrane-
Johnstone, Butt, Sandern, McRae, Holloway and Lyte.   Of
these Cochrane, Cochrane-Johnstone, Butt and Holloway were
"bulling" the Funds.   The others were alleged to be the
persons employed to carry out the deceit.   The indictment
contained seven counts for conspiracy to spread false rumours
and to defraud.   The defendants pleaded not guilty, and the
indictment was removed into the Court of King's Bench.

The trial began on June 8th, 1814, before Lord Ellenborough, the Chief Justice, and two puisne judges, le Blanc
and Bayley, sitting with a special jury.   Mr. Gurney led for
the prosecution, though he had settled Cochrane's affidavit.
Moreover he permitted himself to indulge in severe animad-
versions on that affidavit.   The Chief Justice sat until 3
next morning, and resumed on the same day at 10 a.m.

Evidence was called to trace du Bourg from Dover to Green
Street, and to establish that he was the caller on Cochrane,
and in fact was de Beranger.   So far as Cochrane was concerned the critical witness was Crane, who said he drove du
Bourg from Marsh Gate, Westminster, to Green Street.   Du
Bourg had a red uniform coat on under his great coat.   Now,
if that were true, Cochrane's affidavit was perjured.   De Beranger, according to him, was dressed in the uniform of Lord
Yarmouth's volunteers, and it was said that no change was
made or could be made on the way to the house.   Though the
defence did not know it, Crane was of bad character.   He had
been guilty of shocking cruelty to horses, and, by the time a

new trial was asked for, Cochrane was prepared with affidavits clearly showing, if believed, that Crane was a deliberate perjurer and indeed was the man who drove de Beranger away from, and not to, Cochrane's house. Crane was afterwards transported for theft. The red coat and decorations had been found in the Thames at Wapping. The man who sold them was called, but could not identify de Beranger.

Other evidence was called to prove that de Beranger had boasted that there was a scheme on whereby many thousands were to be made by stock jobbing. The witness was a colonel imprisoned for debt. He wrote to Cochrane before he volunteered to help the prosecution, and, not receiving a reply as soon as he expected, wrote again to say that, being treated with silent contempt, he would make his information public, and on receiving a civil rejoinder wrote proposing a loan to himself of £3,000. These were put to him. De Beranger said that the conversation deposed to did take place, not as to stockjobbing but as to a gunpowder invention.

The witness proved that de Beranger's acquaintance with Cochrane was recent and slight, but that Cochrane-Johnstone called almost every day. Evidence was also called to shew the profits made. Cochrane made £1,390. His transactions had begun on Feb. 14th and ended on the 21st. Cochrane-Johnstone had made several thousands, Butt and Holloway much less. These four were the speculators, and their transactions commenced on February 8th and ended on February 21st. Unlike Cochrane, the three others had been in the city on the day of the boom, and were able to take advantage of the rise during business hours. The other evidence to implicate Cochrane was that two notes for £100, which he had had on February 19th, were changed on February 24th by Butt for one pound notes. Butt handed them to Cochrane-Johnstone, and when de Beranger was arrested sixty-seven were traced to him or were in his possession. Other notes formerly in Butt's possession were traced to de Beranger. The explanation of the two one hundred pound notes was that Butt had advanced some money to Cochrane on the 15th and these were given to him by Cochrane in repayment. It is certain that Butt and Cochrane-Johnstone had given de Beranger money.

The evidence as to the other two men did not implicate Cochrane.

Serjeant Best led for all the prisoners. So far as Cochrane was concerned the defence rested on his affidavit and upon the evidence of his servants. It was suggested that if he were guilty he would not have allowed de Beranger to call in his absence and be seen by the servants. Rightly or wrongly, the defence decided not to call Cochrane's servants, who saw how de Beranger was dressed. We need not trouble about the evidence for the other defendants.

Lord Ellenborough summed up on the assumption that Cochrane was the chief mover. He suggested that he revealed de Beranger's name only after he thought the latter was safe out of the Kingdom, and that when he called he must have worn the disguise, and therefore it followed that Cochrane gave de Beranger the clothes which enabled him to discard that disguise. "It is for you, gentlemen, to say whether it is possible that he should not know that a man coming so disguised and so habited—if he appeared before him so habited—came upon some dishonest errand; and whether it is to be conceived a person should so present himself to a person who did not know what that dishonest errand was, and that it was the very dishonest errand upon which he had been so recently engaged and which he is found to be executing in the spreading of false intelligence for the purpose of elevating the Funds. If he appeared to Lord Cochrane . . . with that red coat star and order which have been represented to you, he appeared before him rather in the habit of a mountebank than in his proper uniform of a sharpshooter. This seems wholly inconsistent with the conduct of an innocent man, for if he appeared in such a habit he must have appeared to any rational person fully blazoned in the costume of that or some other crime."

The jury retired, and after several hours' absence convicted all the accused.

On June 14th Lord Cochrane moved in person for a new trial. It was then supposed that counsel could only be heard if all the parties were present. Cochrane-Johnstone had fled the country. Lord Ellenborough insisted on the observance of this rule. The application failed. On June 20th Mr. Gurney moved for judgment. Serjeant Best moved in arrest of judgment. He took four points: (1) that the fact of war had not been proved, (2) that the indictment charged no offence, as the raising of the price of Funds was not necessarily a crime, (3) that even if it were the persons defrauded were not specified, (4) that there was since the Union no "Kingdom of England" as stated in the indictment, but only that part of the United Kingdom called England. He appeared only for Butt. Lord Ellenborough observed that it was a new proceeding that Counsel should renounce some of their clients to save the rest. Best answered that Lord Cochrane was not desirous of moving in arrest of judgment, and Cochrane-Johnstone wasn't there. The objections were overruled. Even in the days when technical points were potent weapons the objections were not sound. The most plausible was the last.

Lord Cochrane addressed the Court, hardly in mitigation, as he insisted upon his innocence and proposed to read affidavits in support, but was stopped. The others addressed pleas *ad misericordiam*. Mr. Gurney pressed the case against Cochrane and de Beranger. On June 21st, le Blanc J., as the senior of the two puisne judges, pronounced sentence. Cochrane was fined £1,000 and sentenced to one hour in the pillory and twelve months' imprisonment. He was never pilloried. Sir Francis Burdett announced that if it were done he would stand beside Cochrane and it was certain that serious disturbances would take place. Cochrane repudiated an attempt to gain remission of the pillory on the ground of his service. If guilty, he said, he deserved it; if innocent, one penalty could not be inflicted with more justice than another.

Further punishment followed. He was expelled from the Commons but immediately re-elected, no one daring to oppose when Sheridan refused to stand. His name was struck off the Navy List and from the roll of the Bath, and his banner was flung out of King Henry VII's Chapel. During this time Cochrane was in prison, perfecting his lamp, which was used in the streets with success. On March 6th, 1815, he escaped and went home, but returned on March 20th, when he went to the Commons intending to move a resolution against Lord Ellenborough. He was seized and taken back to prison. On June 20th his imprisonment ended. He was not entitled to release because his fine was not paid. His health had suffered, and after a time he yielded to persuasion and paid the fine by a £1,000 note upon which he endorsed these words: "My health having suffered by long and close confinement, and my oppressors being resolved to deprive me of property or life, I submit to robbery to protect myself from murder in the hope that I shall live to bring the delinquents to justice."

In March, 1816, he moved his resolution against Lord Ellenborough, but only Sir Francis Burdett supported him. He continued his political career, attacking the Government, which probably had some part in his prosecution in May, 1816, for his escape from prison. He was fined £100. He refused to pay, and in November, 1816, he was arrested for non-payment. In a few days he was free, the fine having been paid by a penny subscription among his admirers of the working classes to raise the amount of the two fines. No less than 2,640,000 contributions were made and the list had to be closed.

During the next two years he continued as an ultra radical, but politics was not his real love. He longed for sea service, and in 1818 he began a new career. He accepted the command of the Chilian Navy, a small, ill-equipped force, against the Spaniards, who were then attempting to crush the rebellion in South America. His exploits there were so marvellous as to exceed romance. Some of them may be recalled. The superior Spanish Fleet was based on Valdivia. In 1820 Cochrane entered the harbour, drew the fire of the forts, so as to learn their position, and withdrew with a treasure ship and other prizes. Returning, he used the information thus obtained to capture the forts with all their stores and material. On another occasion he cut out the *Esmeralda* from under the guns of Callao. So great were his successes that the Spanish Navy disappeared from those waters. In July, 1821, with 600 men he captured Lima.

In 1823 he entered the service of Brazil, then at war with Portugal. With his flagship and one other warship and a few fire ships he blockaded 17 warships and 70 transports at Bahia. During the blockade he entered the harbour and so frightened the foe that the whole fleet set sail for Europe, followed by Cochrane, who chased them with two vessels as far as Cape Verde. In July he captured Maranha and then Para. The independence of Brazil was assured and in 1825 he came home and resigned.

He was at once invited to help the Greeks in their struggle with the Turks. He set to work to build a fleet, but the Foreign Enlistment Acts impeded his efforts and he could not sail until 1827. His attempts to discipline his seamen were not successful, and the Greek Navy did little or nothing. After the battle of Navarino he returned to England. Cochrane's fighting career was over, but he had powerfully aided in the formation of four new countries, Chili, Peru, Brazil and Greece.

He now devoted his life to obtaining redress in his own country. His utmost endeavours failed to move George IV. On the accession of William IV Royal opposition ceased, but the opposition of some members of the Cabinet still foiled his endeavours. His succession to the earldom in 1831 made no difference. At last, on May 2nd, 1832, he was granted a free pardon and re-instated on the Navy List. On May 8th he was promoted to be Rear-Admiral, and thereafter received his due promotion as he gained seniority. He was not employed for a long time, and spent his time and energies in promoting the use of steam power and urging the adoption of the screw propeller. He was also the author of a secret war plan, about which from time to time rumours have spread that it was too horrible to use though its success was inevitable. It was even thought by some that the Germans discovered poison gas by stealing the plan.

There was one indignity that he felt severely. He had been expelled with ignominy from the Order of the Bath, but not until 1844 did he gain reinstatement, and even then his banner was not replaced. In 1848 he flew his flag as a British Admiral, being appointed to command the North American Station.

It was his last service. After that he wrote his autobiography, and eventually died on October 31st, 1860, and was buried in Westminster Abbey. Not until his death was his banner replaced in its proper position, but Queen Victoria saw to it that when his body was brought to the Abbey his insignia appeared among those of his fellow knights.

Such was Cochrane, a man of infinite courage, resource and daring; not given to placate those above him, an unpleasant insubordinate to men who could not emulate his deeds. Having earned fame in the hardest school, he was suddenly when in the prime of life snatched with ignominy from his chosen career, prevented from serving his country at a time when the whole energies of the nation were called for. Many men would have sunk under the blow, but he rose superior to his fate, and, commencing anew, earned equal fame in foreign service. To him four nations beside his own owe a debt of gratitude. Then, having won a new reputation, and vindicated himself in the eyes of his own race, he regained his position at home and was awarded the last honour that this realm can bestow—a place among the great dead who lie in the Abbey of Westminster.

Was he guilty? I cannot—I do not—believe that he was. His whole life negatives the suspicion; but for suspicion there was ground. If not he, yet his uncle and associates did plan and carry out a nefarious plot. It was inevitable that his conduct should be scrutinised. It is not a matter of surprise if a jury, faced with convincing evidence of a plot, some of which pointed to Cochrane, should have yielded to a common failing of all juries who are apt to condemn without distinguishing between those charged with an offence when they are convinced that that offence has been committed.

THE SOUTHERN RHODESIA
LAND CASE

THE SOUTHERN RHODESIA LAND CASE

No apology is needed to excuse my reviving this case. A land case usually has only a legal or antiquarian interest to anyone but the parties concerned. We have, however, a habit of raising large Constitutional questions in the course of a lawsuit, and this particular controversy involved matters of the greatest interest to all who take an intelligent interest in the expansion and administration of the Empire.

The dispute was as to the ownership of the unoccupied lands in Southern Rhodesia. These lands consisted of enormous areas which had not been assigned to the natives or granted to any settler or company. The mineral rights clearly belonged to the British South Africa Company, but the value and importance of these districts to Southern Rhodesia lay in the immense possibilities of their agricultural development, a matter which demands the closest attention from those who have the welfare of the Empire at heart. Southern Rhodesia is a country eminently suitable for white people, and consequently is one of the few remaining countries where Europeans may make their home. Who owned these unoccupied lands? There were four points of view that might be adopted, if the solution of despair that there was no owner at all be rejected. The British South Africa Company claimed that these vast areas were their private domain. The natives asserted that they were entitled to the benefit. The white settlers set up the case that, whoever was the owner—the Crown or the Company —the lands were the heritage of the community of Rhodesia, and lastly the Crown contended that, on the true principles of law, these areas belonged to the King, not in his private capacity, but as the head of the State.

In order to solve the question, the history of Southern

Rhodesia had to be studied, and incidentally the methods and aims of the concession hunters who forty years ago were contending for the wealth of Africa at the Courts of native potentates were fully revealed. Northern Rhodesia has a different history and administration, and did not come into the problem under discussion.

As a rule, the settlement by white people of a country already occupied by natives raises problems of extreme complexity. The relations between settlers and aborigines must be placed on a fair and equitable footing, and this involves the accommodation of native laws and customs to the needs of a society which henceforth will consist in part at least of persons accustomed to a developed system of jurisprudence, the very elements of which are strange and may even be repellant to the native mind.

The problem was complicated by the fact that after 1894 there was no sovereign to whom could be unhesitatingly attributed the ownership of lands to which no claimant can shew a clear title. Rhodesia as a Protectorate was technically not within the Empire, and consequently not part of His Majesty's Dominions. This circumstance had not prevented the Tudors and Stuarts from making the grants which originated so many of our colonies, but there was the difficulty of applying outside H.M.'s Dominions the legal principle that the King is the ultimate owner of all lands within his realms. The fall of Lobengula had led to the total disappearance of the native sovereigns, so that no easy way out was possible. There was ample room for difference of opinion as to the right solution, but all were agreed that the time had come when it was urgently necessary to arrive at an authoritative settlement.

The way in which the dispute arose was shortly as follows:

In 1890 Southern Rhodesia was under the rule of Lobengula. There were two areas, Matabeleland and Mashonaland. Several native tribes lived a pastoral life on the land. Agriculture was in its early stages, and the pasturing of cattle and hunting formed the avocations of the inhabitants, when they were not engaged in the more congenial pastime of war.

The Matabele were the dominant tribe. They were an offshoot of the Zulu invaders of South Africa, who had conquered the other tribes at a comparatively recent date. The subject tribes, the Mashonas, Makalakas and others, were peaceful folk who lived a troubled existence harried from time to time by the Matabele. The people lived in *kraals* under local chiefs, the more powerful of whom were called *indunas,* who in war-time commanded the *impis,* as the local levies were termed. The king, who owned the wealth of the natives, that is the cattle, was expected to consult the *indunas* on important matters, but whether he was bound to do so remained uncertain, and it was also quite unsettled whether he was bound to follow their advice. Probably a strong ruler, as Lobengula and his ancestors were, could over-ride all opposition, which indeed was dangerous to any chief who advocated views unacceptable to the king. There were also traces of a national assembly or *pitso.*

There was hardly a trace of land law. Probably it had never occurred to the native mind that land was capable of ownership. Whatever principle may be deduced from the position of the king and his people and their subject tribes and the way in which they lived, is after all an effort of the white man's brain.

When the scramble for Africa began, there were three European communities who might covet these lands—the British Empire, Portugal and the Boers of the Transvaal. The ultimate success of this country was due in no small measure to Cecil Rhodes and his colleagues, who, foreseeing the menace to South Africa if the territory of Lobengula fell to others, took effective steps to safeguard Imperial interests.

By 1890 Lobengula's *kraal* was a curious sight. It was beset by a horde of adventurers, some desiring legitimate facilities, many only striving for a concession that could be turned into money. All kinds of inducements that might appeal to the greed or intelligence of the native monarch were being thrown at him, and it may well be imagined that he was bewildered by importunities and that his awe of the European was considerably abated. The disorders likely to arise from the contentions of the rival suitors at Lobengula's court had already caused grave apprehensions both at the Cape and at home, and much thought had been given to the devising of plans to diminish or prevent them. One scheme, intended both to prevent these scandals and to secure that British influence should be paramount in Lobengula's dominions, was the formation of the British South Africa Company, incorporated in October, 1889, with two main objects: commercial exploitation of the wealth of the territory; and the exercise of effective control over the many whites who had come there and were not under the restraint of native customs.

The problem before the Company was a difficult one. The country had immensely rich mineral resources which were quite undeveloped and needed European capital and direction if they were to be made available. The competition of concession hunters bade fair to ruin all prospects of proper development for many years, for the native mind was being subjected to temptations which its previous training did not enable it to resist; the destruction of settled native customs coupled with the presence of many white men, over whom there was no effective control, might easily have led to complete anarchy. The industry imperatively demanded an orderly government. Agricultural development too required the attracting of a class of European with brains and capital; but this class would never come in sufficient numbers unless assured of adequate protection and security for their lives and their crops and herds. Obviously, some organisation had to come into being with authority and power to control the white population and to deal with Lobengula, so that both the white and the black population could live together under peaceful conditions.

The Company was entrusted with this duty. The system of creating a commercial corporation with administrative powers is familiar to Englishmen. Our Indian Empire was founded by the East India Company, and in more modern times there have been a number of such companies, notably the Royal Niger Company and the British North Borneo Company.

In 1890 the Company began its task.

Leaving on one side the Tati Concessions, there were two important concessions, which the Company acquired. One, known as the Rudd Concession, gave the right to prospect for and win minerals throughout the country. The other, the Lippert Concession, gave the right to grant land in Lobengula's name. It was granted in 1891, and the Company were obliged to acquire it, for if it passed into hostile hands the position of the Company might easily be rendered untenable. The High Commissioner for the Cape, who exercised in South Africa the Crown rights to legislate for Protectorates, issued a proclamation to provide laws for Europeans in the land. Among these provisions were clauses requiring land grants and concessions to Europeans to be approved in a particular manner and making essential for the validity of all concessions that the consent of the Colonial Secretary should be obtained. With the formation of the Company and the Colonial Secretary's approval of their concessions, the court of Lobengula ceased to be the happy hunting ground of adventurers, and he naturally soon perceived that his appetite for European commodities, including drink, was in future not easily to be satisfied. No longer could he obtain the things he coveted by putting his mark to a document which, though he did not realise it, expressed in the language sacred to Lincoln's Inn that he had bartered his birthright for a mess of pottage, that he had granted rights the very possibility of which was beyond his conception.

In 1890 the Company's pioneer force marched to Mashonaland. For 1,000 miles the way was impassable for horses and cattle, and four hundred of these miles were through virgin forests. Hardly had they arrived when they were cut off by floods. However, they persevered, and the Company commenced to form settlements and roads and organise a police force and magistracy. The project was on a fair way to success when trouble began with the Matabele.

It must be remembered that, although the Company owed its existence to the Crown, it derived all the rights which it exercised from Lobengula. The Matabele did not consider that the advent of the white settlers had made any difference so far as concerned the subject races or that the towns and farms of the Europeans were exempt from the rights of passage of *impis*. They continued their seasonal raids upon the Mashonas and failed to see how such raids could concern the Europeans, whose servants and neighbours were being hunted, or how there could be any objection to armed hordes stalking through the towns and across their lands, murdering as they went.   Objections to these time-honoured customs were to the native mind puerile, and they resented interference; and to Lobengula remonstrances were a flat denial of his kingly power. Friction increased and the Matabele became more and more threatening, while the settlers saw before them the grim prospect of being isolated in the midst of a country laid waste by raiders.

Threats grew to violence, and violence led to war.   All efforts to obtain a peaceful solution of the difficulties proved useless.   In 1893 the Company's forces, aided by Imperial forces from Bechuanaland, met and defeated Lobengula's *impis* in three pitched battles, and that monarch fled.   He was pursued, and one of the columns, the Shangani patrol under Major Wilson, was surrounded by an overwhelming force, and after a heroic resistance perished to the last man.   This was the end of the fighting.   The Matabele scattered, and as a nation thenceforth ceased to exist.

Lobengula by the end of 1893 was skulking behind the Shangani.   His exact whereabouts could not be ascertained though he was being diligently sought for, but eventually reliable information came that he had died in January, 1894.

His death ended the native monarchy.   It is true that he left sons, but no one claimed the vacant throne, and the arrangements made for the future of the country ignored any pretensions that might possibly have been put forward.

The only way in which the Company could thenceforth derive any rights over the territory was by way of grant or permission from the British Crown.   An Order in Council of 1894 set up an administration.   The Government was vested in an Administrator and a Council of four members.   These officials were appointed by the Company, which was also charged with the duty of providing for justice and police.   A land commission was appointed to provide land for the natives while reserving the Company's mineral rights.   A system of land registration was also put into force and in the Ordinance the unoccupied lands were termed the Company's lands.

The administration of the country was therefore entrusted to the Company, and, as the revenues were not sufficient to meet expenditure, the annual deficits were made good by the Company, so that the commercial profits were eaten up and no dividends paid. At first the accounts made no distinction between administration and commerce, but after 1896 the distinction was clearly shewn, in accordance with the requirements of the Colonial Secretary. Land receipts were carried to the administration account. The Company had a dual function, and it was not always easy in the daily routine to make a distinction between its governing and its commercial activities.

In 1896 an abortive native rising in Mashonaland was put down, and shortly afterwards the country had so far progressed that a Legislative Council was set up consisting of elected members as well as others nominated by the Company. Almost immediately the Company's land development schemes came into question. The waste spaces were suitable for the raising of cattle and crops, and outside markets became available with the improvements of communication, notably the railway which the far-seeing Cecil Rhodes planned to extend from the Cape to Cairo. Immigrants were attracted, and land began to have a considerable and growing value. Besides the land granted to these settlers, the Company set apart large areas for cattle farms for its own benefit. When its rights to the unoccupied areas came into question, the Company began to consider protecting its proprietary rights, and as a measure of precaution transferred its land revenues to the commercial account. It was abundantly apparent to all that responsible government would soon be conceded, and the Company was as anxious to preserve the return from land development for its shareholders as the elected members were to secure that the land should belong to the nascent state. The Company had spent immense sums in rendering the country available for European settlement; its expenditure had never produced any return to the shareholders for the immense sums they had invested in the

Company, and not unnaturally the Directors considered that the undeveloped lands were part of the Company's assets.

The dispute grew into a matter of the gravest constitutional importance to Rhodesia, but fortunately there is a means of settling such questions authoritatively and without heat. The King is empowered by a Statute of 1833 to refer a matter of this kind to the Judicial Committee of the Privy Council for its opinion, and in 1914, at the request of the Legislative Council, the reference was made. Unfortunately, owing to the War, it was found impossible to fix the hearing before 1918, but in April of that year the arguments on behalf of all the persons interested were presented during a ten days' hearing.

There could be neither plaintiff nor defendant, but by mutual agreement counsel for the Company began, then came the case for the natives, thirdly the contentions of the elected members of the Legislative Council, and lastly the Crown, for whom I held the leading brief with the Solicitor-General (now Lord Hewart, the Lord Chief Justice), Mr. (now Sir Thomas) Cunliffe, K.C., and Mr. (now Mr. Justice) Branson.

The Company endeavoured indeed to suggest that the Matabele campaign of 1893 did not result in a conquest, but this contention could not succeed. Before the hostilities began Lobengula was the acknowledged sovereign. He was overcome and immediately afterwards the Company assumed the sovereignty.

The Company's sheet anchor was the Lippert Concession, but the difficulty that proved fatal to that grant was that it had never been acted upon nor did it give the concessionaire any of the rights of ownership. Moreover, the stipulated payments had never been made, nor had the conditions been fulfilled. Substantially, then, the Company relied upon undisputed possession. Its title could not be put upon conquest, as acquisitions made in that way can only be made on behalf of the Crown. The Company's case was therefore vested upon a plea of acquiescence on the part of the sovereign. No document could be adduced to shew an express grant, and if the Crown did acquiesce, then it acquiesced in the Company being there as the government as well as a commercial concern;

so far as any facts could be shewn telling against the Crown's case, they were consistent with the Company's position as the ruling authority.

The natives had a weak case. Not only were they unrepresentative of the dominant Matabele, but their claim was inconsistent not only with the legality of all the land settlement that had taken place under legislative sanction but also with European settlement altogether. Many changes had taken place since 1893. The Matabele had ceased to exist as a tribe. The subject tribes had escaped from thraldom and immigration, and emigration had altered the black population almost as much as they had the white.

The elected members' case was consistent with the Constitutional practice, but they were not in a position to shew that there had been any limitation of the Crown's rights. As a result, the Judicial Committee acceded to our argument, that the only satisfactory legal solution, looking at the question both historically and practically, was to hold that the unoccupied lands of Rhodesia were vested in the Crown. We therefore succeeded in preserving for the community of Rhodesia these vast areas with their promise of untold wealth. Existing holdings, of settlers, of natives and of the Company were not affected.

Such a decision of itself would have worked injustice to the Company, which had spent enormous sums in preserving Rhodesia for the Empire and in developing its communications and resources. I had conceded in the course of the argument that the Company was entitled to reasonable compensation and the Privy Council so held. This was assessed by a Commission, presided over by Lord Cave, which went out to Rhodesia and examined the facts on the spot. The sum awarded was charged on the local revenues. Southern Rhodesia now possesses a vast estate, which is proving, and will in time increasingly prove, an immense national asset.

And so this case too, decided in an obscure little room in Downing Street, made history.

THE PLOT TO MURDER MR. LLOYD GEORGE

PUBLIC memory is notoriously short, and probably many have now forgotten the thrill of horror and surprise that was caused in the first days of 1917 by the news of the arrest of several persons for plotting the death of the Prime Minister and other Cabinet Ministers. It is true that there were Communist tendencies in some centres, and also that a number of individuals who objected to being called to their duty in the Army were resisting the Military Service Acts, but the nation as a whole was so determined to persevere to the bitter end, and so confident in the driving power of Mr. Lloyd George, that it was difficult to realise that such a plot could really have been seriously contemplated, especially when it was found that the conspirators had no encouragement or assistance from the enemy. Indeed, I believe that these misguided individuals never stopped to consider what effect their success would have had in encouraging the Germans.

Mr. Lloyd George is the last person to think that he alone stood between his country and defeat, but no one who realises his courage and determination and the power he had of calling forth from the nation the utmost effort, can fail to perceive how great and irreparable a disaster his death at that time would have been to the cause of the Allies.

What the conspirators thought they would secure by murdering him, if indeed they thought at all, was never made clear. They hated him and all his works, and it may be that his death was all they wanted. *Finis coronat opus.* They were not persons accustomed to reasoning, and the most probable explanation is that they hoped that his successor would be terrified into abandoning conscription, though how anyone out of a lunatic asylum could have believed that such a result could be so achieved passes comprehension. Yet none of these persons was insane.

The discovery of the plot came about by accident. There was a certain amount of Communist activity upon which the Government was bound to keep a wary eye, and many of that way of thinking had taken, or attempted to take, advantage of the exemption from military service conferred upon "conscientious objectors." I do not wish to cast aspersions upon those who honestly and conscientiously believed that service in the Army was a sin. Parliament had recognised that there were such people and that they had a claim to consideration. Many of them recognised that objection to warfare was not incompatible with noble service in succouring those who had fallen victims to the ravages of war and with preventing or mitigating the avoidable evils that follow upon hostilities. Nevertheless "conscientious objectors" were subjected to great and not unnatural opprobrium, and this was intensified by the fact that others attempted, often with success, to take advantage of the exemption, though their objection was rather a matter of politics or spleen than of conscience. Such persons only objected to war when it was waged for a purpose other than the furtherance of their own perverse and peculiar ideas of politics. Many of them were under detention, having given in certain cases unmistakable proof that they could nerve themselves to fight not to fight; others were at liberty, but a close watch was kept upon them. The curious masking of Communism under the guise of Pacifism made the manifestation of their proceedings extremely puzzling, and necessitated a close watch being kept upon the individuals concerned.

Towards the end of 1916 Alec Gordon, an enquiry agent of the Government employed on this work, was in Derby. He was, for the purposes of the duty entrusted to him, posing as a conscientious objector "on the run," and in that capacity made the acquaintance of Mrs. Wheeldon, a widow who carried on business as a second-hand clothes dealer. Mrs. Wheeldon had several children. One son was a conscientious objector; a daughter, Hetty, aged twenty-seven, who lived with her, was a teacher at one of the local schools; and another younger daughter, Winnie, was married to a man named Alfred George Mason, with whom she lived at Southampton. Mason was exempt from service, for he was in an employment of national importance, owing to the fact that he had a knowledge of drugs and was an expert in chemistry. The whole family shared the same political views.

Mrs. Wheeldon was apparently on the look-out for a suitable instrument for some service at which she darkly hinted, and her approaches to Gordon led him to think that something sinister was being planned. He called in his immediate superior, Herbert Booth, to take over the investigation, for he was getting beyond his depth. Booth was well known in the Temple as clerk to the late Mr. E. D. Purcell, a barrister who in his day had an extensive criminal practice, and therefore Booth knew most of the tricks and turns of those who pit themselves against the law. After consulting his superior, Booth went to Derby. On his arrival, on 27th December, 1916, he posed as a more suitable desperado than Gordon, who introduced him to the Wheeldons as a deserter in imminent danger of arrest and consequent execution and as a member of the International Workers of the World, a curious organisation of Communistic tendencies, which would now be described with sufficient accuracy as Bolshevist. Its activities during the war were confined to quarters where any advantage they gained would assist the Germans.

The newcomer was received by the Wheeldons with open arms. He was so apt to their purposes that they accepted him without enquiry. They were persons of some education but of little refinement, and liable to act on impulse rather than on the solid ground of reflection and moral principles. Such people are peculiarly liable to the pitfall of talking themselves into a belief that whatever they think fit to do is for some indefinite reason entirely justifiable and will in some indefinable way lead to the advent of some vague Millennium. Mother and daughter both claimed to have been Suffragettes of a very extreme and unusual type; during the war they had become pacifists of the familiar belligerent stamp. As Mrs. Wheeldon in her obscure abode in Derby was of a different opinion from Mr. Lloyd George, it was obvious to her, for reasons which she never did and probably never could give in intelligible form, that he should be removed and with him, of course, the Labour Ministers, who, having the misfortune to assist their country, were naturally "traitors to the cause" which for the moment had captured the support of these ladies.

They had from time to time given aid and comfort to certain individuals who, having failed to convince the Tribunals of their conscience, were seeking safety in flight. Gordon, so they thought, was one of these and Booth even more desirable, for his offence was much graver. Any person who came to them as a fugitive from justice because he desired not to do his duty to his country was sure of a welcome in at least one English home.

Mrs. Wheeldon did not delay to confide in Booth. She expressed her views in terms more remarkable for their blasphemous indecency than for any other quality. Her daughter faithfully copied this language, though she should have known better, for at her school she was responsible for the religious education of a class of small boys entrusted to her care. On the first evening Booth heard enough to justify the obtaining of an order to examine the correspondence of the pair, who possessed neither the information nor the opportunity to acquire the materials necessary for the accomplishment of their ends. They possessed in Winnie's husband an accomplice who had both the knowledge to instruct and access to the materials which they desired to use.

By this means it was found that Mrs. Wheeldon was corresponding with Mr. and Mrs. Mason in a code based on the sentence, "We'll hang Lloyd George on a sour apple tree." It was an easy cypher and was at once unravelled by our experts, who were set much more difficult problems by the Germans. Evidence was thus obtained that poison was urgently desired for some unlawful purpose, and that Mason was expected to provide it.

The parcel tarried, but Mrs. Wheeldon did not slumber. She became reminiscent and entertained Booth with an account of the burning of Breadnall Church, which had been destroyed some little time before from a cause which had never been satisfactorily established. She remarked, "We were nearly copped, but we —— well beat them." It is by no means certain that the Church was deliberately set on fire.

Meanwhile practical proposals were being discussed. The third meeting was on 1st January, 1917, when Mrs. Wheeldon recalled an expenditure of £300 by Suffragettes designed to poison Mr. Lloyd George by means of a nail in his boot, and also a proposal of hers to send to Mr. McKenna a skull with a poison needle, which had been rejected because the wrong person might be killed. It is only fair to add that these particular Suffragettes were never identified and after the trial Mrs. Pankhurst was allowed by the Judge to repudiate the suggestion that the Suffragettes had ever contemplated murder. Mrs. Wheeldon when giving evidence denied that any of the conversations relating to her activities as a Suffragette had ever taken place.

The parcel still delayed, and this caused acute anxiety, and no wonder, for, as Mrs. Wheeldon remarked, "it has all the incriminating evidence in it." She, however, did not waste her time, for she gave advice to Booth, to whom she had by now revealed the names of the intended victims, recommending Walton Heath as the best place for him "to get Lloyd George with an air gun" and offering to procure him microbes for subtler forms of murder.

At last, on 4th January, 1917, the parcel arrived. Mason had been more subtle in covering his tracks than his mother-in-law thought, for he addressed it to a relative of the Wheeldons, living in Derby, who had no idea of its contents, and no sympathy with the Wheeldons' views. The parcel contained four phials and a paper of directions for use. One phial contained enough strychnine to murder fifteen people; another contained a solution of strychnine; a third phial contained a substance which resembled curare, the Indian arrow poison. Curare, unlike strychnine, can be swallowed with impunity, but if introduced into a wound, or even an abrasion, it causes inevitable death. A bullet steeped in this preparation and fired from an air gun would kill anyone who was struck. Now Mason had taken elaborate notes about curare and was known to have had some in his possession.

Things had gone far enough. The design had been made clear. Some man was to be found to administer poison—by whatever method he might find convenient. The victim had been named, and other victims had been chosen to follow him. The poison had been procured. All that remained was to carry out the project, but Booth, of course, was not the man they thought. The authorities were in possession of the evidence. I advised a prosecution. It is always a matter of grave anxiety for an Attorney-General who is called upon to decide whether a prosecution shall be instituted, especially when the offence in question is closely connected with politics. To commence a prosecution and then withdraw it inevitably causes a loss of prestige, which may have disastrous consequences. To remain inactive while crime is being planned, and may at any moment be committed, is impossible. To risk a prosecution failing ignominiously is one which a Law Officer ought not to run. This plot at first sight seemed too melodramatic to be really serious, but there is no doubt that in this case the conspirators were in earnest and might at any moment find a man who was willing to carry out the plan. Then it would probably be too late to prevent the consequences.

There was nearly a hitch over the arrests. Someone had informed Mason that their letters were opened, but luckily, instead of taking to flight, he cycled to Derby to warn his wife's relations. Obviously he thought the puerile code was not easy to read. However that may be, all four were arrested, taken before Justices and committed for trial. It was originally intended to try the prisoners at Assizes, but it was thought to be fairer to them to bring them to London.

On 6th March, 1917, the day appointed by Mr. Justice Low, who was the presiding Judge, the four were arraigned at the Old Bailey on charges of conspiring to murder and of inciting Booth to commit murder. They all pleaded not guilty and the trial began. It lasted five days, because on the third day an unfortunate juror was found to be seriously ill and proceedings had to be begun all over again.

I led Mr. Hugo Young, K.C., and Mr. (now Sir Archibald) Bodkin, and Mr. (now Sir Henry) Maddocks for the prosecution. Mr. Riza defended all four.

The defence was ingenious. It was suggested that Gordon and Booth had made up the story and fastened it upon the defendants, whose loudly proclaimed dislike of Mr. Lloyd George made the accusation plausible. What they really desired, it was suggested, was to rescue conscientious objectors under detention, and the poison was merely for the police dogs who guarded these gentlemen.

A great deal of capital was sought to be made out of the fact that Gordon was not called. He was not a material witness, as he dropped out at the very beginning. The extraordinary suggestion was made that he was Steinie Morrison, a man who was then serving a life sentence for murder. What good it could have done the prisoners if Gordon had been called and admitted that he was Morrison (though in fact he was not) one cannot imagine.

The difficulty of the defence was two-fold. First, there never were any dogs to poison. Conclusive evidence was called on this point. Moreover, the prisoners could not have thought for a moment that dogs were so employed. They were in close touch with conscientious objectors both at large and under detention, and it would have been the easiest thing in the world for them to have acquired accurate knowledge of the guard over those in prison: indeed, if that had been the plan, such enquiries must have been made, and witnesses would have been available who could have proved that they had told the Wheeldons of the dogs. Needless to say, no attempt was made to call evidence that they ever were informed of these non-existent dogs. Secondly, even if dogs had been so employed, some of the poisons could never have been intended for use upon them, for these poisons would be useless for putting a dog out of the way quickly and without noise. But the directions for use, meaningless for the suggested purpose, were extremely apt if the murder of a human being were the object. Once the defendants' explanations were rejected, the only possible defence was that the Crown witness, Booth, could not be believed on his oath. I omit the particular case of Hetty, who was only proved to have posted letters (but not proved beyond doubt to have known of their contents) and to have taken part in the conversations at Mrs. Wheeldon's salon. Booth was strenuously cross-examined, both to destroy his credit—for it was suggested that his previous employment as a barrister's clerk had made him an expert in concocting evidence, a suggestion obviously ludicrous—and also to show that he was committing perjury. He had no difficulty in meeting the cross-examination.

The jury believed the Crown witnesses and convicted Mrs. Wheeldon and the Masons, but acquitted Hetty Wheeldon, who died not long since. Mrs. Wheeldon was sentenced to ten years' penal servitude, Mason to seven and his wife to five.

It is only due to the prisoners to say expressly that there was no trace of their ever having had any communication with the enemy, who indeed did not suborn assassination. They acted as a result of impulses due to ill-considered notions of what ought or ought not to be done, and had no intention to assist the enemy. What they wanted was to inflict punishment upon people who would not do what the prisoners thought they ought to do, though why they should constitute themselves a tribunal to return a verdict in the teeth of the feeling of the nation, or deem themselves competent to impose and carry out a sentence of death upon persons who had never even heard of them, and were merely carrying out a duty imperatively cast upon them, is a mystery which is probably best left to the psychiatrists.

The trial is noteworthy from the fact that it was the only instance of its kind during the war. It served to emphasise the unanimity of the nation to prosecute the war with the utmost vigour to its successful conclusion.

THE FRAUDS ON THE BANK
OF LIVERPOOL

THE FRAUDS ON THE BANK OF LIVERPOOL

The great criminal trial of 1902 was that of Goudie and a number of other men for extensive frauds upon the Bank of Liverpool. The story is a remarkable one, for Goudie, who was a bank clerk, was, when the frauds commenced, one of that unfortunate class of men who had been unable to withstand temptation, and had committed embezzlement. His crime at first in no way differed from that of many others who have found themselves in like case. What made the trial so interesting was that he was found out, not by his employers, but by two unscrupulous persons who terrified him into more extensive depredations to satisfy their greed; then other men, abler and more greedy, had ferreted out the cause of the sudden access of wealth of the former two, and themselves fastened on to the unfortunate man, who was driven by two sets of merciless taskmasters acting independently into committing for their benefit frauds on a scale hitherto unknown and deemed impossible. All his skill and ingenuity in the committing and cloaking of his crime were exercised to the full, not for his own benefit, but for that of his blackmailers, who thought that they had so arranged matters that, when the discovery inevitably came, they would be able to escape all consequences, leaving their unfortunate tool to his inevitable fate, so artfully did they believe they had planned and carried out their nefarious schemes.

I propose in the following pages to tell the story of these colossal frauds and to show how these bloodsuckers failed in their calculations and shared their victim's fate.

Although the actual frauds were committed at Liverpool, the scheming was done for the most part in London, and thus it came about when others were arrested and charged with

Goudie, the trial was appointed to take place, not on circuit at Liverpool, but at the Old Bailey.

The case marked an important development in my career. I was established in practice at Liverpool, but naturally had then but few opportunities of appearing "off my circuit" and becoming known to a wider clientèle. I had been retained for Goudie, and at the trial I appeared in London in competition with the established leaders of the Bar in a case which riveted the attention of the whole country. It was such a chance as may make or mar a man.

To return to the story:

On 21st November, 1901, there was a scene of great excitement and grave anxiety at the head office of the Bank of Liverpool. Facts had come to light which seemed to point inevitably to defalcations on a large scale which would involve the Bank in heavy losses. The accounts had to be investigated, and it was found that the ledgers in which those accounts were written were in the charge of Thomas Peterson Goudie. He was invited into the office to give an explanation. He had none. He broke down and confessed to a series of forgeries and embezzlements to the extent of some £160,000. As his story was being told, some point was raised which gave him the opportunity of going to his place in the office to fetch the books in his charge. He took advantage of his momentary absence to abscond from the building. For some days he was missing, searched for high and low. Then he was found in hiding near Liverpool in a state of abject destitution. Whoever had profited, he had not, for he was penniless. He was arrested, and while in custody made statements which completed his confession, and led to the arrest of three of those who had driven him on. The delay had, however, enabled two others to abscond, and they were never brought to justice.

Until the fatal day, so long dreaded by him, when he was called into the office, he had never come under any suspicion. He was trusted by the Bank, and seemed to have deservedly earned the confidence reposed in him during his eight years' service. He was then twenty-nine years of age, was a native of Shetland and well educated. To all appearances he was a decent, hard-working young man of no particular note. He had no marked peculiarities or expensive tastes, and lived so simply and quietly that his board and lodging cost him no more than a pound a week. He had attained a position of responsibility for which he received a salary of £3 a week. In those days, bank clerks received comparatively small pay and only achieved promotion slowly and by degrees. They had, of course, a secured position, and the prospect of a pension.

Such a man, whose modest budget appeared to show a steady surplus, should have been saving money. Yet he was penniless. He ought to have had no motive for committing his crimes. He had no obvious extravagance, was not given to folly, and probably was the last of their employees of whom the Bank would have entertained suspicions. Yet he had a secret vice, one which no Bank can afford to countenance. He had taken to betting on horse races. As so often happens, he lost, and lost so heavily that he was unable to meet his obligations to the bookmakers. About 1898 he was faced with exposure and consequent dismissal unless he made due payment of £100. To avoid the consequences of his foolishness, which he had brought upon himself, he yielded to the temptation of stealing from the Bank. He forged a cheque for £100, and, unfortunately for himself, escaped detection at the time. But there was the shortage, and sooner or later it had to be made up. Like so many weaklings, he increased his betting, so as to free himself from the toils. He lost again, and more and more money had to be found. Once he had succumbed to temptation, he yielded more readily, and so he went on, embezzling more money, until such time as the sudden turn of fortune's wheel would enable him to replace the money and again become an honest man. Luck did not change, and perforce he continued his evil courses.

From 1898 to 1901 is a long period, and it may be asked how it came about that, with the constant checking and audit that goes on in a Bank, his misdeeds, trifling only in comparison with what followed, remained unobserved.

As might have been expected, the Bank had an elaborate system, whereby it was thought that mistakes and defalcations could readily be detected. Not only was there a weekly system of checking, in addition to the ordinary supervision, but also frequent audits. Yet Goudie defeated the system by a very simple method. As ledger clerk, he was responsible for posting into the ledgers the accounts of customers whose surnames began with the letter H to K. One of the customers, Mr. Hudson, of Hudson's soap, had an important account, through which large sums of money were continually passing. At that time when a cheque was paid an entry was made in a journal, and the journal and the cheque were taken to the ledger clerk concerned, who marked the journal, took the cheque, which went on to other officials, and made the necessary entries in the ledger.

Cheques, of course, are usually issued in books with serial numbers, and Goudie had no access to customers' cheque books. He opened an account at the Bank, and thus got the right to obtain cheques without arousing any suspicion. He bought cheque forms at the counter like any other customer. He filled up a cheque, forged Mr. Hudson's name, and the cheque was duly presented and paid. To deceive a bank cashier implies that he had great skill as a forger. Of course, if that cheque went through the ordinary routine, the fraud would not remain undiscovered for a single day. It was duly entered in the journal, and with that book it in due course came into Goudie's hands. Then he destroyed the cheque, and marked the journal as if the ledger had been duly posted, but carefully omitted to make any entry in the ledger, where Mr. Hudson's account always showed that customer's actual drawings and payments in.

Obviously, if anyone checked the ledger with the journal, the discrepancy thus created would come to light. There were three ways in which this might happen. First, an occasion might by chance arise which would lead to a casual checking of the items. Goudie never devised any way of avoiding this flaw in his scheme. The other two ways were inevitable. There was a weekly sheet and the recurrent audit. These he did effectually guard against by a system of false entries, which it is perhaps as well not to explain in detail. He could do this the more easily for the reason that it was part of his duty to assist the auditors, an arrangement which should not have been made. It may be well to add that the system then in force was changed by the Bank.

So far Goudie's offence resembled that of most dishonest employees. He had taken the Bank's money, and had guarded himself from discovery in the usual investigation, though, like all others, he remained at the mercy of chance. Even giving him due credit for his misguided skill and ingenuity, it is nevertheless remarkable that he continued so long without being found out.

After a time, however, some members of the bookmaking fraternity became aware of his identity. As bank clerks are not allowed to bet, he was peculiarly liable to blackmail, and two men named Kelly and Stiles took advantage of this to involve him deeper and deeper, but with this difference, that he had to commit the frauds for their benefit, not his own. He was compelled to make larger and larger bets, which he was never allowed to win, and his defalcations rapidly grew larger. These two men were making too good a thing of it for the matter to escape the attention of others of a like occupation. They were growing wealthy and scattering money about, though the source of their means was not obvious. How did they get it? There seems to have been a system of intelligence whereby men of bad character engaged in betting on horse races got to know of one another's doings, and another set of men named Burge, Mances and Marks set to work to find the hidden source of wealth. They soon discovered and thus became aware of the possibilities of enormous gains to be obtained by terrorising Goudie.

In October, 1901, the second gang got to work. They came upon the scene on the 18th of that month, and so skilful and greedy were they that within three weeks £91,000 was extracted from the coffers of the Bank.

Whether their gains would have been larger had they been less grasping may be a tempting speculation; but at all events the scale on which the defalcations were conducted was stupendous and could not be expected to last long without discovery.

On 23rd October, 1901, a forged cheque was cashed for £5,000. On the 28th another for £9,000. On the following day there were two, one for £9,000 and one for £7,000, and on 6th November there was a fifth cheque for £30,000, and on the 12th the sixth and last for £31,000.

Nine days later the discovery was made, and there was a hue and cry after Goudie and those who had battened upon him. Mances and Marks disappeared and were never charged, but Goudie, Kelly, Stiles and Burge were arrested and committed for trial, which was fixed for 17th February, 1902.

The presiding judge was Mr. Justice Bigham, afterwards President of the Divorce Court, who is now living in retirement, a most distinguished lawyer, afterwards raised to the peerage as Viscount Mersey.

Three counsel appeared to prosecute for the Bank. The late Mr. (afterwards Sir Charles) Gill, K.C., led Mr. Charles Matthews and Mr. Graham Campbell, who were both well-known members of the Criminal Bar. Mr. Matthews was knighted when King Edward opened the new Central Criminal Court, and after a noteworthy career at the Bar became Director of Public Prosecutions, in which capacity he instructed me on many occasions when I was a Law Officer. He was made a baronet for his public services, and was a man of singular charm and versatility. Mr. Graham Campbell is now one of the magistrates at Bow Street.

Kelly was defended by Mr. Rufus Isaacs, K.C., (afterwards Lord Chief Justice, Viceroy of India, and now Marquess of Reading), and the late Mr. S. W. Lambert; Stiles retained Mr. (now Sir Edward) Marshall Hall, K.C., and Mr. Moyses; Burge, Mr. Avory, K.C. (now Mr. Justice Avory), and Mr. Biron, who, as Sir Chartres Biron, is well known as the Chief Magistrate of London. I led Mr. Hemmerde for Goudie.

There were a large number of charges, for Goudie's offences had been numerous. He was charged by himself with all of those which the prosecution had elected to rely upon. With Kelly and Stiles he was jointly charged with the forgeries which concerned them, and they were charged with conspiring together. With Burge he was similarly indicted for the group of offences relating to them.

He had no possible defence. The evidence against him was conclusive, and, moreover, he had made statements admitting his guilt. He therefore bowed to the inevitable and pleaded guilty.

Before he could learn his fate, he had a final ordeal. Mr. Gill had very properly decided to call him as a witness against the others. So soon as he had pleaded guilty, and the others had pleaded not guilty, he was available to give evidence.

Burge's case was taken first, and soon Goudie was called into the witness-box. There he was subjected to a searching cross-examination by the acute and experienced Mr. Avory, at the height of his powrs. But notwithstanding all that counsel could do, Goudie stood the test. The jury accepted the evidence given by him and the other witnesses, and Burge was convicted. A curious feature of this case, of which Mr. Avory made the most, was that up to the time of Burge's arrest Goudie had never even seen him. The men who had applied the pressure were the two who were not forthcoming. The prosecution alleged that in this group of offences, whereby the Bank had been defrauded of a total of £91,000, Burge had received £38,500, Mances £36,750, and Marks £15,000. This only leaves a balance of £750 for Goudie, who got no benefit, even from the money he was allowed to retain, as he lost it in the same way as he had lost so much before.

Burge's trial had lasted for three days, and counsel who represented Kelly and Stiles had been watching it carefully. They were men of the greatest experience and realised that if Goudie could survive cross-examination at the hands of Mr. Avory there was no chance for their clients. Accordingly, when the remaining prisoners were put up for trial, they withdrew their pleas. They admitted their guilt, and nothing remained but to sentence them.

It is the practice of English judges to allow counsel for convicted prisoners an opportunity of addressing him in mitigation of punishment. This was the only way in which I could do anything for my client. The trial had begun on Tuesday,

17th February, 1902, and it was not until Saturday, the 22nd, that the final stages were reached. Speeches were made on behalf of all the four. I had been waiting all this time, during which the details of Goudie's crime had been discussed and re-discussed, without a chance of a word being put in for him. Naturally enough, after all that time the quick-witted Judge had formed his own judgment, and if it were unfavourable there was little or no chance of bringing him round.

In any event, whatever might be said, Goudie's offence was deliberate and long-continued. Before ever the others had fastened upon him he had betrayed his trust. There was no hope of a light sentence. Nevertheless there was something to be said for him. But for the others, he would have been a criminal of a very ordinary type. It was as a tool in their hands and for their benefit that he had committed the series of crimes which had made the total loss so great. But for them, his crime would not have been so serious; most of his offences were committed under their compulsion, in abject fear of exposure. With all the force at my command I urged upon the Judge the factors which told for leniency. It is not for me to comment upon my speech, but I may perhaps be permitted to recall a remark made by a member of the Old Bailey Bar, who had come to see the closing scenes of the trial, that unless that Bar did away with me it was all up with them, for I would get their work.

Mr. Justice Bigham was unmoved. He had made up his mind to make an example of the prisoners. He sentenced Goudie to ten years' penal servitude and the others to long periods of penal servitude. Goudie died in gaol. The others have long since served their time, and one may hope that they have retrieved their position and characters. For this reason, as they have expiated their offences, I have omitted to give details of their careers which might identify them.

The Judge was careful to point out that no blame attached to the Bank, which was a heavy loser, for it had to make good all the money that could not be recovered from the prisoners.

The fate of Goudie was hard, yet it must be remembered

that before he fell into the clutches of the others he had shown himself to be an able and deliberate criminal, and, but for his own previous misconduct, would never have been subjected to the terror and degradation into which they forced him.

FIRE AND EARTHQUAKE
IN JAMAICA

FIRE AND EARTHQUAKE IN JAMAICA

IN the course of 1908, soon after I had taken silk, I was engaged on a most important appeal to the Privy Council. Following upon an earthquake, the business quarter of Kingstown, the chief town of Jamaica, had been destroyed by fire. The insurance policies, as is usual in countries liable to earthquakes, contained a clause relieving the companies from liability for fire due to earthquake or similar convulsions of nature.

If the companies were right in their contention that the fire, which caused the greater part of the loss, was due to the earthquake, then the sufferers would have to bear the whole of the loss—a burden which would have caused a most serious financial crisis. On the other hand, if the fire was not so caused and the companies were bound to pay the amounts secured by the policies which they had issued, they would be severely hit, for the damage done amounted to many thousands of pounds.

As so many were affected, there were a large number of actions, some commenced in England, for most of the companies affected were English companies, but the majority were proceedings commenced and tried locally. In any case, the evidence had to be taken in Jamaica, and a number of English barristers were retained to conduct the proceedings in Jamaica, where they were entertained with that hospitality for which the West Indies are so honourably renowned. I had been asked to form one of the party, but a multiplicity of professional engagements here forced me to decline.

By arrangement a number of cases were taken as test cases. In the appeal I am now mentioning, some premises in Harbour Street, Kingstown, had been burned down, though they had escaped serious damage in the earthquake. The trial was before judge and jury in Jamaica, and after a protracted hearing, during which many witnesses were called, the verdict was in favour of the policy holders. An appeal to the local Court of Appeal had been brought, but failed, and the companies concerned appealed to the Privy Council.

That appeal was heard in London, and I was able to accept a brief with other counsel for the policy holders. The main question was whether the verdict could be justified by the evidence given. The whole of the story was discussed at great length.

It is impossible to set out at length the volumes of evidence that were before the Court; but, shortly, the story disclosed was that which follows:

Monday the 14th January, 1907, at Kingstown in Jamaica was a delightful day. The sun shone in a cloudless blue sky and light airs tempered its rays. In the afternoon, the heat increased: most people rested in their houses, while those whose business or duty called them out kept to the shady side of the street.

Alongside the wharf lay moored the s.s. *Port Kingston*. On board, there was nothing to do, and Mr. Little, the chief officer, leaned on the ship's rail contemplating the quiet town. About half-past three he noticed near the parish church that a column of smoke had begun to rise. If, as he at once decided, this meant that a house was on fire, he had to take steps to safeguard the ship, for houses there contain much wood, which in the tropics burns even more readily than here, and what wind there was set towards the wharf. He called the third officer to him to discuss the matter, but before they could take action, the town was shattered by a violent earthquake. Many houses were down. A thick cloud of dust rose and hung overhead like a black fog. As the cloud dispersed, Mr. Little saw again the column of smoke, thicker, blacker and taller than before. As he and his men set to work to preserve their craft other fires broke out. The business quarter of Kingstown had caught alight and by next day the heart of the town was destroyed by fire.

The shock that caused the damage occurred at 3.35 p.m.

During the night there were other shocks, followed next day by a second very severe convulsion, but the damage that was done was mostly caused by the first shock of all.

Nothing is so well known as the terror caused by earthquakes. In all misfortunes we rely upon the solid earth, but if that moves, our whole confidence is dissipated and panic treads fast on the heels of fear. Yet the shock itself generally causes little damage. The greatest have passed unnoticed save by nomads in the wide deserts or by some ship at sea and by scientists watching their instruments. It is when a town is shaken and its buildings fall that an earthquake becomes known to fame, and even then it usually owes its sinister reputation to some supervening calamity to which it has given rise rather than to the direct and obvious damage. Thus, at Lisbon the fame of the earthquake rests upon the tidal wave. At Tokyo, upon the conflagration which slew its thousands when the earthquake was content with hundreds. So, too, at Kingstown, the shock caused many houses to fall. The fire destroyed a whole quarter. How many were the victims will never be known.

Nothing is more difficult than to obtain a clear statement of events from eye-witnesses of such a disaster. In the first place the cataclysm comes without warning, and the sufferers are naturally bewildered. As soon as they have realised what has happened, they obey the imperative call for rescue and salvage. Not until a long time has elapsed can they spare time to arrange their thoughts and, as no one can see the events as a whole, the history of the calamity must be pieced together from numerous and often inconsistent narratives.

What was made clear was that after the earthquake, first one, then two and then three columns of smoke arose, spread and joined in one mass of flames. The companies, not unnaturally, said that the town was safe before the shock and that the fire came after. What could be more obvious than that a fire used for cooking or some business purpose in a house that fell should have caused the damage? Besides, even if there were a fire before the earth moved, soon after there were three, and those destroyed in the track of the other two were clearly not covered.

It was curious that before the earthquake this fire was not noticed by the inmates of the house or by the passers-by until after the tremor was over. Those who would naturally see first, did not see at all. The inference was that the shock had upset some chemicals or drugs on the bunsen burner—the house was in part a doctor's surgery and in part a wholesale chemists—and thereby caused the fire. But the maid said she had put out the burner, and though the drugs were inflammable, no one could say that they would set themselves on fire.

Great controversy raged over this part of the case. Counsel discussed at length questions such as how long the burner was needed to sterilise instruments, and how a maid could know when an instrument was properly sterilised without being told, and also what chemicals and drugs were there, and their nature, and whether they could or would ignite if they were suddenly thrown down when the house was shaken.

Besides, there were two circumstances to negative the company's contentions. The smoke had been seen by a number of people before the earth moved. Captain Munro of the *Lady Shea* was bringing his vessel to anchor when he noticed the smoke. Five minutes afterwards came the shock, and then his anxiety for his wife, for she was at home in the town, sent him ashore as fast as he could row. Two negro boys, servants to the German Consul, were at his house in the hills six miles away looking for German vessels entering the harbour. The Consul, when he was at home, used to tip them for reporting such ships. He was not at home, but yet they kept a look-out, and as they watched they saw in the town a column of smoke rising high in the air. Then came the earthquake. Other observers nearer the town saw it too. One of them was of a scientific turn of mind. He noticed how high it was compared with the church tower, and months later took angles from which he was prepared to swear that the column rose exactly 205 feet. He would not admit an error of more than five feet either way. The nearest of those who had seen the smoke was a neighbour's wife. She sent one of her twelve children to call his father so as to make sure, but before the message was delivered the house was thrown down, and the severely injured mother was searching for her children. She found them all, but one so injured that it only lingered for a while to die of a broken back. She was attacked in cross-examination because she told her story months later and her husband had tried to keep her out of the box. One would have thought that her absence for months, recovering from injuries and nursing her frightened children, one of whom was slowly dying, amply accounted for both of these facts and should have prevented the severe attack upon her veracity. Of course, her evidence was vital; if she were believed, a great part of the company's case utterly collapsed. These witnesses had seen a fire which had already started.

The evidence did not rest there, for many saw the column as the dust-cloud cleared away. It was well established that the cloud only overhung the place for at most five minutes—too short a time for a freshly started fire to reach up a pillar of smoke to heaven. Even witnesses who thought the earthquake caused the fire admitted that the smoke was thick and high a bare five minutes after the shock. And Mr. Duperly, one of the neighbours, acted in a way that shewed what he believed; for, being caught by the arm under a beam in his fallen house within the shortest time after the earthquake, was so convinced that to remain would mean his being burned alive by the fire next door that he tore himself free, leaving flakes of his flesh behind, so that his arm had to be amputated. If there had been no fire a few moments before, his fear would have been foolish. But if there were a fire which had got a good hold his action was natural.

But, even then, accepting a fire raging in King Street, how about the fire in Harbour Street, some four hundred yards away? The case was, as I have said, a test case about a shop, No. 104 in the latter street. The second fire was at No. 92 Harbour Street, a shop known as the Army and Navy Stores, and the company contended that this fire at least followed the earthquake, as indeed it did. Now the owners of No. 104 and in consequence all those in like case, answered the contention in two ways; first, by claiming that the Army and Navy Stores caught light from the King Street fire; the wind set that way and blazing embers and sparks could do the damage; secondly, by contending that the evidence shewed that both fires were spreading towards No. 104 but that the King Street fire got there first.

The Company was confident of their case on this point. When the Stores fell, a number of men were imprisoned under the ruins. A quantity of safety matches had been stored by a door, and near them wine and oil. The upper floors and beams had fallen upon them. One man, Captain Davies, escaped in a few minutes or so and climbed out over the place where the door had been. The others of whom anything was heard again were caught further away—in twos and three, near enough to talk but in inky darkness. One by one, they ceased to talk, and just as the three nearest the street began to feel heat and smoke, rescuers arrived and they were saved. How long had elapsed, the survivors could not tell. They were in utter darkness, and time passes slowly in such a plight. Mr. Henriques thought he was imprisoned from twenty to thirty minutes. When they emerged into the daylight, the débris had caught fire. The others could not be reached, and it is to be hoped that they died before the flames reached them. The flames came up from quite another part of the shop. The Company's theory was that the safety matches caught alight, but it called no scientific evidence to shew that that was even probable.

Captain Davies could not have escaped over the place where the matches were lying, if they had fired. The alternative theory was that one of the entombed struck a match. No witness said so, though several were there, and it is a singular fact that none of those who complained and then ceased to speak ever mentioned fire, heat or smoke. Yet they complained of pain. Besides, if a fire were caused by the lighting of a match, the earthquake did not cause it, and the companies would be liable.

The second contention, that the original fire got there first, depended upon dry facts. A most important factor was the wind. It was light and variable, but the witnesses differed so much that if all were believed, there never was so variable a wind. Mr. Little on this point was an invaluable witness, not so much for what he said but for what he did. He observed the fire and the way it spread, and with the wind he noticed the peril to his ship to be so grave that he bent his energies to saving her from fire. An experienced seaman would not so waste his time unless the wind did set his way, and his photographs, for later on he found leisure to use a camera, shewed the way the flames spread.

The fire brigade was called, and gave most contradictory evidence. This is not to be wondered at. Working singly and by twos and threes, they were overwhelmed by competing demands upon them, and they worked where and as they could, striving, not to observe, but to quench the flames. The superior officers, with more opportunity to watch in order to fulfil their duty to direct, believed in the spread of the King Street fire. Their men in the streets, working first here and then there, believed that fires broke out all round. There were some curious incidents. At the Central Station the coachhouse was damaged, and as they set to work to release a horse, in the nick of time a horse cantered up from the sub-station, where its stable had fallen, but so as to leave it free. Feeling the need for companionship, it set off home, and by this chance a horse engine was sent out at once. The Governor, Sir Alexander Swettenham, was in the streets urging on the work of rescue. He did not give evidence, but a witness spoke of receiving directions from him.

The evidence called at the trials was a mass of contradictions not to be wondered at. The shock had imprisoned many, and the fortunate, so soon as they realised the plight of others, were at once absorbed in the work of rescue. Husbands sought wives, wives their husbands, parents their children, and friends their friends. To add to the confusion looting began, and had to be suppressed quickly and sternly. Few could have had a clear idea of those awful moments and those crowded hours.

It is the task of juries to find the truth from the oral testimony of witnesses on both sides. It is the duty of the lawyers to urge upon the judge and jury those circumstances and con-

SIR ROGER CASEMENT

SIR ROGER CASEMENT

On August 1st, 1913, Sir Roger Casement, C.M.G., His Majesty's Consul-General at Rio de Janeiro, retired after twenty-one years' public service in Africa and South America. It is not often that a Consul comes so prominently before the public as he had done, for on two occasions he had been engaged on prolonged and difficult investigations in unhealthy tropical districts on matters which had gravely troubled the public conscience—the Congo and Putumayo rubber atrocities—and his name had thereby become a household word.

After his treason there was manifested a disposition to minimise the importance and accuracy of his reports, but there is no reason to doubt the reality and value of his public work. He was, therefore, a man who had fully earned his honours, and the right to retire.

I cannot say why he chose to quit his duties when he was just short of fifty, but, if one may conjecture, it was probably due to the fact that he had spent nearly all his official life in tropical regions and had been continuously engaged in unusually hard work, which would tax the strength of any normal individual working in a temperate climate.

After his retirement he appears to have taken an interest in politics. He was of Irish birth and parentage, his father having been an officer in the Antrim Militia.

At first, if I remember rightly, he was engaged in an unsuccessful attempt to recreate the Liberal party in Ulster, but by 1914 he is found to be actively employed in the organisation of the Irish National Volunteers. In connection with that work he asserts that he visited the United States, and he may have been there when the War broke out. He drew his pension down to the end of September, 1914, and, as he is not known to have had any considerable private means, it is a matter for conjecture how he managed to live afterwards.

It will be remembered that at the outbreak of the War there was a very serious crisis in Ireland, which was at once suspended by a kind of mutual truce. Casement was following a course of his own. From a public servant remote from domestic politics, he had been gradually becoming more extreme, and, by some process which it is impossible to trace, he had determined to throw in his lot with Germany.

There is nothing in his career to explain or justify this. He had recently retired, and there can have been no grudge or fancied slight which would have turned him against his duty to the King, at whose hands he had gratefully received the signal honours bestowed upon him. He has left no statement which enables us even to guess.

At his trial, he claimed that he was actuated by a burning and exclusive desire to serve Ireland, but his interest in his native country was of recent origin, and others who had spent their lives in furthering Irish aspirations took a saner and more statesmanlike course. It may be that he allowed himself to be seduced by one of the German agents who swarmed in the States at the period.

However that may be, by December, 1914, he was in Germany, moving about the country in a way which proved that he enjoyed the countenance and support of the German authorities.

The first manifestation of his enmity to this country was one of the meanest, and particularly so when it is remembered that he had been himself a public official. He was employed to seduce from their duty the Irish soldiers who had been taken prisoners by the Germans.

It will be remembered that in the earlier stages of the War many of our troops had been captured, and these were scattered through the prison camps in Germany. In December, the Irish soldiers were collected together in a camp at Limburg, in the Ruhr area, and given better rations and lighter duties. At the same time Casement was engaged in addressing them in speeches breathing hatred towards this country and trying to persuade them to join an Irish Brigade. He set up the contention that this brigade was only to be used in Ireland after the War, but it may be doubted whether he expected anyone to believe this. The German Government had never been conspicuous for altruism, and still less would it be expected that, in the course of a struggle which called for the utmost effort, they would allow time and money to be spent with the object of forming a Volunteer force for use after the War, when, if they won, they could have a decisive voice without needing the brigade, and, if they lost, could not influence the course of events. It is obvious that trouble in Ireland during the War was the only factor that would further Germany's aims, and the evidence was clear that the brigade was to be used at once— at least, as soon as the expected naval victory, which never came, enabled the Germans to get into effective touch with Ireland.

"Now is the time," said Casement, in one of his speeches, "for Irishmen to fight against England."

To the honour of the Irish prisoners, Casement failed. Only some fifty men joined, and several of them, if not the majority, were actuated by the desire to escape from the monotony and hardships of prison life. The remainder, in spite of pressure brought to bear on them in every conceivable way, stood firm, and Casement was forced to come to the camp under the protection of German soldiers, so that he could escape the just resentment of the prisoners at his disgraceful and unmanly attempts to divert them from their duty. His visits were frequent until February, 1915, when it became more than certain that this treasonable intrigue was a hopeless failure.

What happened to the brigade we do not know, but one may be sure that the fifty lived to repent in bitterness the day when Casement led them astray.

Between February, 1915, and April, 1916, it is impossible to say what Casement was doing. He may have visited neutral countries near Germany, but, whatever form his machinations took, he was continually during this period in close communication with the enemy.

In 1916 Good Friday fell on April 21st. On the night before Good Friday, persons in Tralee saw a light at sea, and during the night a boat came to the shore containing three men. One was Casement, and another was Bailey, a member of the Irish Brigade who had joined with a view to getting back home if he could. When they landed, the boat was abandoned on the shore, and Bailey buried there some weapons, some maps of Ireland of foreign origin, and three coats, one of which contained Casement's diary.

The names of persons and places in this diary were fictitious. We know that Casement came on a German submarine from Wilhelmshaven. The entry of this voyage reads: "Left Wicklow in Willie's yacht." There appears to have been a mistake as to the rendezvous, for a motor-car had come to the coast a short distance away but the driver miscalculated his position and drove into the sea, whereby his passengers were drowned.

It was not long before the police were informed of the suspicious visitors; and, though they had gone inland and separated, both Casement and Bailey were arrested during Good Friday. On the way to the police barracks Casement dropped a paper. It was seized, and on examination proved to be a code relating to warlike supplies, with a note that it was in force only for a short time. Clearly, therefore, Casement was on an expedition which was to become immediately effective.

Nor was that all. On Good Friday, *H.M.S. Bluebell* sighted, off south-west Ireland, not far from Tralee, a vessel disguised as a Norwegian tramp steamer, the *Aud,* on a voyage to Genoa. She was escorted to Queenstown, but, just before reaching there, she stopped and hoisted German colours. The crew, who proved to be all in the German Navy, took to their boats and surrendered, but, before anything could be done, an explosion was seen on the vessel, which sank at once.

It was proved that this ship belonged to the firm of Wilson's and had been taken by the Germans at the outbreak of war. A diver went down and had no difficulty in establishing that she was laden with rifles and ammunition, some of which he brought up. The coincidence is too remarkable to be accidental. Casement came by arrangement with the Germans, accompanied by a shipload of munitions of war. At Easter, the Irish rebellion broke out in Dublin, and it is easy to picture what might have happened had Casement's scheme not gone awry.

He was brought to England for trial. There are many peculiarities about the law of treason, and one is that treason committed abroad is triable before the Courts in England. Casement tried to make capital out of the fact that he was brought here for trial, but there was no other course open. Moreover, so far as one can tell, his usual abode was in England. The prosecution went through the usual stages. As Attorney-General, I was in charge of the case throughout. First he was brought up at Bow Street before Sir John Dickinson, and was committed for trial on May 17th, 1916.

The trial was at Bar. In such a trial three judges at least sit, and in this case Lord Reading, the Lord Chief Justice, was assisted by Avory and Horridge, JJ. The counsel associated with me were the Solicitor-General (now Viscount Cave, L.C.), Mr. Bodkin (now Sir Archibald Bodkin, the Public Prosecutor), Mr. Travers Humphreys (now Sir Travers Humphreys, Senior Treasury Counsel at the Old Bailey), and Mr. (now Mr. Justice) Branson.

The prisoner was most ably defended by three junior members of the English Bar, Mr. Sullivan, who at that time was also one of the prominent leaders of the Irish Bar holding the rank of Second Serjeant, Mr. Artemus Jones, and Mr. Morgan, the Professor of Constitutional Law at University College, London. All three have now "taken silk." His solicitor, Mr. Gavan Duffy, shortly afterwards went to Ireland and was one of the signatories to the Treaty. Mr. Doyle, of the American Bar, was also present, assisting in the defence.

An untoward incident occurred very early in the case. A juror fell ill, and the case had to commence again with a new jury. I need not go into the details of the evidence. The witnesses were hardly challenged, except on the point whether the brigade was to be used during or not until after the War, but they remained unshaken.

The real interest to a lawyer was the point whether any

offence had been committed.   Mr. Sullivan took the point
before the prisoner pleaded, but the court thought the best
course was to hear the evidence first, because then the facts
would be fully before the Court.   Consequently, when I closed
the case for the prosecution, the legal argument began.   It
was necessarily long, technical and intricate.   It involved the
true meaning of the Statute of Treason, passed in 1351, which
was drawn up in Norman French.   It necessitated a minute
examination of a number of musty Statutes, long since repealed,
and many cases, both old and new, in which various persons,
some of the greatest eminence and others of very humble
rank, had become involved in accusations of treason.   To
understand the precedents, it was essential to grasp the details
of antiquated procedure and to have a clear idea of the Constitutional position of England in regard to Wales, Scotland,
Ireland, France and the Colonies, at the various dates when
the precedents came into being, and to examine and discuss
the opinions of many bygone judges and legal writers of the
greatest eminence and reputation.

Casement was charged with that kind of treason which is
described as "adhering to the King's enemies."   Strange as it
may seem, it was contended that this offence could only be
committed by a person physically present in this country.   If
this were the true meaning of the words of the Statute, then
Casement had committed no offence, for he had done nothing
in the realm of England.   The defence were confronted by the
fact that not only was there an unbroken current of legal
opinion, from the sixteenth century onwards, dead in their
teeth, but such decisions as there were, necessarily few because
such offenders take care to remain out of reach, were also
against them.

I had little difficulty in disposing of the legal objection.   Casement made a statement, but did not go into the box to give
evidence, and, after counsel's speeches and a judicial summing-
up by Lord Reading in terms most scrupulously fair and impartial, the jury convicted and Casement was sentenced to death.

An appeal was at once lodged and heard, as criminal appeals
always are, within a short period.   Mr. Sullivan did his utmost

to convince a strong Court, presided over by Mr. Justice (now Lord) Darling, that the point he had taken was good law, but without success. His argument was, in the words of the judgment, "exceedingly well considered, well delivered, and in every way worthy of the greatest traditions of the King's Courts," and the prisoner's counsel can justly claim that all that human skill and ability could do for him was done.

Then came an attempt to appeal to the House of Lords. This placed me in a singularly delicate position. By the Criminal Appeal Act, no such appeal can be lodged without the consent of the Attorney-General. I had throughout argued that there was no substance in the point raised by the defence. I had to consider the position from a different point of view. It would have been easy to have consented, but that would have been a negation of my duty. After the most careful and anxious reconsideration, I came to the decided opinion that I ought not to shrink from the responsibility of refusing the application, and accordingly no further appeal took place.

It was no part of my duty to consider whether the King should show any leniency to the prisoner. There can be no question that the decision not to interfere with the execution of the sentence was right. Casement, blinded by hatred of this country, as malignant in quality as it was sudden in origin, had played a desperate hazard in our hour of need. He had lost, and his life was forfeit.

It was, however, still his destiny to raise doubts in legal circles. The Act of abolishing public executions did not apply to treason, and it was asserted that the execution must, therefore, be in public. It is doubtful in the extreme whether there ever was any rule that a death sentence must be carried out in public, but in any case an Act of 1887 had authorised sheriffs to execute any death sentence in a prison within their jurisdiction. Casement was accordingly hanged in Pentonville Prison on August 3rd, 1916. The day after his execution it was announced that the King had, before then, deprived the traitor of the honours that he had earned and of which he had proved to be unworthy.

THE GERMAN HOSPITAL SHIP

THE GERMAN HOSPITAL SHIP

THE Prize Court is a very special tribunal which only comes into existence in a country which has embarked upon a war, and its main jurisdiction is to determine whether ships or cargoes belonging to enemy or neutral subjects have been properly captured in the due exercise of belligerent rights.

The law it administers is International Law, and it follows, from the origin and nature of its jurisdiction, that the outbreak of war often finds both judges and advocates without practical experience in the conduct of prize cases. Fortunately, the Universities and the Inns of Court provide instruction in International Law; so that we are assured in any event of a supply of lawyers who have a sound theoretical knowledge which they can readily turn to practical advantage.

When I became a Law Officer in May, 1915, I found the Prize Court in full swing. The President, Sir Samuel Evans, had already laid down the main lines of that marvellous adaptation of ancient rules to modern conditions upon which his fame as a judge so securely rests. Nevertheless, as the blockade tightened, and Germany's needs grew more and more urgent, and supplies harder and harder to obtain, many difficult and intricate cases arose which called for close detailed study of a multitude of commercial doctrines and facts.

There had been built up a system of recording information which placed at the disposal of the Procurator-General, who acted as Crown Solicitor in all prize cases, a mass of information about persons, places and commodities from which his skilled assistants could prepare the evidence upon which the Crown relied.

Volumes could be written on the various crafts and subtle devices to which the Germans resorted. Rubber, for example, was misdescribed, then disguised. Our naval authorities found books, soap, fruit and almost every conceivable commodity which when closely examined proved to be rubber intended for German use. We succeeded in stopping the supply.

All the ancient methods of secret communication—messengers, secret writing, codes, false names, and covert allusions—were revived and placed on a scientific basis with the aid of the new methods of telegraphy. It was unceasing labour, for no sooner had one device failed than another was adopted, and these not one at a time but many simultaneously.

And with all this task of investigating details and unmasking fraud, the principles of International Law had to be borne in mind and applied steadily to the cases. The nation is not aware of the immense labours, or of the unceasing vigilance, of those upon whom fell the task of justifying the seizures which the Royal Navy made.

It is not easy to select from the many cases that fell to my lot to conduct one which stands out in interest and importance beyond all others. I have selected the case of the German Hospital Ship, because, on the one hand, not only does it illustrate the work both of the Royal Navy and of the lawyers, but also because it throws a light upon German habits of thought, and shows how it was that they falsely concluded that we for our part were habitually abusing the Red Cross.

The ship in question was the *Ophelia*. She left the Thames on 3rd August, 1914, a date just before the War, when the Germans were holding up our ships in their ports. She was a German-owned merchant-ship built and adapted for the carrying of merchandise. She reached Germany in safety. On arrival she was ordered to a naval dockyard, underwent a thorough overhaul, and was then equipped and painted as a hospital ship.

Under the Hague Convention such ships, if built or adapted wholly and solely with a view to aiding the wounded, sick and shipwrecked, are absolutely immune from capture, provided they are not used to commit acts harmful to the opposing belligerent power.

Although the case was in its main features not a very difficult one, it was unusually troublesome because of the mass of detail. The equipment and arrangements of the vessel had to be considered in the light of her alleged employment as a hospital ship and of the charge that she was in fact used for scouting purposes, and in both those matters she had to be compared with properly equipped hospital ships. Her movements had to be traced not only from observations made by the witnesses on board British warships, but also from such of the ship's papers as fell into our hands, and the varying statements of her crew compared with the Crown evidence in the light of the information painfully pieced together from such documents.

It called for the closest co-operation between the Crown lawyers and their technical advisers from the Admiralty, and for much hard work on confused and intricate details before the main outlines could be established and clearly stated before the Court. Yet this task was indispensable for the double purpose of establishing the case for the Crown and demolishing the case set up by the Germans.

The captain attended the Court and gave evidence, a comparatively rare event in a prize case.

She came under naval observation on two occasions. The first was on 8th October, 1914, when she was seen by a submarine which was on patrol outside the mouth of the Ems. On the 6th a German torpedo-boat had been sunk by a submarine off the Ems. The *Ophelia* was then lying off the Weser, and, so it was alleged, was ordered to the Ems for duty.

The mystery as to her orders was never solved. Her captain "thought" he was told the boat had been sunk, and he also "thought" he was told there were survivors, but it is certain that no one told him where the sinking took place, and he did not know it on the 8th. Yet on that day, much too late to be of any legitimate service, the vessel was cruising off the Ems and a long way from the scene of the disaster.

The submarine commander observed her movements for some time, and, as a result, he became suspicious. He followed her and she ran away. Although he had only some four miles to make up, and his craft was going at eleven knots, he could not overtake her before she got too near the shore to be safe for him to follow, and so she got clear away. It was alleged that this must be a mistake, as she could not do more than nine knots an hour, but I disproved this objection by producing her log for other voyages which she made before the War, when she constantly averaged eleven knots. It may be remembered that though a hospital ship cannot be captured, she may be inspected. No hospital ship legitimately employed should have any need to run away.

The fact was that this hospital ship, under orders which were never produced, was cruising at a place where she could do no proper work, and, when sighted by a British submarine, went off home at full speed, though it was broad daylight and she had not finished the task in which, as she alleged, she was engaged.

When that is coupled with the fact that on the 6th a flotilla of torpedo-boats had made a dash from the Ems, had been intercepted and one of them sunk, and the rest had since been keeping safe within the river, it is certainly open to suggest that her real object was to ascertain whether British submarines were about, her status protecting her from the fate which might befall a torpedo-boat on scouting duties. The suspicions of the submarine commander were, at least, extremely natural. On this occasion she got clean away. Taken by itself, her behaviour might not have been conclusive of her guilt, but it was not the only time she was seen. Her second appearance was not so successful, and her career came to an end. It happened in this manner.

On October 17th, 1914, the *Ophelia* was ordered to the Haaks lightship to obtain further orders. A fresh disaster had occurred. The four torpedo-boats in the Ems on 8th October had been sunk by a British squadron earlier in the day. The lightship was a convenient place at which to report for duty, but the *Ophelia* appears to have gone to the scene of the disaster. Her presence was revealed by the fact that in the afternoon she was heard sending code messages to Norddeich station, the great German wireless installation.

No small mystery envelops the orders which she received, or the question how she obtained the information of the disaster, or knew where to go, for her record of messages received and sent did not, as it should have done, disclose any such information. Nor was it ever shewn what message it was that she was sending in code, for the time did not correspond with the story that she was asking for instructions; that request having, on her own story, been made at noon, whereas the message was being sent some hours afterwards. Moreover, there are no circumstances which would justify such a ship sending messages in a secret code, however reasonable it may be for her to receive them.

She could do no good in her proper capacity where she was, and after being watched for some time her actions were found to be so suspicious that she was seized. A captain who could, with such vague information, proceed so expeditiously to the place where his vessel might be wanted, but had not been sent, would have been wasted in command of a hospital ship, but on the 8th his skill, so convincing on the 17th, had not been of such outstanding merit.

When search was seen to be inevitable, she committed a serious breach of International Law. The secret codes were thrown overboard, which may be justified, and her other records were jettisoned, which may not. This was sought to be explained by saying that they acted on the principle that it was better to throw away too much than too little, but if the story told be correct, it was the very evidence that would establish her innocence which was so carefully destroyed. It is certain that if such evidence existed it would have been flourished before the search party, and one can safely assume that the messages were such that they could not be allowed to remain.

There would naturally be a record of these messages kept by the others with whom she was in communication, so that even if the *Ophelia's* records had legitimately been destroyed, it did not prevent the messages being produced. Needless to say, no attempt to bring any such evidence was ever made.

But that was not all. After the seizure, the accounts of

the stock and consumption of searchlights were surreptitiously thrown overboard. They had not been asked for, nor any mention made of them. If there was no evidence against the ship to be deduced from the book, it was mere waste paper, and yet it was destroyed.

This brings me to a most important and damning part of the case.

When the *Ophelia* reached port, Commander Newman, an officer of great experience in fitting hospital ships, was asked to report on her suitability as a hospital ship. He was not told why she was detained, and was allowed to think that he was reporting upon a proposal to use her in the British service, so that his report should be absolutely fair. He reported that she was unsuitable for a hospital vessel, but was fitted and intended for signalling work. As a hospital ship she would, of course, require signalling apparatus, but not extensive fittings. The fact that such a vessel may cruise with impunity in places where she could obtain information useful to her country, but not otherwise obtainable, renders such a vessel peculiarly open to the abuse of being used as a scout.

She was found to have had fitted an unusually large number of signal halliards working on brackets from the funnel. These had been recently fitted, on an occasion when her masts had been lengthened, so as to increase her wireless range. It was explained that this was quite innocent; the halliards and wireless, as originally fitted, had interfered with one another and so had to be altered. But the international commercial code flags were stowed away in a place not easily accessible, though the halliards were kept for obvious immediate use. Unless there had been special German flags, which had been done away with, the new fittings were a pure extravagance.

It is idle to suppose that a mere inconvenience, operating only very occasionally, would be remedied at such trouble in a naval dockyard overwhelmed with really serious war activities. The new fittings, increasing her signalling efficiency, must have been made because there was an urgent naval purpose to be served, and that purpose one which could not be, in the circumstances, innocent or capable of explanation. They were of no possible advantage to her for her legitimate use as a hospital ship.

She had also an enormous number of Verey lights on board. These are fired from special pistols, of which she possessed two; and there were 600 green, 480 red and 140 white lights. How many she originally had and how many she had used could not be shewn, for the record was carefully destroyed, as I have mentioned. A British hospital ship, with its immensely greater chances of service, carried normally about twelve of each kind.

Naturally, the carrying of such an extraordinary stock called for explanations and several were put forward. One was so extraordinary as to be almost humorous. The captain said that, having no searchlight, they were used to illumine the sea at night. The two pistols firing white lights would be almost useless and the red and green lights of no earthly use whatever for that purpose. The excuse served only to emphasise the fact that if she were seriously intended for her ostensible purpose she would have had a searchlight.

Another explanation was that they used to acknowledge Morse signals at a distance greater than their Morse lamp would carry—an explanation possible, but not probable, and certainly not calling for such numbers. It was also stated that they were used to identify her on entering German harbours at night; but, if that were so, no information was given as to the identification signal or to show how many it would require.

The fact was that the lights could not be explained innocently, nor, we may conclude, could the book be produced without disproving innocence; and so at all risks it had to go.

This vessel, therefore, ill-adapted and hardly even capable of hospital service, well adapted and most elaborately fitted for signalling, was found on two occasions, each immediately after a German naval disaster, cruising near the scene of the conflict, in pursuance of orders which were never properly disclosed, upon an alleged errand which was so useless as to be idiotic; for she could serve no useful purpose whatever for saving or succouring sick, wounded, or shipwrecked German mariners, the only possible justification for her presence. On the other hand, cruising where she did on those occasions, she was in a position to obtain information about the British Navy of vital importance to the German forces, which could only be obtained by legitimate scouting at the risk of almost certain disaster, and she was sending messages in code which she never succeeded in explaining.

It is, of course, quite unnecessary to bring captured enemy warships before the Court in order to obtain a decision that they have been lawfully taken, but this was an exceptional case. Although belonging to the German Government, she was ostensibly engaged on service which exempted her from seizure. It was necessary to establish that she had forfeited the protection conferred upon hospital ships by the Hague Convention, and for this purpose a judicial investigation by the Prize Court was essential.

As the claimants were our enemy, the difficulty was surmounted by the captain making the claim on behalf of his Government. English counsel were engaged to argue the case on behalf of the ship, and they discharged their duty with that zeal and ability which is rightly expected from counsel. They put forward and strenuously maintained every argument and every fact that could tell in their client's favour.

Sir Samuel Evans unhesitatingly held, after an exhaustive review of all the facts and circumstances, first, that the *Ophelia* was not adapted and used for the special and sole purpose of affording aid and relief to the wounded, sick and shipwrecked; and, secondly, that she was adapted and used as a signalling ship for naval purposes. Each of these findings deprived her of the protection of the Hague Convention. Moreover, she had been guilty of the serious offence of destroying her papers.

An appeal was lodged and the Judicial Committee of the Privy Council reconsidered the whole case and independently came to the same conclusion. I had argued that there was a finding of fact against the appellant and that he could only succeed if he showed that there was no evidence to support it. The Court did not accept this argument as the President sat without a jury; but, apart from that, I argued that the case was conclusive.

The attempt to use the Hague Convention as a cover for naval operations ignominiously failed; and the British Navy was not again indulged with the sight of a German hospital ship. The lawyers had rendered, without distorting in the letter or the spirit any doctrine of International Law, a great service to the Navy and to the Allies.

THE "VERONICA" MURDERS

THE "VERONICA" MURDERS

On 11th October, 1902, the *Veronica,* a British wooden sailing ship of 1,000 tons burthen, sailed with twelve men on board from Ship Island, in the Gulf of Mexico, with a cargo of timber for Montevideo.

The twelve men were the master, two mates, a negro cook and eight men. The master, Alexander Shaw, was a man of mature years, somewhat deaf, who on occasion wore glasses. He had been in command for several voyages with the same officers, both of whom had served in her before the mast. Only two of the others had been on her before. These were two German lads named Morisson and Flohr. The ship was seaworthy and properly provisioned. Being laden with timber she was practically unsinkable.

The *Veronica* was never seen again and the first news of her was received when one of her lifeboats, manned by five men, reached Cajueira Island on Christmas Day. This island lies off the Paranhyba River in South America, not quite 150 miles south of the Equator, and is owned by Liverpool shipowners who have a warehouse there. The five men were Rau, Smith, Morisson, Flohr and the cook. Three were Germans, one English and one Dutch. The boat was in good order but was without food, chart or compasses.

The s.s. *Brunswick* arrived a few days later, and to her master, Rau, who claimed to be the second officer of the *Veronica,* told a sad but not improbable story of disaster. He said that while in Florida Straits, one man had died of fever and that shortly afterwards the chief mate was killed by an accident which also caused injuries to Smith, whose head bore two serious wounds and whose eye was cut. In consequence of the mate's death, the master had made Rau the second officer

About seven or eight weeks out, one night when Flohr was on the look-out, gossiping with Morisson, Rau, who had not spoken to him for a week, came along and told the two boys that they would soon be overboard, as he had heard the mates arranging to do it. He suggested that they should throw the officers overboard first, and, saying that Smith and Morisson agreed, asked Flohr to join in. Flohr said that he refused and wept; but ultimately agreed to join the mutineers.

The mutiny was arranged for the night of the first Sunday in December. At midnight the first officer's watch, Smith, Flohr, Paddy and Johanssen, went on duty; and at two o'clock Paddy was on the look-out and Johanssen at the wheel. Flohr went to call Rau and found him conversing with Smith. After hesitations and delays, Rau went to Paddy and asked him if he could see the North Star. As the ship was heading, this meant that Paddy had to stoop to look under a sail, and as he did so Rau hit him twice with an iron belaying-pin. Paddy dropped bleeding and insensible, but not dead, and was dragged to the foc'sle and put in a locker.

Morisson had been set to watch Julius, who was on the watch below; but what Alec, the remaining man on the watch, was doing then, or at any time during that night, no one ever told.

The chief mate came forward and at once missed Paddy and called for him. Rau replied that he must be about as he had been fighting there. The mate came in the dark to the foc'sle and Rau hit out, but struck Smith, who naturally called out and dropped his revolver. Rau kept his head; he said, "Is that Paddy again?" and having made sure of his victim, struck the mate, who dropped with a deep groan. He was promptly put overboard, the first of the seven to die.

Rau and Smith went aft, leaving Flohr guarding Paddy. Two shots range out and the second officer ran into the navigation room calling to the captain. Rau was then heard shouting at the cook, who was in his cabin. The negro had been awakened by the shots and had heard a man run past the door, calling out "Oh Lord, Captain, I'm shot." Next Rau came to the door saying "I've killed the captain, the chief officer and the

second officer. Come out you black son of a bitch." The cook
barred the door and remained there till morning, Rau coming
at intervals to abuse and threaten him.

Rau then ordered Flohr to finish off Johanssen, who was
still at the wheel. Flohr went and struck the man, who ran
forward and begged his life at Rau's hands. Rau relented, but
only for a time. Flohr went to the wheel and on the way saw
the captain on the deck, looking at the topsails. No one knows
what he was doing all this time; probably his deafness had
prevented him from realising what was afoot. Rau came aft,
threw an iron belaying-pin at him and shot him twice. The
captain fell and crawled to his cabin, where Rau locked him
in. The two surviving officers were both wounded and secured.
Rau knew that they had weapons, so it may be assumed that
he would not risk going in to finish them off.

Julius was dead by then. He had tried to climb out of the
foc'sle window and Morisson had killed him with one blow.
He had been thrown overboard, and only a pool of blood
remained to show where he had fallen.

Paddy then revived sufficiently to get out of the locker.
He staggered, with his head covered with blood. He begged
for water. Rau said, "I'll give you a good drink of water,"
and struck him dead. He too was thrown overboard, the third
and last to be murdered that night.

In the morning the negro emerged and begged his life.
Smith interceded with Rau, who gave way, but said, "Don't ask
any damned questions." He was set to make coffee under the
guard of Flohr, but, before it was taken, the negro was forced
to drink some to prove that he had not poisoned it. The spar-
ing of the cook was almost the only serious mistake Rau made.
In such a case you must be thorough if you are to cheat the
gallows.

The next task was to barricade the cabins and to discuss
what was to be done. The negro said that he was shut up in
the old sail room; but Flohr asserted that he went on with his
duties as cook all the time. It was decided to prepare a lifeboat
and the negro was set to caulk it. Meanwhile Rau wanted a
chart and some instruments . The captain was called through

the skylight. Both he and the second mate were there, each had two wounds and unless there was food in the cabins, neither had any food during the rest of their lives. Rau got his chart and other things in return for a drink of water. The master reproached him for having made no complaint and begged for his life. Rau told him they were going to Pernambuco.

Then the discussion continued while the lifeboat was being got ready. At first the ship was to be taken to St. Paul's Rocks and there destroyed, but the risk of being spoken to was too great and it was decided to destroy her in mid-ocean. She was headed south-east at the time of the mutiny; but her course had been altered to south-west, so that during the fortnight or so they remained on board she was approaching South America. Three tasks remained: to prepare and provision the lifeboat; to destroy the vessel, having first finished off the two wounded men; and, lastly, to agree upon a convincing story which they could all learn by heart.

The officers were soon settled. The mate was called up on deck and sprang overboard. He swam alongside and was fired at and soon disappeared. Alec was set to hunt the captain out with an axe, and when this unhappy and, as far as we know, blameless man appeared, Rau shot him dead on the spot. Five had now been murdered, and here the slaughter was to stop. There was, however, an unexpected hitch. Johanssen, the Swede, and Alec, the Indian or Eurasian, who were both men of some age, failed to learn their story. At intervals every day each had to say over his piece until he was word perfect. Johanssen was a hopeless pupil. The desperate situation of the mutineers could not afford the survival of an evident incompetent. So Smith shot him and his body followed the five others. Half the ship's complement had now been murdered.

For some days they persevered with Alec, but one day he bungled the handling of a sail and part of the tackle swung round and cut Smith's eye. Rau ordered Alec's execution. Flohr and the cook were detailed for the job. Flohr said he fired and missed on purpose. The cook was sure that Alec was shot. Whatever were the facts, the unfortunate man went overboard, the seventh and last victim.

The survivors had been methodically preparing the ship for destruction and the boat for their departure. Rau had assumed command, calling himself, or being called, "Captain Bung-starter." On 20th December all was ready. The men got into the boat, Rau remaining till last to fire the ship, and as soon as the fire took hold, they set out for the coast. There had only been one hitch. The other lifeboat was to have been capsized in the story, so as to drown the others, but she would not capsize and had to be burned, so that in the story the other boat was afloat somewhere in the ocean. It could not decently be said to hold seven, as it was the smaller; and so Julius died of fever and the first officer of accident, which also neatly accounted for Rau appearing as a ship's officer.

The voyage was uneventful, but when they sighted land misgivings arose. They were much too well provided for. Overboard went the charts, the compasses, the food and one of the weapons—the captain's—and the boat came to land. As they approached, a new misgiving affected these guilty minds; and another revolver was jettisoned. Once on the wharf, Rau parted with his in the same way—and then found that he had the cartridges. These Flohr buried and the men were then sufficiently destitute for their story at the warehouse.

The defence challenged the story thus told. Not that the murders were denied or the fire alleged to be accidental, but all the blame was put on the cook. Rau and Smith gave evidence lamely and unconvincingly, and in spite of all that their counsel could do, the jury had no hesitation in finding the three guilty of murdering their captain, brutally, callously and without reason or motive that can be suggested.

This drama of the sea proves once again that when men brood on trivial matters they may commit enormities so totally out of proportion to the provocation or hope of gain that the only rational explanation is that they must have been insane. Yet these men were sane. Why they began, no one may tell. Once started, fear and the desire to save their own wicked and worthless lives accounts for what followed, but the mutiny remains and must remain for ever an unsolved mystery of the sea.

Its master spirit was Rau. His only chance would have been to kill all his fellow-criminals before he landed. For he alone had supreme wickedness, supreme daring and supreme resource.

THE MARCONI SCANDAL

THE MARCONI SCANDAL

THE TRIAL OF REX V. CHESTERTON

I DO not intend to write a history of the Marconi controversy which embittered politics during the course of 1912 and 1913, but only to tell the story of the prosecution of the late Mr. Cecil Chesterton for publishing criminal libels on the late Mr. Godfrey Isaacs in the course of attacks upon the contract for the Imperial Wireless Chain made by the Postmaster-General with the Marconi Company in 1912.

I must, however, sketch the outline of the main events, in order that the way in which the mass of erroneous deductions and inferences from mere coincidences came into being can be understood. This outline may, however, serve to clarify ideas on the political controversy, of which echoes are even now occasionally heard.

Signor Marconi is still comparatively young, a fact which enables us to realise how rapidly wireless has developed, for he was well known in electrical research before he began wireless experiments. Like most useful inventions, wireless telegraphy passed through many stages between the times when it was a laboratory toy and when it became a business proposition. By 1897 sufficient advance had been made to justify forming a company, and contracts were made with the Government in 1903 and 1909. By the last date the invention was chiefly used for communications between ship and ship, or ship and shore, besides being used over comparatively short distances on land. It may be remembered that the apprehension of Dr. Crippen in 1910 was due to the fact that the s.s. *Montrose,* on which he was sailing for Quebec, was fitted with wireless, then a somewhat unusual circumstance.

By 1910 further progress made it feasible to communicate

across oceans. In this year Signor Marconi found that the business had so expanded that it interfered with his scientific work, and he ceased to be managing director. He was succeeded by Mr. Godfrey Isaacs, a brother of Lord Reading, then famous as Mr. Rufus Isaacs, K.C.

In the same year the Marconi Company applied to the Government for a licence to erect a chain of wireless stations which would enable them to send messages round the world. It was entering the field as a competitor of the cable companies. The proposal being to erect these stations in lands situated within the British Dominions, a licence was necessary before the scheme could be put in hand.

Such applications were, as a matter of course, referred to the Cable Landing Rights Committee. This was a standing body presided over by the Parliamentary Secretary of the Board of Trade, and its members consisted of representatives of the Admiralty, War Office, Foreign Office, Colonial Office, India Office, Post Office, and the Treasury. Its duty was to examine and report upon such applications from all points of view—Imperial, strategical, technical, commercial, and financial. Its origin was naturally to examine the applications of cable companies, but when this application was made in respect of a wireless system—a completely novel project—the Committee was, by its nature and functions, competent to deal with the matter.

This committee ultimately reported that such a chain was feasible and necessary, but that it was not in the public interest to allow it to be in private hands. It was too vitally important to allow the Marconi or any other company to control such a service.

About the same time Sir Joseph Ward, then Prime Minister of New Zealand, had carried a motion at the Imperial Conference in favour of such a scheme. The preparation of an actual proposal was referred to the Committee of Imperial Defence, which delegated the preliminary inquiry to a sub-committee of experts. By June, 1911, these bodies had decided that the matter should be taken in hand as a matter of urgent public

importance, and the execution of the project was entrusted
to the Post Office.

Mr. Herbert Samuel (now Sir Herbert Samuel, and lately
Governor of Palestine), who had just become Postmaster-
General, formed a third committee, known as the "Imperial
Wireless Committee," from the various Government Departments concerned. This Committee decided after much discussion that the equipping of the stations should be put out to
contract, and that the Marconi system should be adopted. They
had considered the rival systems, of which there were several,
and had rejected them. The Marconi system alone had given
practical demonstrations over the required distances, and the
company alone had the necessary experience. Naturally the
companies which owned and were developing the other systems
were disappointed, for the obtaining of such a contract was an
unmistakable testimony to the pre-eminence of the system
selected.

In December, 1911, negotiations were opened with the Marconi Company. Mr. Samuel represented the State, and was
aided by the assistance and advice of experts from a number
of Government Departments. There were in the service of the
Admiralty, the War Office, and the Post Office a number of
experts who had great practical experience of wireless telegraphy and a competent knowledge of all the rival systems.
The company was represented by Mr. Godfrey Isaacs and his
staff. It was during these negotiations that Mr. Samuel first
met Mr. Isaacs, and they had no private intercourse at all.
Mr. Rufus Isaacs had become a Law Officer and been knighted,
but took no part in the negotiations, of which indeed he was
entirely unaware. It is no part of the work of a Law Officer
to take part in such matters.

Eventually, after hard bargaining, terms were arranged, and
the company sent in a tender which was accepted on 7th March,
1912. Shortly, the scheme was that the Government should
build, and the company should equip, six stations at a cost of
£60,000 for equipping each station. The company was to give
the Government licences for all existing and future patents, and
its advice and assistance, and to receive during the terms of

the contract a royalty of ten per cent. The contract was to run
for twenty-eight years, with a "break clause" at eighteen
years, and the royalties were to cease if the Postmaster-
General decided at any time to discontinue the use of the
Marconi System.

Mr. Isaacs had in vain tried to secure that the "break
clause" should be kept secret. The day after the acceptance
of the tender he issued a circular to the shareholders, announc-
ing that the tender had been accepted, but he did not mention
this provision. A great deal was afterwards made of this
omission.

It must be borne in mind that the company had two master
patents, one expiring in 1914, and the other in 1918, unless
renewed. There were, however, many subsidiary patents, the
numbers of which were being constantly increased.

The next stage was to draft the contract, and this was left
to the legal and technical advisers. Many points arose on the
draft, and these were considered and settled in the same way
as the questions which had arisen in the first negotiations.
The contract was finally agreed and signed on 19th July, 1912,
and on the same day placed on the table of the House of Commons. No such contract can be made without the sanction
of the Commons, and this necessarily involves the publication of the terms before any motion for such sanction is
debated.

The fact that it had been decided to negotiate only with the
Marconi Company was of course well known, and after the
acceptance of the tender the general lines of the agreement
were made public. But up to the signature of the contract
the actual terms remained a secret, so that until the contract
was laid on the table informed criticism was impossible.

Before dealing with the course of events in the House of
Commons, it is necessary to go back and explain some other
vital factors in the agitation.

The company had by this date become a dividend-paying
concern. The first declaration was in July, 1910, and by 1912
all preference arrears had been paid and 20 per cent. was being
paid on the ordinary shares. Of course, none of these profits

was due to the Wireless Chain contract, which still awaited confirmation.

Mr. Godfrey Isaacs, on assuming the managing directorship of the company, had taken vigorous steps in England and America to restrain infringements of the company's patents, and immediately the tender was accepted he sailed for America to fight the actions there, and accordingly took no part in settling the draft of the contract. He was accompanied by Signor Marconi and other experts and a member of the Stock Exchange, who had managed the issues of the company's shares.

Not only were the actions successful, but important business arrangements were made with American cable, telegraph and telephone companies, which made it necessary to reorganise the American Marconi Company. The English company was a large shareholder in the American company and therefore directly interested in its profits, but the latter had no interest whatever in the English company, and could not benefit, except in prestige, from the contract with the Post Office. This fact is of the greatest importance.

The *Titanic* disaster had excited extraordinary interest in wireless telegraphy, so that the English company's prospects were very bright.

One thing that the English company was forced to do was to undertake to place the American company's additional capital—1,400,000 shares at $5 each—rather over £1,500,000. The reason was that wireless finance in the States had been so shamelessly conducted by certain rival companies that the whole industry was under a cloud. It was therefore deemed impossible to place the shares in the States. Mr. Isaacs agreed to be responsible for 500,000, and while still in America placed 350,000 with the company's jobber.

On his return he offered some to his brothers. He thought that they were a good thing. Sir Rufus declined, but the other took 56,000 altogether, and persuaded Sir Rufus to take over 10,000 of these. This transaction was not influenced by the contract, nor had it any influence upon it. The American company had nothing to do with the contract. Sir Rufus parted with 2,000 to two of his colleagues in the Government, and some of the purchasers afterwards bought more on the market.

The shares were introduced on the market with some apprehension, but at once a boom began, and prices soared. Both companies' shares went to high premiums, and with an excited market full of speculators the terms of the contract were published, and the proposal to confirm the contract came before the House.

Some members considered the terms unduly favourable to the company; and Mr. Samuel, though anxious to give effect to the decision that the matter was urgent, was forced to postpone consideration until after the Recess. Newspaper attacks began, and Mr. Chesterton made himself conspicuous by articles published in the *Eye Witness* and the *New Witness,* which were weekly journals edited by him.

In some way the dealings in American Marconis by Ministers had become known, and were confused with the English company and connected with the contract. By the time Parliament reassembled serious allegations were flying about, and there was nothing for it but an inquiry. A Special Committee was set up. The ratification was necessarily postponed and one consequence of this was that the War found us without this urgently needed wireless chain.

The setting up of a Committee did not silence Mr. Chesterton. The attacks continued. He had taken a decided stand against party politics and had evinced an aversion to the influence of Jews. He was entirely ignorant of the way in which Government contracts were negotiated and drawn; and being struck by the boom and convinced that the contract was a bad one for the nation, leaped to the conclusion that it must have been privately arranged between Mr. Samuel, Sir Rufus Isaacs and Mr. Godfrey Isaacs, so that the public treasury should be raided for the benefit of the Marconi Company.

Primarily he was attacking the Jews and their political and financial influence. However misguided, he was completely honest. The contract offered a popular theme, and, almost without thinking, Mr. Godfrey Isaacs was included in the diatribes, and to reinforce them the files of Somerset House were searched. It was found that Mr. Isaacs had in years gone by been concerned in a number of unsuccessful companies— most of them were private ventures—but Mr. Chesterton saw fit to call upon the Attorney-General to do his duty and set the law in motion agaist his brother.

Such attacks are usually ignored, and so were these for a time, but they were pressed in such a way as to amount to actual persecution. Wherever Mr. Isaacs went he was pursued by placards. Street vendors with copies of the journals and large posters were stationed outside his offices and other places where he was to be expected, and his life became unbearable. He took advice, and resolved to prosecute. Mr. Chesterton had acknowledged that he was responsible for the publication of these attacks. Leave was obtained to institute a prosecution. He was brought before a magistrate and committed for trial at the Old Bailey.

The prosecution relied upon six charges of libel, contained in as many counts of the indictment. Five the defendant claimed were true, and their publication to the public interest. The sixth, he said, did not refer to Mr. Isaacs, and on this one count the jury upheld his contention. Once a person charged with libel justifies, the rôles are reversed. He becomes the accuser, and must establish the truth of his accusation or be found guilty.

The trial lasted ten days, from 27th May to 7th June, 1913; Mr. Justice (now Lord) Phillimore, was the judge. Sir Edward (now Lord) Carson and I led the late Sir Richard Muir for the prosecution. Mr. Wild, K.C. (now Sir Ernest Wild, Recorder of London), and Mr. Rigby Swift, K.C. (now Mr. Justice Swift), led the late Mr. Purcell and Mr. Gordon Smith for the defence, which was conducted with ability and pertinacity.

All the prosecutor has to do is to show that the words were published by the defendant, that they are defamatory and refer to him. It is usually prudent, however, for him to meet the justification in advance and allow himself and his witnesses to be cross-examined before the defendant is called on for his defence. Such a course was followed in this case.

We called evidence showing exactly how the negotiations were conducted, and thus made it plain how ludicrous was the ignorance that had inspired the attack. Mr. Samuel, Sir Rufus Isaacs, Mr. Godfrey Isaacs, and Signor Marconi were all called and cross-examined at great length.

The defence had assumed that a great point could be made if they were able to show that the defendant acted in good faith, but he was not charged under the section dealing with the more serious offence of publishing a malicious libel. The judge pointed out that it is no defence of a libel to prove that the defendant honestly believes it. A man is only entitled to publish such allegations if they are true, and if it is in the public interest that they should be published.

Then it was asserted that the politicians were the sole objects of the attacks on the contract. Certainly it was the main object, but even if it be laudable it only makes it worse to drag in the name of one who is not a politician.

Again it was suggested that there was no imputation on Mr. Isaacs over the contract, as he was entitled to do his best for the company, and drive as hard a bargain as he could. But, then, how explain the use of such words as "corruption," "conspiracy," "abominable business," "hands in the till," and other choice expressions which were put in the articles? They are not capable of such facile explanations.

When, however, the defence came to Mr. Isaacs' past record, they pressed the attack with vigour and venom. The allegations could not be explained away. They were either true or else foul libels. There was no alternative. I will not gratify the defendant's supporters by reviving these allegations. The evidence and the verdict are sufficient to satisfy any unprejudiced reader that the attacks were as false as they were despicable.

In the event, the justification of the five counts failed miserably. The jury, after listening carefully to the arguments put forward on defendant's behalf, and to an able and impartial summing-up by the Judge, convicted the defendant, and thus finally gave the lie to the campaign of abuse that had been levelled at the prosecutor.

The vindication of Mr. Isaacs was all that he desired. He had no desire to see his libeller in prison.

In pronouncing sentence, Mr. Justice Phillimore stated that he had been troubled in his mind whether, in view of the methods adopted, he ought not to send the defendant to prison. The libels were due to ignorance and prejudice. However, as the attacks, although wrong-headed, were honestly believed, he decided to let Mr. Chesterton off with a fine, but ordered him to pay all the costs of the prosecution.

The verdict of the jury thus put an end to this particular crusade against Mr. Godfrey Isaacs—a crusade due to ignorance and confusion of mind, aided by unreasoning prejudice. With regard to the Ministers concerned, I need only refer to the War for readers to realise how disastrous for the nation it would have been if they had been driven from public life as a result of what was termed the "Marconi Scandal."

ETHEL LE NEVE:
CRIPPEN'S MISTRESS

ETHEL LE NEVE: CRIPPEN'S MISTRESS

It will be many years before Dr. Crippen, whose trial was the great criminal sensation of 1910, will be forgotten. His crime was remarkable in many ways. It seemed incredible that the little insignificant man should have been capable of such an unusually callous, calculated and cold-blooded murder. It is not very surprising to find him using hyoscine, a poison new to the annals of crime, for he was a medical man. But the systematic mutilation of the body rendered the crime particularly beastly, and it is a curious circumstance that both Crippen and Mahon managed to dispose of the main organs, though one organ, the head, is particularly difficult to destroy. The method of mutilation and destruction shows that Crippen was skilful, but that Mahon was a miscalculator. Unlike the medical man, the latter had no conception of the magnitude of his task.

The most surprising feature of Crippen's case is that but for his senseless flight the crime might never have come to light, and it would have been told of some other criminal that in his case for the first time wireless telegraphy was employed in the apprehension of a fugitive.

The telegraph was first used to secure the apprehension of a criminal when a man named Tawell, who had committed a murder near Slough, succeeded in boarding a train for Paddington. Before the telegraph system had been installed he would have vanished in the crowd, but unknown to him the police at Slough were able to telegraph his description to Paddington, and on the train's arrival he was arrested. Thus the invention of railways, which facilitated the criminal's escape, was countered by the telegraph, which outstripped him in his flight. The submarine cable was first used in 1864 to capture a murderer named Franz Muller, who had shipped on a steamer bound for America before his guilt was discovered.

As in Crippen's case, the police were able, by taking a fast liner, to outsail the vessel he was on and to meet and arrest him on his arrival. It may also be remembered that a year or two ago a man, who was afterwards acquitted, was arrested at Croydon aerodrome just as he was on the point of leaving England by aeroplane. Bevan got away by aeroplane and eluded capture for months until he was run to earth at Vienna.

My own part in the proceedings had nothing to do with Crippen. I was retained to defend his unfortunate companion, Ethel Le Neve, who was charged with complicity in his crime. In order to give a clear idea of her trial and of her acquittal it is, however, necessary to tell the story of Crippen's crime.

It was the outcome of the old familiar matrimonial tragedy.

The little man was nearly fifty. He had qualified in medicine in the States, and in 1900 had come to London to assist a firm of patent medicine vendors. During the ten years that followed he made the round of the patent medicine firms, one of which, the Drouet Institute, had in their employment a young girl, Ethel Le Neve, as a typist. She was under Crippen's orders, and their association continued even when they were not in the same employment.

Crippen was a married man living with his second wife, whom he had married in America. She was half German, half Pole, whose maiden name was Kunegunda Matamotski, though she preferred to be known as Cora Turner at the time of her marriage, and afterwards called herself Belle Elmore. Her ambition was to be a music-hall artiste, but she failed dismally, and had to be content with membership of a benevolent association to assist needy artistes. She was a woman of a flamboyant type, loud in her tastes and extravagant in her personal expenditure, but a parsimonious and slovenly housekeeper. Crippen's life with her must have been one long period of discomfort broken at intervals by outbreaks of violent disturbance.

It is not very surprising that he sought elsewhere the peaceful affection of which his wife was incapable, but for which he longed. He turned to his typist, whom he found an easy victim. She came from the lower middle classes; Crippen was her superior, and in her eyes a man of great education and of position. She was young, a gentle, affectionate girl, not unattractive, though anæmic and liable to neuralgia. She lodged with a Mrs. Jackson and inspired such mutual love in the mind of this woman that their relations soon ripened into the affection of mother and daughter. Sent out into the world at a tender age, condemned to earn her living in a monotonous avocation and to spend her leisure in drab, uninteresting lodgings, it is not surprising that the opportunity offered by Crippen to this soft and ductile young woman proved a temptation which she could not resist.

By 1907 or 1908 she had become his mistress while remaining his clerk, but to a girl of her ideas there was a dreadful drawback—the union was unlawful. So long as Crippen's wife existed her relations with him could never be open and honest; and to her respectability was a fetish. At times and seasons she fell intelligibly ill, and then her position caused acute anxiety. This worry and the fact that the wife was entitled to her paramour's society and affection aggravated her condition, and she was often wretched and ailing.

In 1905 the Crippens had moved to Hilldrop Crescent, a road in North London, where they lived in increasing discomfort. The wife's ambitions had definitely failed and she scarcely concealed her predilections for other men. By 1910 matters were reaching a crisis. At the beginning of February, Crippen announced that his wife had suddenly gone to America, and shortly afterwards he published the news of her death. On the twentieth of that month he went to a dance with Le Neve. It was a function which he knew would be attended by his wife's friends, and they noticed with disfavour that his companion was wearing a brooch belonging to his wife. At this time Crippen gave her a good deal of that lady's clothes and jewellery, some of which she presented to Mrs. Jackson. On 12th March, Le Neve took up her abode at Hilldrop Crescent, telling her people that she had become the housekeeper, and there she lived, but for a short holiday with Crippen at Dieppe in March, until July.

Mrs. Crippen's friends were not satisfied and talked the

matter over, until at last their suspicions grew so grave that they communicated with the police.

Inspector Dew was entrusted with the enquiry and, on 8th July, went to Crippen's offices, and afterwards searched the house. At the office, Crippen met him with the greatest apparent candour. He said his wife had bolted with a man, and the story he had told was a lie to cover up a scandal. At the house, Miss Le Neve had received him frankly and placed no obstacle in his way. The inspection revealed nothing suspicious, and the matter would have probably dropped but for the murderer's panic.

On 11th July, Dew went to the office to make a trifling enquiry and found the bird flown. His suspicions reawakened. He went to the house, and found it deserted. For two days he searched, and then discovered what proved to be the remains of the miserable Elmore buried under the brick floor of the cellar.

He at once prepared a case for a warrant, which was issued on the 16th, and then came the question: Where were the fugitives? Their description was circulated and a great sensation filled the newspapers.

Dew knew that on 9th July, Crippen had disguised Miss Le Neve as a boy and had gone away, but where he did not know. They had, in fact, gone to Rotterdam and Antwerp under the name of Robinson, passing as father and son. On the 20th they sailed in the s.s. *Montrose* for Quebec.

The captain was attracted by the unusual caresses of the man for his apparent son, and at once perceived that the boy was a disguised woman. He had read of the missing couple and communicated by wireless. His ship happened to be fitted with that recent invention, which was still in its infancy. Their identity was quickly established, and the vessel proceeded with the two lovers dreaming of a future all gold, quite unconscious that they had been discovered and that the police were racing across the Atlantic to meet them. They were arrested, brought back and committed for trial.

Crippen was tried first. His case lasted a whole week. He

was eventually found guilty and sentenced to death on 22nd October.

The trial had many noteworthy features which did not concern me, as they were not in any way part of my defence of Le Neve. The case will be for a long time the leading authority on the rule that a jury trying a charge of murder must not separate, for a juryman who felt ill was taken by the jury-keeper into the courtyard for fresh air and then returned to his fellows. It was held that there had been no separation of the jury so as to invalidate the trial. The scientific evidence both as to the detection of hyoscine and the identification of the body by a small mark on a tiny piece of skin aroused great interest and controversy. The medico-legal aspect of the evidence is of the greatest importance to all experts and lawyers who may be concerned in similar cases in future.

To complete the story of Dr. Crippen. He appealed and, after the dismissal of his appeal, was executed, denying his guilt. His only thought was for Le Neve, and the only time that he broke down was on receiving her telegram of farewell the night before his execution. At his urgent request the letters that he had from her and her photograph were buried with him. He never ceased to declare her innocence and his love for her. In a statement made for publication he said, "In this farewell letter to the world, written as I face Eternity, I say that Ethel Le Neve has loved me as few women love men, and that her innocence of any crime, save that of yielding to the dictates of the heart, is absolute. To her I pay this last tribute. It is of her that my last thoughts have been. My last prayer will be that God will protect her and keep her safe from harm, and allow her to join me in Eternity. . . . I give my testimony to the absolute innocence of Ethel Le Neve. She put her trust in me, and what I asked her to do she did, never doubting. . . ." He was at least a brave man and a true lover.

And now to return to Miss Le Neve. She had been charged with being an accessory to murder after the fact. For this purpose it is sufficient to explain that this charge would be satisfied by assisting Crippen to escape from justice knowing that he was a murderer. She was tried on 25th October, 1910, at the Old

Bailey. Lord Alverstone was the presiding judge. Sir Richard Muir led for the prosecution and I led Mr. Barrington-
Ward for the defence.

Sir Richard knew that he had not a certain case and, like a
wily old campaigner, tried to put me in the position of proving
that my client was not guilty. I saw the snare and declined
to be caught. It is an elementary rule of English law that the
prisoner has to be proved guilty. It is only when the evidence
for the prosecution has established a case that the defence is
forced to give an explanation. In my opinion the Crown did
not prove their charge, and I took my stand accordingly. My
attitude was abundantly justified by the summing-up and the
verdict.

Sir Richard laid stress on these points. There were guilty
relations between the two. About the date of the murder the
prisoner, who had been looking ill and troubled, suddenly
became very ill in a way which showed that she had been
overcome with horror by a sudden shock. She had said that
she was feeling her equivocal position, and that she could not
bear to think that the wife was living with her lover. This,
said Sir Richard, must have been untrue, for the situation had
lasted for years. Immediately afterwards she recovered her
spirits and began to wear the dead woman's jewellery and gave
her clothing to Mrs. Jackson. She attended the dance wearing
the wife's brooch. She went to live at the house. She fled in
disguise. She must have seen the newspapers at Antwerp.
The only inference was that she had a guilty knowledge. What
explanation had she to offer?

Now immoral life is no proof of complicity in murder, and
I was able to establish that the illness so relied upon, in fact,
occurred during Mrs. Crippen's lifetime, when she was visiting
her friends. The mistake was due to Mrs. Jackson's haziness
as to dates, but in cross-examination the fact became clear.
I was also able to show that the recovery was about the date
of the murder, and that it was due to Crippen having said that
his wife was gone. He made this statement everywhere and it
is not wonderful that, with the suggestion of a divorce, Miss Le
Neve recovered her spirits at the prospect of regaining not only

respectability, but also of acquiring a status in life far above any she had ever dreamed of.

It is inconceivable that Crippen, who was taking the greatest pains to conceal the truth from the world, should have said to her in effect: "I have murdered my wife. Now come and take her place." In July, Miss Le Neve had frankly explained her position to Inspector Dew, and had said that she had first heard of Mrs. Crippen's death on her return from Dieppe. This again was the story which Crippen was spreading. Dew was satisfied at the time that she was telling the truth.

Then there was the flight in disguise, but this was sufficiently explained by her admitted knowledge. The police were making enquiries. Crippen was morbidly afraid of arrest. He had, so far as she knew, done nothing, but arrest meant certain ruin. No jury could be asked to draw the inference that the prisoner knew that Crippen had committed murder and was fleeing to avoid the just punishment of his crime.

Lastly I dealt with the suggestion that she must have seen the English newspapers at Antwerp. If they were available the prosecution could easily have proved the fact. There was cogent evidence that she had not seen them. At her arrest the captain asked her, not whether she had seen in the newspapers that their flight was discovered and that a warrant was out for murder, but whether she had not seen her father's letter in the newspapers. With her mind directed only to her parents, she replied that she had seen no newspapers since she left London. She had said that she knew nothing of the murder. Dr. Crippen had said so, too. There was no reason why he should entrust his guilty secret to her at the risk of losing her who was the prize that he hoped to gain. There were many reasons why he should not impart to any living soul a secret which might cost him his life.

I submitted that the case had wholly failed. The judge's summing-up was a fair and judicial statement of the case, leaving no doubt as to the verdict, and shortly afterwards Miss Le Neve was acquitted by the unhesitating verdict of the jury.

Some readers may say: "Yes, but all that amounts to is that the evidence was not enough. For all that, she may have known." That is true within limits. Nevertheless, I am convinced that she was innocent in every sense of the word. I had the advantage of a close study of all the facts and circumstances of the case, including a great deal that was never in evidence. She was a girl whose character for truthfulness had never been questioned. She denied all knowledge of the crime, and I am convinced that she told the truth. I am fortified by the knowledge that the late Dr. Scott, who had charge of her during her detention for the weeks that elapsed between her arrival in England and her acquittal, shared my belief in her innocence.

Frail she was and of submissive temperament, but not an accomplice in murder nor an ally in its concealment.

I was told that after the trial she left for America. But I never heard of her again.

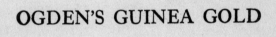

OGDEN'S GUINEA GOLD

A GENERATION is now rising to whom the name of Ogden's Guinea Gold has no appeal. Yet there was a time when this brand of what were then termed "fags," and I believe are now called "gaspers," was known throughout the length and breadth of the United Kingdom. The causes of its rise to fame and sudden extinction remain vividly in my recollection; during four very important years of my professional life, from 1902 to 1906, hardly a day passed without my being engrossed in one aspect or another of the innumerable lawsuits brought against the Company.

When I was first retained in 1902 I was practising at Liverpool and my prospects were as bright as that of a "local" may well be. When the proceedings came to an end in 1906, I had been elected to Parliament and had "come to town," where I had acquired a substantial practice which bade fair to justify my applying for silk in the near future. Every young barrister dreams of being engaged in heavy litigation, but few can ever have had the fortune which came to me, at a time when I had only been called for four years, of being retained in an unprecedented series of actions arising out of the same events, and thus of gaining in a short space of time that indispensable knowledge and experience of practice and procedure which can only be acquired by a busy junior.

The cases in one form or another, including the applications made in the course of framing the issues to be tried and of preparing them for trial, came before the Courts on more than 1,200 occasions. The arguments before the House of Lords occupied four days; in the Court of Appeal twelve days; and no one ever computed the number of days of judicial time taken up before the Judges of the High Court and the Masters.

Company at all; and, secondly, what was the amount of damages he should have if he succeeded on his claim. Obviously, however, the issues had been considerably simplified. For some time longer the actions were pressed, but eventually wiser counsels prevailed.

There were two considerations, in addition to the failure to obtain damages for the loss of the promised share of profits, which considerably affected the retailers' dreams of substantial gains. One was that the costs were heavy. The other was that in the winding up of a company, the creditors could only obtain payment out of the company's assets. These, however, were subject first of all to the liquidator's costs and charges, so that in effect the litigation was carried on at the expense of the retailers, since it was obvious that the assets would not permit payment of the creditors in full. With all these actions coming on for trial, it was quite on the cards that, when the liquidator had taken his costs of fighting them, the surplus assets might even be exhausted, so that the retailers would be left with judgments of no value to them, and would have spent their money for nothing. It was wiser to take what they could get before the money was all gone. Otherwise, they would have paid dearly for providing a new illustration of the fable of the lawyer and the oyster. On the other hand, the Imperial Company realised that the retailers were essential to their business and it was important not to render future business relations impossible. There were still a number of manufacturers who had stood outside the amalgamation and consequently a retailer could always obtain supplies.

Considerations of this kind always appeal, sooner or later, to business men, and negotiations were opened with a view to a comprehensive settlement. After all, the actions were only the clearing up of the tobacco war, which was over and could not break out again, and all branches of the trade had to readjust themselves to altered conditions. The negotiations were necessarily very complicated and took much time and anxious thought before they reached a successful conclusion. Eventually, on 19th September, 1906, they were brought to an agreement and the trade settled down to new and amicable relations with each other.

The chairman of the Retailers' Association celebrated the consummation of these efforts by presenting to all those engaged in the litigation a souvenir, illustrated by portraits of the Judges, counsel and others who took a prominent part in these events. A copy of this hangs in my old chambers to this day, a memorial to four years of hard work which materially assisted my advance in the profession. Soon after the settlement, I was given silk and took my place within the Bar.

THE END